D0899196

The Magic Zoo
The Natural History of Fabulous Animals

PETER COSTELLO

ST. MARTIN'S PRESS
NEW YORK

In memory of my father
JAMES CORMAC COSTELLO
(1906–1977)
who introduced me to
THE HUNTING OF THE SNARK
and taught me the real
meaning of nonsense

Library of Congress Cataloging in Publication Data

Costello, Peter.
  The magic zoo.

  Bibliography: p.
  1. Animals, Mythical.   I. Title.
GR825.C53   398.′469   79-22880
ISBN 0-312-50421-7

'But I, for my part, Phaedrus, consider such things as pretty enough, but as the province of a very curious, painstaking, and not very happy man, and for no other reason than that after this he must set us right as to the form of the Hippocentaurs, and then as to that of the Chimaera; besides, there pours in upon him a crowd of similar monsters, Gorgons and Pegasuses, and other monstrous creatures, incredible in number and absurdity, which if anyone were to disbelieve and endeavour to reconcile each with probability, employing for this purpose a kind of vulgar cleverness, he will stand in need of abundant leisure.'

Socrates, in Plato's *Phaedrus*

CONTENTS

Acknowledgments		xiii
Preface		1

Part One: Animals and Man

1	Animals and Man	7
2	Shaman into Scientist	10
3	The Science of Unknown Animals	17

Part Two: The Magic Zoo

4	The Beast of Lascaux	27
5	The Minotaur	30
6	The Mermaid	34
7	Sirens, Centaurs and Satyrs	59
8	The Phoenix	63
9	The Griffin	71
10	The Roc Bird	83
11	The Giant Ants of India	90
12	The Unicorn	94
13	The Manticora	104
14	The Catoblepas	111
15	Leviathan and Behemoth	115
16	The Dragon	119
17	Basilisk and Salamander	127
18	The Barnacle Goose	135
19	The Vegetable Lamb	148
20	The Carrabuncle	159

21 Heraldic Creatures   163
22 Literary Beasts   166
23 Modern Monsters   171

Part Three: Man and Animals

24 The Fauna of the Mind   177
    Bibliography   183
    Index   217

ILLUSTRATIONS

List of Plates (between pages 106 and 107)

Seal in mermaid pose
Man-headed monster from Persepolis
Centaur from Parthenon
Modern phoenix : Niger advances towards the fire
Niger rises phoenix-like from the flames
Origin of the griffin : monster from Persepolis
Pair of griffins from Cashel Cathedral
Forehead of Dr Dove's unicorn (*photo: Dr F. W. Dove*)
Skull of unicorn showing horn buds fused (*photo: Dr F. W. Dove*)
Modern unicorn at 2 years old (*photo: Dr F. W. Dove*)
Origin of the manticora : the Indian tiger
The gnu, the origin of the Catoblepas
Dr Bernard Heuvelmans, 'the father of cryptozoology'
A triumph for cryptozoology : *Homo pongoides*, a surviving
Neanderthaler, photographed in ice
Reconstruction by Alika Watteau
The ultimate monster – the Boojum Snark surprises his victim

List of Figures

Evidence of man's aquatic past : hairs tracts on the human
fetus (from F. W. Jones, *Man's Place Among the
Mammals*)   52
Griffin from an Assyrian ivory, 8th century BC   72
Wandering Albatross   88
Kaffirs manipulating cattlehorns   98

xi

Manticora from bestiary   105
The salamander of medieval legend, from Gesner   130
The Barnacle Goose tree, from Gerard's *Herbal*   141
How the barnacle turned into a goose (from Ray
Lankester, *Diversions of a Naturalist*)   142
Barnaculised goose from Mycenean pot (from Schliemann)   144
The Scythian Lamb, from Claude Duret   152
Chinese 'vegetable lamb' described by Hans Sloane   152
Toy dog from South China   155
The original Barometz – the cotton plant   156

ACKNOWLEDGMENTS

In preparing this book I am grateful for the kind assistance of many people.

From the beginning Dr Bernard Heuvelmans has been a source of great encouragement, providing me with information, references and photographs. My wife and I have happy memories of our stay in the Dordogne where I had the opportunity of being one of the first to use the materials which he has gathered in his unique Centre de Cryptozoologie at Verlhiac. I only hope that the result is something like the book he expected.

I am also grateful to John Litton for recreating several unicorns in all their colourful detail; to Professor Carleton Wells and Professor Frank Brownlow for sending me materials from America; to Cecil Gould for advice about the background to some paintings, and for the photograph of his father, Rupert T. Gould; to Dr Maurice Burton and Dr W. F. Dove for supplying me with photographs of their experiments.

I am also grateful for their ever-ready assistance to the staffs of the libraries where I worked : Trinity College and University College in Dublin; the Chester Beatty Library and the National Library of Ireland; and the various library departments of the British Museum and British Library in London.

I would also like to thank Nick Austin for his interest in my cryptozoological researches, and his patience in waiting so long for this sequel to the Loch Ness monster to surface. Nor should I forget my wife Mary for making me finish this book, and my son Timothy for not tearing up *this* work in progress.

The author and publisher express their thanks for permission to use copyright material as follows : The Hogarth Press and W. W. Norton & Co. for *Sonnets to Orpheus* by Rainer Marie

Rilke, translated by J. B. Leishman; The Dolmen Press for 'The Last Monster' from *Poisoned Lands* by John Montague; and The Folio Society, London, for 'The Barnacle Goose' from *Riddles of the Book of Exeter* translated by Kevin Crossley-Holland.

PREFACE

I should like to make clear, at the very beginning of this book, just exactly what I mean by 'magic' in the title.

I do not mean the magic of the anthropologist, a form of pseudo-science used to claim control of events by witch-doctors and shamans. Though this is the common, technical meaning, it is too limited for my purposes.

By magic I mean the other realm of meaning which lies between man and nature, that world of mystery and enchantment that we first recognise as children in fairy tales. All the animals in *The Magic Zoo* are magical in this sense, though some of course have been used for magic in the anthropologist's sense as well. The unicorn, for instance, was thought to have special powers in its horn : in Europe these horns were used to detect poison, in China to restore the waning virility of aging mandarins.

Such creatures as the unicorn are not purposeless fantasies. They all have some special meaning. They are all cultural artifacts, as much so as the flint knife of the early shaman, or the space-probe of the modern scientist. They are 'man-made' in a very special sense.

The unicorn, as the Chinese knew, is in some ways as 'domesticated' an animal as the horse. Both have changed during their long association with man. We have varieties of unicorns, just as we have types of horses; all are adapted to the cultures that created them. But though the horse is found working in field, farm and circus, the unicorn is merely *'une chose à penser'*, an object to think about and think with, a kind of intellectual conversation piece. These animals are, in a cultural sense, mediators between man and nature; in the case of the unicorn, between man and the strange wild beasts of the Indian deserts, between man and defilement, between man and impotence.

The natural history of these magical creatures – and I emphasise

1

that this book is about their natural history only – is bound up with man's experience of animals, wild and domestic, through the centuries. In the first three chapters, which make up the first part of this book, I shall try and outline man's changing relationship with the animals around him. How the purely magical needs of the early shamans gave rise to an ever increasing scientific knowledge of animals. And more recently, with the realisation in the last century or so that there might well be a great deal of truth in ancient myths and legends, how the remaining mysteries of the animal world are being explored by the novel science of Cryptozoology – the Science of Unknown Animals. Behind the magical beasts of myth and the monsters of folklore there may well be hiding real creatures of flesh and blood.

In the second part of the book I have collected together some of the fabulous animals of Western man over a long period of time. No attempt can as yet be made to deal exhaustively with every magic beast: such a work would need to be an encyclopedia in ten or twelve large volumes. At a later date I plan to write about lesser-known monsters, and about the fabulous beasts of non-Western traditions. Detailed bibliographies for each creature are given at the end of the book for those who may want to explore further for themselves.

Though most of this book deals with the *natural history* of fabulous beasts, the last part takes a brief look at the magical dimensions of man's experience and knowledge of these animals. Art, literature and folklore have become almost the last refuges for these creatures. The mind of man has become the ultimate Serengeti, the imagination the last great game park where man's destructive urges cannot reach them.

> Somewhere on the ultimate scarp
> The last monster watches
> With hooded eyes,
> While tiny men trek urgently towards him
> Armed with strange supplies.

So writes the Irish poet John Montague, who warns that forlorn creature in advance:

Stay hidden wherever you are
The Abominable Scientist is after you.

Here then are a very few of the 'beasts of strange pattern and birds past belief' that can still be found at large in some imaginations.

PART ONE
Animals and Man

The people who expect the Natives to jump joyfully from the stone age to the age of motor cars, forget the toil and labour which our own fathers have had, to bring us all through history up to where we are.

Karen Blixen: 'Of Natives and History' in *Out of Africa*

CHAPTER ONE

ANIMALS AND MAN

The animals in the magic zoo are the beasts of myth, folklore and fantasy. They are creatures of man's imagination. Once they haunted the empty spaces of the world. But as the world grows smaller, and the last realms of mystery and romance are opened up for development, they have found their final refuge in the human imagination.

But these animals are not completely imaginary. They have their own natural history. Behind even the mermaid, the phoenix and the unicorn, there are real animals, and real biological facts.

Because man himself is both human and animal, his relationship over the centuries with the animals around him has been an ambiguous one; changing through history from awe to fear to contempt, until today, when the need to cherish and protect whatever remains of the natural world has brought a return of a sense of wonder at the mystery of creation.

At some as yet unknown date over three millions years ago, a group of hominids in central Africa ceased to be animals and mysteriously became men. This change would not have been sudden, but the result of a long, slow, evolutionary process lasting perhaps a million years or more.

Yet speech, fire, murder, all the trappings of civilisation, have not quite suppressed in any of us the biological urges and responses of our animal nature. Desmond Morris, the British ethologist, was able to score a great literary success a few years ago by setting down in plain prose what modern biologists had discovered about the make-up of modern man. His news surprised the ordinary reader.

But in fact we are far from being merely 'naked apes' as the title of his book suggested. Between us and the animals we have placed our culture, the accumulated actions and beliefs of centuries, creating a half-world in which wander (among other things) the

7

strange beasts of our imagination, which are at once animal and human, natural and artificial.

In the dark beginnings of our race there was no difference between men and beasts. The primal hordes from which we are descended lived in complete harmony with their environment on the open plains of Africa.

So too did our own earliest ancestors. The first real men, *Homo sapiens* and *Homo neanderthalensis*, were hunters, only a short way removed from the animals they killed and ate. Even today, the primitive groups that remain in the world show us how early man must have lived in unity with the natural world around him, as simply and completely as the animals themselves.

During the millennia since the Old Stone Age began, man's experience of the animal world has been varied and diverse. The men of the Stone Age held animals in awe – the evidence is in the paintings and engravings which still survive in the caves of Western Europe, such as those at Lascaux, Font-de-Gaume and Altimira. Then the animals were more than beasts: they were gods. And in some cultures, they have remained gods, or at the very least, very sacred beings.

With the coming of the Neolithic Revolution, as it has been called, man ceased to be nomadic and began to grow crops around permanent settlements. From these villages – the earliest of which have been found in the Balkans – the earliest cities – those of the Middle East, along the Nile and the Euphrates – eventually developed.

To the earliest farmers animals were of two kinds; those they reared and those they feared: the cattle, sheep and goats; the lions, wolves and vermin which preyed upon them and the farmers' crops.

In the *Epic of Gilgamesh*, a Babylonian poem of about 2000 BC, the contrast between the warrior hero and the wild man Enkidu describes this cultural passage. Enkidu runs with the wild animals, but having been tempted to have sexual intercourse with a harlot from the city, he finds that the beasts flee from his smell. He has lost his birthright, and has no other choice but to join Gilgamesh on his quest for the herb of immortality.

To city dwellers, such as those who first heard the poem, all animals were more or less alien. They fled from the smell of man.

8

As cities came to depend on trade and industry, and the farm became, in its turn, an alien realm, the role of animals changed again. No longer of prime social and economic importance, animals were reduced to entertainments. Wild beast shows and zoos had their origins in the temples and arenas of the ancient world. These were bloody spectacles. Thousands of creatures were slaughtered annually in the Colosseum of Imperial Rome. The keeping of animals for hunting in parks (originally called paradises) gave rise to menageries, and so to zoos. But the scientific interest in animals came only much later.

The growth of cities, and the long historic movement of people from the country into the city, has meant that fewer and fewer people have any direct experience of animals, either as wild beasts or domestic creatures.

Hunting, when it ceased to be for survival, became the only way that some men encountered animals. From the lion hunts carved on the monuments of Babylon to the paintings of George Stubbs and Edwin Landseer, animals and hunting have inspired marvellous works of art. So while he hunted some creatures – such as the auk, the American bison, and the whales – to extinction, man also celebrated their mystery and strange appeal.

To early man the animals had been super-beasts. To the Egyptians they were the great gods themselves; to the Greeks the bodily forms of the Olympians; to the Buddhists the possible incarnations of their ancestors. To some primitive tribes they were sacred totems, to others tabooed monsters. But always the sense of mystery persisted, and from this sense of mystery the animals of the magic zoo arose.

As the men of Europe explored the unknown world, they found the creatures of the New World, of the Orient and Australia and Africa even more mysterious. As we shall see, many of the animals in the magic zoo arose from tales of the bizarre creatures and monsters to be found in India or Africa. But as the real world came to be better known, the mysteries disappeared; the monsters dwindled down to ordinary creatures. As man's direct experience of animals waned, his exact knowledge of them expanded. The great gods dwindled into mere zoological specimens. For the shaman of early man had by this time changed during the intervening centuries into the modern scientist.

9

CHAPTER TWO

SHAMAN INTO SCIENTIST

On 8 November 1896, on a remote stretch of river in the Chaco
wilderness of Paraguay, then an almost unexplored area of South
America, a Cambridge scientist, John Graham Kerr, went fishing
with a local witch doctor, or shaman, named Waikthlaling-
mayalwa.

On reaching the fishing place the shaman broke up a large
water snail and threw it into the river as ground bait. Another
piece of snail he used to bait his hook. They fished for one and a
half hours, the scientist standing patiently beside his friend the
shaman in the river water up to his waist. Friends though they
were, the two men were separated by ten thousand years of history,
as Kerr realised.

> As I waited patiently I could not help passing back in imag-
> ination to the early times of man's communal evolution and
> realising that the witch doctor of those far-off days was the com-
> mon ancestor of our scientist, priest and physician. The witch
> doctor's authority rests primarily on his scientific knowledge of
> his environment – its rational phenomena and its fauna and
> flora – but with it goes the knowledge accredited to him of the
> supernatural and his consequent power over evil beings that
> cause misfortune and disease.

This knowledge of his environment is 'the science of the concrete'
described by Claude Lévi-Strauss in his book on 'the savage mind'.

Graham Kerr was in the Chaco hunting specimens of the primitive lung-fish *Leipidosiren*, which was to be used for genetic research in the laboratories of Cambridge university. The shaman
was hunting for his dinner. So when they did catch a lung-fish
they ate it for dinner : this sacrilegious treatment of a precious
specimen astonished Kerr's colleagues in Cambridge. The shaman

and the scientist, even when in pursuit of the same animal, see it differently.

This difference in world-view lies at the heart of many of the problems we will have in dealing with the natural history of the magic animals later in this book. To a shaman a species of bat may be a blood-sucking monster; to the scientist merely a curious disease-spreading creature. That the incidence of rabies might be a quite sufficient reason for the dread in which the bat was held by the natives might not strike the scientist with such great force.

It took mankind many millennia to move from the magical to the scientific view of the world. But we should remember that the scientific view is not superior, it is merely different. And that in any case, behind the mumbo-jumbo of the magic, there is often a stern practicality and an exact knowledge of the real world. Perhaps too there is also a touch of the magical in the scientific outlook as well – certainly the world of modern sub-nuclear physics is a very strange place, as strange as any enchanted forest in a fairy tale.

The story of man's scientific knowledge of the animal world begins in the caves of Western Europe some 25,000 years ago. The painted caves of France and Spain record man's passionate involvement with the natural world around him. His experience with animals (as we saw in the first chapter) led to a slow increase in man's actual knowledge of animals and their ways. The history of zoology moves from the ideas of the early shamans making hunting magic to a modern biologist pondering the strange mysteries of genetic variation, the key to evolution.

Histories of zoology usually begin however with Aristotle, who died in 322 BC. But we should recall that behind him lay millennia of accumulated practical experience of animals. This knowledge, sometimes exact, sometimes absurd, passed from mouth to mouth for centuries, even after Aristotle's death. Behind the absurdities (as they may seem to us) of the early naturalists, there is the real knowledge of hunters, farmers, gamekeepers and falconers.

What Aristotle first achieved was some sense of the pattern of natural life, though his thoughts on this did not go very far. But he was an original and patient observer of animals, whose work was admired by Charles Darwin and by William Beebe in our own day. He also dissected animals, which was new. But the great difficulty which he faced, and which affected zoology until the eighteenth century, was the lack of standard names for plants and animals. This led to confusion between familiar creatures and the weird wonders travellers met in India and Africa.

Aristotle had little time for mere travellers' tales, such as those which delighted Herodotus and Ctesias. The Roman writer Pliny the Elder was more credulous and provided posterity with a great variety of strange lore about animals, little of which was up to the scientific standard set by the Greeks. However it was from Pliny, rather than from Aristotle, that much of what passed for zoology in the Middle Ages derived. Much of what appears about monsters in the *Bestiary* comes from Pliny by way of later writers and commentators such as Solinus and St Isidore of Seville. This is the source of the classic monsters and imaginary animals dealt with in this book.

Originating in Alexandria about the fifth century after Christ as the purported work of Physiologus, or the Naturalist, the *Bestiary* in its several forms spread throughout the civilised world. Copies continued to be circulated until the eighteenth century; a manuscript of one bestiary, now in Trinity College, Dublin, was made in Iceland as late as 1724. The basic arrangement of the book remained unaltered during all this time. First an animal was described, and then its moral or theological significance was expounded. This gives the book a somewhat sententious air, which is well preserved in T. H. White's remarkable translation. For example, the phoenix (which had begun as a sacred bird of the Egyptians) became in the bestiary a symbol of the Resurrection and immortal life; the mermaid of the snares of lust; the unicorn of the virtue of chastity.

Much of what the Naturalist says about more ordinary animals was ancient folklore, ancient even in Cro-Magnon times, such as the legend that hedgehogs carry off apples on their spines. (Long disbelieved, this hardy legend has been supported by recent researches by Maurice Burton.) But a large amount of the material was derived from Isidore's *Etymologies*, a major source of lore in the Middle Ages. Behind him lie Pliny, Herodotus and Ctesias, names which will be very familiar by the end of this book.

The medieval bestiaries with their delightful pictures have been described in the past as indicative of the ignorance of Europe during the dark ages between the fall of Rome and the Renaissance.

Yet in reality they were efforts to place some sort of pattern over the bewildering variety of nature. Any pattern is better than none. The great fault of the compilers was to rely on authority rather than on experience. They would consult Isidore or Pliny about the birds, rather than look at the birds themselves.

Even so there were some individuals who did look at the birds, and at other animals, but their practical knowledge was not often recorded by the literati of the day. The Holy Roman Emperor Frederick II (1194–1250) did more than look at birds, in his case his beloved falcons and their prey, very carefully. He thought about them as well. The results of his lifetime's interest were incorporated in his magnificent book *The Art of Hunting with Birds*, a remarkable intellectual achievement for the thirteenth century. He dismissed the myth of the Barnacle Goose growing from barnacles after sending some of his men into northern Europe from Sicily to investigate the matter at first hand.

Another example of medieval exactness : there is a passage in the English poem *Sir Gawain and the Green Knight* which deals with a deer hunt. After the kill the butchering of the carcase is described in such exact technical detail that it has puzzled many translators, who have been forced to brush up their biology and anatomy in order to deal with the passage. So much for medieval ignorance.

Hunters knew things unknown to the savants of the day. So too did painters. In a sketchbook of about 1400 (now in the Pepys Library, Cambridge) there is a page of birds, all drawn from life it would seem. And in the Sherborne Missal, the small birds among the marginal decorations are models of exact observation. But as Kenneth Clark observes, these little images, fresh and delightful though they seem, turn out to be largely derivative from earlier works. And yet at some point somebody did observe the birds. So medieval men were not quite so removed from the real world for all that the strange things in the bestiaries might suggest they were. Though their preference for the wild fancies of Sir John Mandeville over the plain facts of Marco Polo does suggest a taste for the fantastic and bizarre. But such a taste is far from dead.

So it was with the shaman and the scientist : the expertise of John Graham Kerr was of a different order to that of his Indian friend. But what the shaman knew was real knowledge. As Claude Lévi-Strauss points out, the 'science of the concrete' is more widespread among 'primitive' peoples than we might suppose. This long tradition of exact knowledge among ordinary people (hunters, fishermen, farmers) is in sharp contrast with the systematised ignorance of the literate. Monsters are not the product of ignorance, but of refined civilisation.

So we should not be surprised to find monsters among the works of the very learned. The first great zoologist of the Renaissance was Conrad Gesner, whose *Historia Animalium* (1551) was to remain a standard work for some centuries. He was rivalled in his wide-ranging knowledge by Ulisse Aldrovandi, writing after 1599. These, and other writers such as Turner, Belon and Rondelet, will often appear in later chapters, for monsters of all kinds and shapes wander quite casually in and out of their pages.

The great natural history encyclopedias of the Renaissance gathered up the traditions of the past, good and bad. Only slowly did scientists begin to distinguish which was which. Sir Thomas Browne's magisterial essay in scepticism, *Vulgar Errors*, published in 1646, and the founding of the Royal Society in London in 1660 represent a shift away from a dependence on authority towards accepting only the evidence of one's own eyes and experiments. So experimental science grew up and zoology came to rely on exact observations only. In Gilbert White's *Natural History of Selbourne* the reader senses a new discipline coming into existence.

Observations from travellers in the newly discovered countries overseas increased, as did the knowledge of animals at home. The bewildering variety of nature presented an insoluble problem. Early writers, such as Pliny, drawing on several sources, often gave several descriptions of the same animals without realising that they were the same. Hence the existence in the *Bestiary* of both the monoceros and the unicorn, both derived from accounts of the one-horned Indian rhinoceros.

It was not until the publication of *The System of Nature* by the Swedish botanist Carl Linné in 1758 that the biological sciences were placed on their modern formal basis. With his original system of two-part Latin names (now three-part) for all animals and plants, Linné provided a scheme by which there could be no errors about the animal under discussion once it had been scientifically described.

There was no room for monsters in this system. Even so Linné included under *Homo sapiens* at the head of his list *Homo sylvestris*, the Wild Man of the Woods, who had haunted the medieval imagination. He was soon got rid of, only to re-emerge in a new form a little later as the modern monster we know as the Yeti.

Zoology expanded rapidly by extending its descriptions of animals and plants, and in theories such as Darwin's and Mendel's, which tried to explain how the great diversity of nature originated and propagated itself. The study by geologists of the fossil record of extinct animals extended our knowledge of the world slowly backwards to the dimmest reaches of the past.

But as zoology became established as the science of the nineteenth century, it became hardened in its attitudes to new ideas, and to new animals. The attitudes of the French anatomist and paleontologist Baron Georges Cuvier provides an example of this. Cuvier was a brilliant anatomist whose work on fossils earned him the popular title of 'father of palaeontology'. His effort to explain the fossil record through a series of catastrophes was soon exploded by the gradualist idea of evolution. He also claimed that 'fossil man does not exist' : a couple of decades later he was found to be wrong. Though his ideas were exploded, his attitude to travellers' tales of mysterious animals became the common one. Though many of the strange creatures reported sounded similar to some known only as fossils, he said the reports were untrue. Such creatures could not have survived through previous catastrophes. Thus the sort of creatures which this book deals with were dismissed as of no interest to the scientist. Such an absurdity as the phoenix could have no real natural history. Cuvier also claimed that a cloven-hoofed creature such as the unicorn was supposed to be could not have a horn growing on its forehead because the divided skull bones would provide no support. He was wrong about the phoenix, and he was wrong about the unicorn. They do have a natural history.

It was to take a further century during which both reports of mysterious monsters and evidence about fabulous beasts increased, before the errors of this one man were admitted by some zoologists more open-minded than others. These were the men who contributed to the growth of a new alternative science. This is cryptozoology, the science of unknown animals. Scientists had turned again to the myths of the shaman.

CHAPTER THREE

THE SCIENCE OF UNKNOWN ANIMALS

With zoology established as the leading science of the nineteenth century, it was inevitable that a few individuals should appear holding notions going against the grain of the established views.

Linné had classified. Cuvier had categorised. To them creation seemed to be static, species fixed, unchanged and unchangeable, except by the intervention of a universal catastrophe. Though the theory of evolution as expounded by Darwin and others was to upset these tidy notions, one idea espoused by Cuvier, that all the great animals had already been discovered, died hard.

His work *The Animal Kingdom* surveyed in 1817 the extent of contemporary zoological knowledge : he described in all some 386 mammals. Seventy years later Leunis and Ludwig in 1886 listed some 2,300. By 1939, when Arndt compiled his listings, the number was 13,000. And that was only for mammals. Cuvier had known some 765 birds; Arndt listed 28,000.

During that century the world continued to be explored. New animals, some of them quite large, continued to be discovered, on average some 5,000 species a year. Many of these animals were, of course, quite small, but there were also very large creatures such as the Panda from China, and the Okapi and the Mountain Gorilla from the Congo. Many other 'new' animals were found to be living fossils, that is creatures thought to have been extinct for many millions of years. The most famous 'living fossil' was perhaps the Coelacanth caught off South Africa in 1938, which was thought to have been dead for seventy million years. Later research established that they were common enough around the Comoro Islands in the Indian Ocean.

These discoveries persuaded some zoologists that rumours and native legends of monsters and weird beasts should be taken seriously. Slowly since 1817, the science of unknown animals has taken shape. The term cryptozoology is much newer. The first use of the term in print was in 1959 by Lucien Blancou in *Géographie cynégétique du Monde*, in which Bernard Heuvelmans was described as 'Master of Cryptozoology'. Heuvelmans, however, had been using the term in his private correspondence for some time before that. By 1968 the term was well enough known for Brian Aldiss to call one of his science fiction novels *Cryptozooic*! A new science had come of age.

In 1818, the year after Cuvier had set bounds to the march of zoology, two long articles on the sea-serpent and on the kraken were published in the Edinburgh review *Blackwood's Magazine*. Their author, who signed himself 'W', reviews the history of both these creatures in some detail. Perhaps there was nothing new in his reports (many of which came from the celebrated Bishop of Bergen, Erik Pontopiddan), but these articles provided the bulk of the material for the anonymous author of an article on 'The Natural History of Apocryphal Beasts' which was published in Paris in the *Revue Britannique* in 1835. The author wrote:

A foreign scholar is reported to be concerning himself with a natural history of apocryphal animals. If the author concientiously justifies his title, he will produce a curious book. We ourselves had the idea for a similar work; and we remember that every piece of new research opened up a whole new world. It was not only from such diverse sources as popular superstition, the poetic inventions of ancient myths and medieval legends, symbolic paintings or heraldry that we claimed to take our evidence. Natural history revealed to us the true origins of what we had once thought fabulous because of the complete extinction of their race; but a learned anatomist [Cuvier] knew how to exhume and reconstruct their real skeletons, thus demonstrating to tradition and to science what the imagination alone seemed to have created.

He went on to point out that the universal legend of the dragon, which had once been thought to be nonsense, had been proved to have some basis in reality by the discovery of the Pterodactyl, as the strange flying dragon of antiquity had been called by Cuvier. The discovery of the Mosasaurus (now the Ichthyosaurus) had shown that there really had once been such giant reptiles of legend

18

such as that in the Rhone, the Tarasque, which St Martha defeated.

He then pointed out that science proper resisted the idea that there was a connection between these fossil monsters and the monsters of myth and legend. It would be necessary for the student of aprocryphal animals to follow a proper scientific method in his researches, classifying according to type and origin the various creatures of myth and legend.

He admitted that this was a large programme, but it is what cryptozoologists have been trying to do ever since. Not all at once, naturally enough, but slowly piece by piece, the evidence has been built up. Evidence not only about the creatures of Western myth which he refers to, but also about the 'unknown' animals which still lurk undetected in the remoter areas of the world.

The foreign scholar he refers to may well have been the German writer H. M. Malten, who published a long article which he styled 'a preliminary discussion' about the existence of such apocryphal animals. Though one of the earliest attempts at cryptozoological research, this essay seems to have been of little influence, as the centres of zoological research were elsewhere at that time, notably in England.

There Richard Owen was laying the foundations for the study of the dinosaurs during the 1840s. Early reconstructions of such creatures as the pterodactyl and the mosasaurus had emphasised their dragon-like appearance. Perhaps in the distant past they might have been the origin of the legends of living dragons. But Owen did not have much sympathy with the idea of surviving dinosaurs. Others were less cautious.

Hugh Falconer, a geologist who had made many important discoveries in the Siwalik Hills in the foothills of the Himalayas, returned to England in 1843. Among the creatures quite new to science which he had discovered in India was a huge turtle-like creature *Colossochelys Atlas*. In lectures during 1844 in London and York, he drew attention to the Hindu myth of a giant turtle which supports an elephant on its back on which the earth rests. Did the fossil creature he had discovered, which was about fifteen feet long, survive into historical times he asked, and so provide the basis for the ancient myth?

This was a daring conjecture, now made more reasonable by

sightings of a huge creature called 'The Father of All Turtles' in Sumatran legend. There have, in fact, been four sightings in recent years in different oceans.

Four years later, in 1848, Charles Hamilton Smith pursued these ideas into other areas, writing about Amerindian legends of the survival of the mammoth, their legend of the 'naked bear', and the East Indian Elephant Horse. Smith was also a keen supporter of the theory that the unicorn was a real animal, and that it existed in the unexplored parts of Africa.

1848 was the year that HMS *Daedalus* sighted a sea-serpent off the coast of West Africa. The heated controversy that followed in England led to an increase of reports of that particular 'unknown'. Indeed all through the last century the existence or non-existence of the sea-serpent was the most hotly debated subject of crypto-zoological interest.

However it was the natural history of mythical animals proper which concerned the German biologist Karl Müller in 1858 when he devoted several numbers of *Die Natur*, the scientific journal he edited at Halle, to the subject. To date this had been the longest essay on the topic. But once again, as with Malten's earlier work, it seems to be little known in English-speaking countries or in France.

One book which was of enormous influence was *The Romance of Natural History* which Philip Henry Gosse published in 1860. Thanks to his son's memoir of their relationship, Gosse today is something more than merely a shadowy Victorian savant. His peculiar genius still lives in the bitter pages of *Father and Son*. A brilliant marine biologist who did much to popularise aquariums, Gosse was drawn to mysteries. The last two chapters of this book deal with 'the Unknown' and 'the Great Unknown' – this was the sea-serpent. Gosse was optimistic about discovering new animals. Among the rumours of unknown animals he mentions were 'a great anthropoid ape' in South America, and reports of 'a unicorn' in Africa. Other parts of the world, such as the East Indies, China, Madagascar and Central Africa, also held great promise of new discoveries. But the depths of the sea were the most promising, with reports of the kraken and the sea-serpent. In the second series of the book, Gosse reviewed the evidence for the mermaid, expressing his hope that it too might one day be found.

Gosse was interested in new zoological discoveries; the other aspect of cryptozoology, the explanation of ancient myths and legends, was taken up by the pioneering ethnologist Edward Burnet Tylor in a book published in 1865 dealing with the development of civilisation. Early myths, he suggested, seemed to contain references to the memory of the huge animals of the Quarternary Period. The survival of the mammoth or elephant in America (a mystery which had interested Alexander von Humboldt), the giant turtle of Hindu myth, and those Brazilian apes were the examples he adduced.

Another pioneer was the Irish geologist Valentine Ball, who had spent many years in India before returning to Dublin to take charge of the new National Museum. In his book *Jungle Life in India* (1882) Ball documented the first modern reports of children reared by wolves. He was impressed after his years in India that the many commentators on classical writers such as Herodotus and Ctesias themselves knew very little about the ancient Orient. He showed that much of what had been thought of as nonsense in classical accounts of India was actually based on fact.

In 1892 the sea-serpent surfaced again. The Dutch biologist Dr A. C. Oudemans published in that year his great book on the creature, which made an heroic effort to be definitive. His work has been the departure point for all subsequent research on the sea-serpent and its kin.

Oudemans was of great influence. In Sweden, Dr Peter Ollsson investigated reports of a monster in Lake Stosjö and his report was the first to put the search for fresh-water monsters on a scientific basis. Oudemans was widely read; Ollsson's small pamphlet lingered unread and gathered dust on the shelves of the institutions he had sent it to. Certainly I believe that I was the first person in a long time to read the copy in the Natural History Museum in London.

The turn of the century saw the controversy about the existence of the giant sloth in Patagonia. Rumours about it were reinforced by the discovery of an amazingly fresh skin on a farm at Last Hope Inlet. But a British expedition to find it turned back even before it reached there, saying it was all a hoax. The mystery remains unsolved.

Then after World War I came the strange affair of the Congo

Brontosaurus, when reports of a living dinosaur in Katanga excited the world press for a few months, and brought into focus reports of other unknown animals from Africa. Writing in 1920 A. F. M. Webster wondered if there might not still be some undiscovered animals. This was the theme of many articles at this time, and the discovery of the gorilla, the okapi and the panda seemed to support the contention. It did not impress many zoologists.

But in 1924 Grafton Elliot Smith returned to the mystery of the elephant in America, producing as his main piece of evidence a carving from a pillar at Copan in Mexico which seemed to show an Indian elephant and his mahout. Like Tylor before him, Elliot Smith saw the question of these mythical creatures as central to the problem of how early cultures originated and spread.

A key figure of this period who also deserves to be mentioned was Charles Fort, the author of four books dealing with mysterious events and peoples. During many years of diligent research, much of it in the reading room of the British Museum and the New York Public Library, Fort amassed an immense number of accounts of bizarre and anomalous phenomena which were enough to shake the scepticism of many of his readers since then.

Another student of unsolved mysteries was Rupert Thomas Gould, a retired British naval officer. His books *Oddities* and *Enigmas* were models of their kind. In *The Case for the Sea-Serpent*, he moved on to a zoological mystery, and he followed that with the first book on the Loch Ness Monster in 1934.

The creature in that isolated Scottish loch was the most notorious creature of its day. Other 'monsters' were overshadowed by its fame. Captain William Hitchens, however, drew attention to several African creatures such as the Nandi Bear of Kenya, and a whole range of strange water monsters in other parts of Africa.

It was from Africa too that the young Ivan T. Sanderson, the leader of the Percy Sladen Expedition to the Cameroons in 1932, reported an encounter with a strange flying creature which sounded suspiciously like a living pterodactyl. (His companion on that trip Gerald Russell did not see it, and ever since has kept a discreet silence about the matter.) In later years Sanderson was to pursue lake monsters and other unknown animals in many parts of the world. He was to have a part in a great cryptozoological discovery in 1969, but his last years were clouded by bizarre behaviour, which was partly explained by his death in 1973 from a brain tumour.

Other African mysteries concerned F. B. Macrae and Frank W. Lane. Lane's book *Nature Parade* brought together a great deal of scattered material, and was in its way as important a landmark as Gosse's book had been. Its publication represented a major step in the gathering of cryptozoological material.

Important also were the various zoology books of Willy Ley, a German writer exiled in America. Ley was a trained scientist who had written a biography of Conrad Gesner. He had been a founder member with Werner von Braun of the Berlin Rocket Society, but when the Nazis came to power and von Braun went to work for the army on the V-1 and V-2, Willy Ley could not follow him. America was a safe haven where he was able to pursue his researches unhampered by politics. His researches into the history of the dragon and the unicorn were important contributions.

These writers, and another German Ingo Krumbiegal, were the immediate inspiration for the work of the Belgian zoologist Bernard Heuvelmans, who has been called 'the father of cryptozoology'. From early childhood he had been enthralled by animals, but especially by the strange and the mysterious. His university thesis classified the hitherto unclassifiable dentition of the Ardvaark. During the war he wrote articles which entailed extensive research into the history of science. This led him on to other problems. In 1955, after four years of research, he published the French edition of his book *On the Track of Unknown Animals*, which has since been translated all over the world. This book placed cryptozoology on a permanent basis at last. His subsequent books have dealt with the involved histories of the giant squid, the sea-serpent and his amazing discovery (along with Ivan Sanderson) of a surviving specimen of the long vanished Neanderthal man.

Currently Dr Heuvelmans works on a remote estate at Verlhiac in the Dordogne near Lascaux where he has established a *Centre de Cryptozoologie*, the first in the world, dedicated to the pursuit of unknown animals of all kinds. Here he hopes to gather all the materials relevant to the subject and provide a base from which others may also work.

Other modern students who should not be forgotten are Odell Shepard, Richard Carrington, Maurice Burton and David Attenborough in Britain; and Tom Slick and Peter Byrne in America.

In recent years the expeditions to look for the Abominable Snowman, the Loch Ness Monster and Bigfoot have attracted a great deal of publicity, bringing cryptozoology very much into the public eye at last.

This book, drawing on the methods of cryptozoology, hopes to go some way to establishing the sort of categories suggested by the anonymous writer in the *Revue Britannique* in 1835. By applying the ideas of this new science, I hope to reveal something of the natural history of fabulous animals, and also something of how man has seen them over the centuries.

PART TWO
The Magic Zoo

But here were animals no man had ever seen before; beasts fierce beyond all dreams of ferocity; serpents cunning beyond all comprehension of guile; hybrids strange beyond all nightmares of fantasy.

Charles G. Finney: *The Circus of Dr Lao*

CHAPTER FOUR

THE BEAST OF LASCAUX

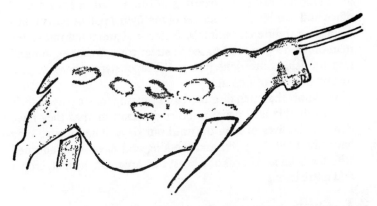

On 12 September 1940, five boys out hunting with their guns and a dog stumbled over the entrance to a cave at Lascaux in southern France. The walls of the caverns they entered that day were decorated with a wonderful series of prehistoric paintings. They had discovered 'the Sistine of the Old Stone Age'.

Among the familiar ponies, horses, stags and bulls that spread over the walls of the main oval hall, there was one mysterious creature, an apocalyptic beast, which has been nicknamed the 'Unicorn of Lascaux'.

As can be seen in the line drawing above, the animal is not actually a unicorn, as it has two long horns rising from its forehead. But it is certainly just as strange, and it has puzzled palaeontologists and commentators ever since its discovery. As Sigfried Giedion writes, 'this creature, its gravid body marked with ring-shaped symbols, imbue[s] the domed hall of Lascaux with an awesomeness which never fails to impress even the most casual sightseer'.

The painting shows a large heavy animal, gravid with young, having thick legs and spotted shanks. The head is also large, with two long, antelope-like horns. 'Some sort of ox, or perhaps a rhinoceros, as the very short tail may indicate,' wrote Alan Brodrick in 1949, 'such a composite monster is not the only one in Palaeolithic art, but it is the most spectacular.' As he observes 'the stumpy legs are stiff and artificial looking'.

It is possible that the painting does not represent an imaginary beast but rather a wizard or sorcerer clad in his robes of office and combining in one set of vestments potent parts taken from several different animals. In fact a shaman not unlike the man-orchestra one used to see at street corners shaking himself into musical contortions. Or is this apocalyptic beast a protecting daemon of Lascaux?

We know that men disguised and wearing masks played their part in the life and ritual of Aurugnancian man as they have done in the lives of men up until our days. The sorcerer may have preceded the priest and the king and have stood adorned with the head and horns of a beast that are mask, helmet, crown and mitre in one.

Actually it now seems, after the survey of prehistoric art in Western Europe published by André Leroi-Gourhan, that this picture is unique.

Imaginary beasts are very rare in prehistoric art, as are the representations of human beings. (Lascaux is one of the few caves in which a human figure is drawn.) What special magic can have been intended by this monster? We do not know.

Already in the very dawn of human history and human art, a fabulous animal shuffles onto the scene. In the case of Lascaux, we can only guess at the origin and meaning of the creature. With other fabulous animals of later periods we will be luckier. But already the special magic and appeal to the imagination of these creatures is apparent. These are not ordinary animals : these are magic beasts.

These early painters were able to portray real animals with amazing grace and accuracy. When they represent the fantastic or the composite it is not from an inability to represent reality. Thus the few instances of 'magic beasts' are all the more important for their rarity. Some are quasi-human, the animal in man already recognised and externalised. Others, such as the beast at Lascaux, are real monsters. These distinctions, made here in the dawn of history, are still with us.

Already in these early days of human history we can see in the art and ideas of Western Europe themes and images which are still extant today in the mythologies of modern man. The magic of animals, the magic beast, the beast in man : all of these ideas will appear in later forms.

These creations are the first of a long series in art : the apocalyptic beast connects with the strange beasts described later in this book; the sorcerers from Lascaux and Trois Frères become in time the Minotaur of Greek myth, and the beast-men of later myth and legend.

CHAPTER FIVE

THE MINOTAUR

The Minotaur was a fabulous beast of Greek mythology, the off-spring of a Cretan queen by a great white bull that had come up out of the sea. This hideous and unnatural monster was imprisoned by King Minos at the heart of the labyrinth, a maze specially built for him by the legendary craftsman Daedalus.

This man-beast, once famous in classical times, and known even to medieval geographers, was eventually dismissed as having no basis in fact. The monster was a fantasy of the lively Greek imagination. But the work of modern archaeologists on the island of Crete has cast a bright revealing light on the real origins and meaning of the Minotaur.

The story of the Minotaur has come down to us only in paraphrases from late classical times, and these may bear little relationship to the original myth. The various strands of the story have been patched together by H. J. Rose and Robert Graves.

King Minos was a great king in Crete in 'the olden days' (possibly about 1500 BC); just and powerful by general repute, he was a tyrant according to the Athenians from whom he exacted a heavy tribute of human lives.

Minos was the son of Europa by Zeus, who, in the shape of a white bull, carried her away to Crete. There the child was born. Minos became king of the island in due course and married Pasiphae. In answer to the prayers of Minos, the sea-god Poseidon sent up from the sea a great white bull. But this creature was so beautiful that Minos could not bring himself to sacrifice it as custom required. Instead he kept it for his own stud.

In revenge, Poseidon inflamed his wife Pasiphae with an unnatural lust for the bull. She assuaged her feelings with the help of the craftsman Daedalus. He built her a wooden cow covered with hide into which she could climb, placing her legs down the back legs of the cow. And so she was mounted by the bull. She gave birth in due course to a bull-headed child, which was called the Minotaur, or the Bull of Minos. From shame it was immured in the heart of the labyrinth.

Minos, who had conquered the Athenians, extracted from them an annual tribute of seven youths and seven virgins, who were shut up in the labyrinth to be devoured by the Minotaur. However, one year, the Athenian hero, Theseus, with the help of Ariadne, a daughter of Minos, killed the Minotaur. Following the thread that Ariadne had given him, he was able to make his way back out of the maze. He sailed away from Crete with Ariadne, but, pursued by Minos, he left her behind on Naxos.

The exact historical origins of this myth are now lost, but some of the sources from which it was built up can now be guessed at. Though it was destroyed about 1400 BC the ruins of the great palace of the Cretan kings at Knossos would have been impressive enough in their complexity to suggest a maze of a very elaborate kind to the invading Greeks who destroyed the civilisation of Minoan Crete. Of Minos himself we have no historical evidence, but he may well have been a real person. The name labyrinth comes from the word *labrys*, the double-headed axe which was the Cretan symbol of royalty.

Bulls played an important part in the culture of Crete. On the walls of the palace at Knossos are frescoes showing young men and girls performing with bulls in some elaborate games.

With this historical basis, other elements – such as the natural fear of freaks and monstrous births, and the perverted cravings which some individuals evince for sexual intercourse with animals – have become confused.

Yet at the heart of this historical labyrinth is the same bull man first seen on the cave walls at Les Trois Frères. Some primitive ritual dance of appeasement to the natural forces of power and fertility which the white bull represented has, in the course of time, come to stand for something different. A little of the genuine fear of the Minotaur which those young Athenians must have felt can be seen in the painting by G. F. Watts (now in the Tate Gallery, London), which shows the Minotaur gazing out to sea towards the approaching Greek ships, a small bird crushed under his fist. A very real fear communicates itself from this painting done some fifteen hundred years after the murder of the Minotaur by Theseus at the heart of the maze.

Sir George James Frazer suggested in *The Golden Bough* that these sacrificial victims might have been burned alive in a bronze image of a bull-headed man. But though there are parallels to be found for such a practice in Carthage and the Near East, there seems to be no archaeological evidence on Crete for this flight of fancy.

It was only at the end of the nineteenth century, when the British archaeologist Sir Arthur Evans began to excavate the ruins of the palace at Crete, that the historical background to the myth became known.

Evans revealed the astonishing riches of the Minoan civilisation where bare-breasted ladies of the court walked serenely among the plants and flowers of long vanished gardens. On the walls of the palace were frescoes of bull-baiting and fierce griffins and other monsters.

In Crete, archaeology has revealed some of the elements from which the myth of the Minotaur was created. Other monsters seemed equally strange to many in the past. But it may be that what seems strange and puzzling to us now may be revealed by patient research to have less mythical origins than is often thought. As Jorge Luis Borges, a diligent student of such mysteries, observes, 'most likely the Greek fable of the minotaur is a late clumsy version of far older myths, the shadow of other dreams still more full of horror'.

The fragmentary story of the Minotaur can be reconstructed

in many ways. Mary Renault, the distinguished novelist, and Geoffrey Bibby, the well-known archaeologist, have each given us views of the monster and the end of Minoan Crete from the poetic and the scientific points of view.

Both suggest that the Minotaur was not an animal, or a mythical monster, but a priest wearing a bull-mask. This modern idea is supported by a late Greek bead-seal of Theseus killing the Minotaur, in which the legendary monster is clearly human. But the novelist and the scholar see the Minotaur in different lights. This should warn us that we should be careful in our use of such meagre evidence as we have from ancient sources while on the track of mythical monsters. We shall have to try hard to keep the poetry and the science apart, though this is not always possible when tracing the history of these creatures. Especially when they are as seductively alluring as the mermaid.

CHAPTER SIX

THE MERMAID

With the mermaid we move on to another kind of imaginary creature, again one which is partly human, partly animal. These creatures mediate between man and the animal world, between nature and culture. And as is often the case, man's cultural ideas affect the facts of nature, for the mermaid may in the end be a far more mysterious creature than we could have guessed.

While the early history of mermaids and mermen can be traced back into the earliest known civilisations, later reports of mermaids, some of them quite recent, often present a problem. Are these creatures figments of the imagination, or reports of seals and manatees as is often said? Or are they really some quite different creature, as yet unknown to science?

The first creature we can call a merman was Ea (or Oannes in Greek), a god of the Accadians who was taken over by the Babylonians. His worship would have originated about 5000 BC. An account of him by Berossus, a Chaldean priest of Bel in Babylon, has been preserved by Alexander Polyhistor:

In the first year [of Babylon] there made its appearance from a part of the Erythrean Sea, an animal with reason, who was called Oannes. The whole body of the animal was like a fish; and had under a fish's head another head, and also feet below, similar to those of a man, subjoined to the fish's tail. His voice, too, and language were articulate and human; and a representation of him is preserved to this day. This Being in the day-time used to converse with men; but took no food at that season; and he gave them an insight into letters and sciences, and every kind of art.

Oannes brought civilisation to Babylon, for 'he instructed them in everything which could tend to soften manners and humanise mankind'. At sunset Oannes would plunge back into the sea and stay in the depths all night.

Early pictures of Oannes show the god in human form with a sort of fish-head cap and cape falling to his feet. This was perhaps the actual costume worn by the priest of his cult. Later, however, in the reliefs at Khorsabad, he is shown as a true merman with a fish's tail. In this shape he was identified both as Ea, the Babylonian god of the waters, and with Dagon, a god of the Philistines mentioned in the Bible, to whom Milton refers: 'Dagon his name, sea-monk, upward man and downward fish...'

For the origins of the mermaid, we must look elsewhere in the Middle East. Lucian tells us that among the deities of Syria was Dercerto. 'Of this Dercerto likewise I saw in Phoenicia a drawing in which she is represented in a curious form; for in the upper half she is a woman, but from the waist to the lower extremities runs the tail of a fish.' She was also known as Atargatis by the Syrians, and she had a temple at Hierapolis in Syria which was destroyed in 55 BC by the Romans. No one was allowed to fish without a licence from the goddess, and fish ponds sacred to her were known in Cyprus and Crete.

Fish-tailed deities and water-gods are known in many mythologies: from India, China, Japan and Greece. The first incarnation of Vishnu was a man-fish. And in Chinese folklore there are the dragon-kings and their wives. In Greek mythology there were the Tritons. The original Triton was a son of Poseidon, the god of the sea, and a nereid named Amphitrite. But eventually a clan of fish-tailed deities were all loosely called 'the tritons'.

At Tanagra, which is on a river in Boiotia, the Greek geographer Pausanias, writing in the second century AD, described the capture of a triton in the local river. The legend need not concern us, but the description of the creature, which was still preserved in the temple of Dionysos, is very curious. Pausanias had seen another triton among the sights of Rome, 'but it was smaller than the triton at Tanagra which would really make you gasp'.

Tritons are certainly a sight; the hair on their heads is like the frogs in stagnant water : not only in its froggy colour, but so sleek you could never separate one hair from the next : and the rest of their bodies are bristling with very fine scales like a rough-skinned shark. They have gills behind the ears and a human nose, but a very big mouth and the teeth of a wild beast. I thought the eyes were greenish-grey, and they have their hands and fingers and fingernails crusted like sea-shells. From the breast and belly down they have a dolphin's tail instead of feet.

There is no doubt about the existence at Tanagra of this pickled merman. A century later it was investigated by Damostratos, who was an internationally known expert on sea monsters according to Aelian, and was the author of a book on the subject which is now lost.

According to Damostratos the creature's head was corrupt and unrecognisable. It had rough hard scales. When he burnt a piece of the skin it smelled very nasty, but not fishy in any way. Alas, as Peter Levi comments, 'this admirable and primitive creature is unfortunately not as yet known to marine scientists'. John Timbs records that in 1774 a 'mermaid' from the Grecian Archipelago was exhibited in London : it was made from the skin of an angle-shark. In the intervening centuries Greek fishermen had not lost their talent for tritons it seems.

If today we wonder why people in the past should have believed in such things as mermaids, it was because of such relics as this triton at Tanagra : they were convinced by the evidence of their own eyes.

What was the creature? At this date we cannot be certain, but from the description (and later events) it may well have been a monster compounded from a dolphin and a skate or shark – the wide mouth and gills certainly suggest a shark. But then again, it might well have been an unknown marine animal.

The sirens, as we shall see in the next chapter, are very different creatures from mermaids, though the distinction is often lost in English and French, for originally they were conceived as birds with women's heads. But in time they became proper mermaids. The picture of the siren in the *Bestiary* shows a creature with both bird's legs and a fish tail. For medieval writers the siren represented the fatal lure of the flesh which would draw good men to their doom.

But for Pliny, writing in the first fifty years of the Christian era, the tritons were as real as the monster at Tanagra. His account of them, in the rich language of his Jacobean translator Philemon Holland, makes curious reading.

> And as for the Meremaids called Nereides, it is no fabulous tale that goeth of them : for looke how painters draw them, so they are indeed : only their bodie is rough and scaled all over, even in those parts wherein they resemble women. For such a Meremaide was seene and beheld plainly upon the same coast near the shore : and the inhabitants dwelling near, heard it a farre off when it was a dying, to make piteous mone, crying and chattering very heavily. Moreover, a lieutenant or governour under Augustus Caesar in Gaul, advertised him by his letters, That many of these Nereides or Meremaides were seen cast upon the sands, and lying dead.

Pliny also reports that in the reign of Tiberius a delegation arrived in Rome from Ulyssipon to report that 'a certain sea goblin called Triton' was found along the coast there. Some Roman knights reported that on the Spanish coast near Gades, they saw a merman which would climb partly aboard their boat at night. At the same period on an island near the province of Lyons, three hundred sea monsters were washed up, among them 'many mere-maids'.

And all across Europe 'many meremaids' are still to be found, carved on stones as in Pictish Scotland, or in the cathedrals of England and France. These mermaids belong more to the history of art rather than to natural history. What interests us here are not representations, but reports of mermaids.

The *Annals of the Four Masters*, compiled in Ireland between 1632 and 1636, records that in 'the Age of Christ 558':

> In this year was taken the Mermaid, i.e. Liban, the daughter of Eochaidh, son of Muireadh, on the strand Ollarbha, in the net of Beoan, son of Inli, the fisherman of Comhgall of Beann-chair.

Liban was the heroine of a romance, and her legend lingered on about Lough Neagh in Ulster until the last century.

In 887 another Irish mermaid was recorded, sandwiched between the holding of a famous fair and the death of a chieftain:

> A mermaid was cast ashore by the sea in the country of Alba. One hundred and ninety-five feet was her length; eighteen feet was the length of her hand, seven feet also was the length of her nose; she was whiter than the swan all over.

The *Annals of Ulster*, however, record this event as well, but under the year 890. And also for the year AD 1118: 'Another wonderful tale from Ireland: a mermaid was taken by the fisher-men of the Weir of Lisarglin in Ossory, and another at Port-Lairge.' One wonders if the white mermaid might not have been a white or albino whale.

Other curious reports of mermaids abound. One, from the *Speculum Regale*, is quoted by Sabine Baring-Gould. A monster was seen near the coast of Greenland, in all respects like a human down to the waist and below that like a fish. 'The hands seem to people to be long, and the fingers not be parted, but united by a web like that on the feet of water-birds.' She had, too, 'a very horrible face, with broad brow and piercing eyes, a wide mouth and a double chin'. This unlovely creature may well have been a large seal or walrus.

But what are we to make of the quite detailed account of the merman captured at Orford in Suffolk on the east coast of England by some net-fishermen in 1197. The original account was recorded by Ralph of Coggeshall in the *Chronicum Anglicanum*, which was retailed by Raphael Holinshed in his *Chronicles* published in 1697. It is a very strange story.

In this first year of King John's reigne, at Oreford in Suffolk, as Fabian saith (although I think he be deceived in the time) a fish was taken by fishers in their nets as they were at sea, resembling in shape a wild or savage man whom they presented unto Sir Bartholomew de Glanville, Knight; that had then the keeping of the Cassel of Oreford in Suffolke. He was naked, and all his lims and members resembling the right proportion of a man; he had hairies also in the usual parts of his bodie, albeit that the crowne of his head was bald, his beard was long and rugged and his breast hairie. The knight caused him to be kept certaine daies and nights from the sea, meat set afore him he greedilie devoured and did eat fish both raw and sod. Those that were raw he pressed in his hand till he had thrust out all the moisture and so did eat them. He would not or could not utter any speech, although to trie him they hung him up by the heeles and miserablie tormented him. He would get him to his couch at the setting of the sunne, and rise again at the rising of the same.

One day they brought him to the haven, and suffered him to go into the sea, but to be sure he should not escape from them, they set three ranks of mighty strong nets before him, so to catch him againe at their pleasure (as they imagined) but he streightwaies diving down to the bottome of the water, got past all the nets, and comming up shewed hiself to them againe, that stood waiting for him, and dowking diverse times under water and comming up againe, he beheld them on the shore that stood still looking at him, who seemed as it were to mocke them, for that he had deceived them, and got past their nets. At length after he had thus sported himselfe a great while in the water, and that there was no more hope of his returne, he came to them againe of his own accord, swimming through the water, and remained with them two monethes after, but finallie, when he was negli-

39

gentlie looked to, and now semed not to be regarded, he fled
secretlie to the sea, and was never after seene nor heard of.

This story, so curiously circumstantial, is in a very different
class to such other medieval tales as that of Melusina of Lusignan,
in whom everyone in France once believed. The details of her
story were collected by Jean d'Arras in his *Chronicle* in 1387.
The legend of Melusina's secret, and how her husband discovered
that she had a fish's tail, became one of the great romances of
Europe. Families even changed their pedigrees to claim her, and
Henry VII, Holy Roman Emperor and Count of Luxembourg,
was only one of many. But such legends tell us little about such
other creatures as the one at Orford.

Or indeed about the mermaid which was captured at Edam in
Holland in 1403. In that year the dykes gave way, and the area
of West Friesland around Edam was flooded. A mermaid came in
on the tide and was found stranded. An account of her was given
by John Swan in his *Speculum Mundi* (1635).

Not finding a passage out again was espied by certain women
and their servants as they went to milk their kine in the neigh-
bouring pastures, who at the first were afraid of her, but seeing
her often, they resolved to take her, which they did; and bringing her home, she suffered herself to be clothed and fed with
bread, milk and other meats, and would often strive to steal
again into the sea, but being carefully watched, she could not :
moreover, she learned to spine and perform other pettie offices
of women; but at the first they cleansed her of the sea-mosse,
which did stick about her. She was brought from Edam and
kept in Harlem, where she would obey her mistris, and (as she
was taught) kneel down with her before the crucifix, she never
spake, but lived dumbe and continued alive (as some say)
fifteen years; then she died.

This again is another strange story, though like the merman at
Orford, this could be merely folklore passing as history. But these
monsters made their way into the works of Conrad Gesner and
Ulysse Aldrovandi. One of these was a monster from the Adriatic
in 1523, which was brought to Rome in November of that year. It
was about the size of a five-year-old child, 'like a man even to the

navell, except the ears; in the other parts it resembled a fish'. Gesner took his sketch of this creature from a painter who had drawn it from life (so to speak) when the object was exhibited at Antwerp.

In this incident we can recognise an old acquaintance: the Triton from Tanagra. Such artificial mermaids played a large part in keeping the legend of the mermaid alive in the popular imagination.

Another source of support for the legend were travellers' tales. Among these was a report from no less a person than Christopher Columbus. On his first voyage to the Americas, on 4 January 1493, he 'saw three sirens that rose high out of the sea, but were not as beautiful as they are represented'. These 'mermaids' are supposed to have been manatees; on an earlier voyage he had seen sea-cows like them on the coast of Africa.

But this neat explanation cannot cover all the cases on record. The Italian lawyer Alessandri quotes an account given by Theodore of Gaza, who said he came upon a nereid on the shore of the Peloponnese. The crowd which had gathered was afraid to touch the gasping, dying creature. But Theodore picked her up and carried her into the sea. In our day this incident impressed even so sceptical a mind as Norman Douglas's.

Another feature of the natural history books of this period were such creatures as the 'Bishop-fish' and the 'Monk-fish'. Though the bishop-fish was supposed to have been found on the Baltic coast of Poland in 1531, there seems to be little doubt that he was a cousin of the Triton of Tanagra. These were soon seen to be absurdities. But there seems to have been a brisk trade in these fakes, called Jenny Hanivers, perhaps because they originated in Antwerp.

Despite the exposure of frauds and fakes, reports of living mermaids were still recorded. In the waters of Rappahanock in the colony of Virginia, a surgeon named Thomas Glover saw a merman:

His skin was tawny, much like that of an *Indian*; the figure of his head was pyramidal, and slick, without hair; his eyes large and black, and so were his eyebrows; his mouth was very wide, with a broad black streak on the upper lip which turned up at each end like mustaches; his countenance was grim and terrible . . . he seemed to stand with his eyes fixed on me for some time, and afterwards dived downe.

Glover's report was published in 1676 in the *Philosophical Transactions* of the Royal Society in London, which was laying the foundations of the New Science. The Barnacle Goose and the Barometz or Vegetable Lamb were only two of the fabled creatures which fellows of the Royal Society briskly disposed of. Credulity would no longer do, only the evidence of experience. But the 'evidence of experience' still brought forth weird animals, sea-monsters and mermaids. But we are coming to a time when the reports become more detailed and exact, even clinical. Such things were no longer folklore, but were still unworthy of scientific investigation.

One report was of the netting of seven mermen and mermaids on the coast of Ceylon in the year 1560. This came from a party of Jesuits and a doctor named Bosquez, who was attached to the Viceroy of Goa. The good doctor dissected the seven creatures, and his report was published among the annual *Relations* of the Society of Jesus. He found that externally and internally the creatures were just like human beings.

Mermaids in Ceylon had been mentioned in the fourth century BC by the Greek traveller Megasthenes. These are likely to have been dugongs, a relative of the American manatee. They have indeed a surprisingly human appearance to those unfamiliar with them.

André Thevet, writing in 1556 about the new worlds then being discovered, mentions similar creatures off the west coast of Africa:

I will not forget what was shewed me to have been seen near to the Mine Castle: A sea monster having the shape of a man, that the floud had left on the shore, the which was heard to crie. In like case the female came with the next floud, crying aloud and sorrowing for the absence of her mate: the which is a wonderful and strange thing. By this may be knowen, that the Sea doeth nourish and bring forth divers, and strange kinds of monsters, as well as the land.

These too are likely to have been sea-cows. And they will have been the source of the mermaid's skin seen by a party of German travellers at Thora on the Red Sea on 18 November 1565. 'In this citie wee saw a mermaid's skinne taken many years before, which in the lower part ends Fish-fashion : of the upper part, onely the Navill and the Breasts remaine; the arms and head being lost.' Which was a convenient accident for the showman, no doubt.

However, explanations are not always so easy. In 1608 the Bristol navigator Henry Hudson was trying to find a route across the northern coast of Russia to the Far East. On 15 June the ship was off the coast of Novaya Zemlya.

> This morning, one of our companie looking over board saw a mermaid, and calling up some of the companie to see her, one more came up, and by that time shee was close to the ship's side, looking earnestly on the men : a little after, a Sea came and overturned her : From the Navill upward, her backe and breasts were like a woman's (as they say that saw her) her body as big as one of us; her skin very white; and long haire hanging down behinde, of colour blacke; in her going down they saw her tayle, which was like the tayle of a Porposse, and speckled like a Macrell. Their names that saw her were Thomas Hilles and Robert Raynar.

This is an extraordinary account, on which the comment of P. H. Gosse is worth quoting : 'Whatever explanation may be attempted at this apparition, the ordinary resources of seal and walrus will not avail here. Seals and walruses must have been as familiar to these polar mariners as cows to a milkmaid. Unless the whole story was a concocted lie between the two men, reasonless and objectless, and the worthy old navigator doubtless knew the character of his men, they must have seen some form of being as yet unrecognised.'

Another remarkable report from the same period was published by Sir Richard Whitbourne in his *Discourse and Discovery of New-found-land* in 1622. Captain Whitbourne was hoping to interest settlers in the attractions of that country, among which was one remarkable beast :

Now also I will not omit to relate something of a strange Creature, which I first saw there in the year 1610, in a morning early as I was standing by the River side, in the Harbour of St John's, which very swiftly came swimming towards me, looking cheerfully on my face, as it had been a woman : by the face, eyes, nose, mouth, chin, ears, neck and forehead, it seemed to be beautiful, and in those parts well proportioned having round about the head many blue straks resembling hair, but certainly it was no hair . . . [It swam] towards the place where before I landed, and it did often look back towards me; whereby I beheld the shoulders and the back down to the middle, to be as square, white and smooth as the backe of a man, and from the middle to the hinder part, pointing in proportion like a broad hooked Arrow; how it was proportioned in the forepart from the necke and shoulders I know not; but the same came shortly after unto a Boat, wherein one William Hawkridge then my servant, was, that hath bin since a Captaine in a ship to the East Indies and is later there imploied again by Sir Thomas Smith, in the like voyage, and the same Creature did put both his hands upon the side of the Boate : whereat they were afraid and one of them strooke it a full blow on the head : whereat it fell off from them : and afterwards it came to two other Boates in the Harbour : the men in them, for feare fled to land : this (I suppose) was a Mermaide.

And perhaps it was, for it certainly recalls no known animal.

In 1614 another British captain, John Smith, saw a mermaid off one of the West Indian islands. At first he thought she was a woman – though she had 'large eyes, rather round, a finely shaped nose (a little too short), well-formed ears, rather too long, and her long green hair imparted to her an original character by no means unattractive'. He was almost ready to fall in love with her, when she moved and he found that 'from the waist down the woman gave way to the fish'.

Another report of an American mermaid : John Josselyn claimed in his account of New England published in 1672 that :

One Mr Mittin related of a Triton or Mereman which he saw in Cascobay . . . encountered with a Triton, who laying his

44

hands upon the side of the Canow, had one of them chopt off with a Hatchet by Mr Mitten, which was in all respects like the hand of a man, the Triton presently sunk, dying the water with his purple blood, and was no more seen.

Mermaids were also reported by another traveller, Father Merolla, a Capuchin missionary, on his voyage out to the Congo. The passengers on his ship saw 'a sort of sea-monsters like unto men' who were collecting herbs with which they plunged into the sea. They gathered some of these herbs, which the 'monsters' took in exchange for coral and other sorts of plants. But they could not catch them in nets. In the Congo kingdom of Malanbe, Fr Merolla found that in the river Zaire 'there is to be found the mermaid, which from the middle upwards has some semblance of a woman, as in its breasts, nipples, hands and arms, but downwards it is altogether a fish ending in a long tail'.

Now there is little doubt that these 'mermaids' were in fact dugongs. A contemporary picture of these creatures shows them as more human in shape than they are. The classical idea of the mermaid was interfering with travellers' observations of real animals.

But once again other reports suggest that something very strange was sometimes being seen. Benoit de Maillet, writing in 1748, claimed that 'a sea-man' was taken at Sestri in 1682.

He in every respect resembled that taken at Martinico [in 1740], except that instead of Hair and a Beard, he had a kind of moss on his head, about an Inch long, and a little very short Down on his Chin. In the Day-time he was placed on a Chair, where he sat very calmly for some time; which evidently proves that his Body was flexible and that he had Joints, which fish have not. He lived thus for some Days, weeping and uttering lamentable Cries, but would take nothing either to eat or drink. I got this account twenty-five years ago at Sestri, where I found a Lady of my Acquaintance of great Wit and Curiosity, and who, as well as I, inform'd herself of these Particulars.

The other 'sea-man' he mentions was shot outside the walls of Boulogne by a sentinel. An account of this creature was published by a naturalist named Mason. Benoit de Maillet felt there was some significance in the hair of these sea-men, and thought (somewhat confusingly) that whites with their long hair and negroes with their woolly hair 'equally derive their Origin from the Sea'. At least one modern naturalist has endorsed a similar view.

The hope of discovering the *real* mermaid died hard. In 1717, the Amsterdam publisher Louis Renard produced a lavishly illustrated work on the fish, crayfish and crabs of the Moluccas, a group of islands in the Dutch East Indies (and now part of Indonesia). The pictures were made by Samuel Fallours from specimens collected by Van der Stell, the governor of the island of Amboine. One of the plates in the second volume showed a 'sea-wyf', the soon to be famous 'Mermaid of Amboine'. This was:

> A monster resembling a Siren, caught near the island of Borne, or Boeren, in the Department of Amboine. It was 59 inches long, and in proportion like an eel. It lived on land, in a vat full of water, during four days seven hours. From time to time it uttered little cries like those of a mouse. It would not eat, though it was offered small fish, shells, crabs, lobsters, etc. After its death some excreta, like that of a cat, was found in its barrel.

The creature was the colour of kelp, with an olive-tinted body with olive webs between the fingers, each of which had four joints. The fringe around its waist was orange, with a blue border. The fins were green, the face slate grey, and a delicate row of pink hairs ran down the length of the tail.

This pathetic parti-coloured creature aroused great intellectual interest in Europe. While the book itself was being prepared, Peter the Great of Russia (then travelling incognito in western Europe) visited Renard and took a great interest in the mermaid. Renard said that Fallours had seen the creature alive for four days in Amboine, but the czar wanted this confirmed. Renard wrote to François Valentyn, a former Superintendent of the Churches in the Colonies. Valentyn, as he recounts in his own book on Amboine, was unable to help. He had not heard of the original mermaid, but thought it was not impossible that such a creature might have been seen by Fallours. He was however able to supply some more reports.

> I may say that I know for certain, that in the year 1652 or 1653 a lieutenant in the service of the [Dutch East India] Com-

pany saw two of these beings in the gulf, near the village of Nennetelo, near the islands of Ceram and Borneo, in the Department of Amboine. They were swimming side by side, which made him presume that one was male, the other female. Six weeks after they reappeared in the same spot, and were seen by more than 50 persons. These monsters were of greenish grey colour, having precisely the shape of human beings from the head to the waist, with arms and hands, but their bodies tapered away. One was larger than the other; their hair was moderately long.

Nor was this all: he had a personal experience to relate. For while on the return voyage from the East Indies:

I saw, on the 1st May, 1714, long 12° 18' and on the Meridian [off the west African coast in the Gulf of Guinea], during clear, calm weather, at the distance of three or four ship-lengths off, a monster, which was apparently a sort of marine-man, of bluish-grey. It was raised well above the surface, and seemed to have a sort of fisher's cap of moss on its head. All the ship's company saw it, as well as myself; but although its back was turned towards us, the monster seemed conscious that we were approaching too near, and it dived suddenly under water, and we saw it no more.

The 'fisher's cap of moss' recalls the 'kind of moss on his head' which de Maillet used of the 'sea-man' taken at Sestri in 1682. A small detail, but it is just such small points of agreement between reports that suggest that some of these reports are more than folklore.

Certainly Erik Pontopiddan, Bishop of Bergin in Norway from 1747 to 1764, thought so. In his *Natural History of Norway* published in 1752 he stoutly defended, and provided evidence for, the existence of the kraken, the sea-serpent and the mermaid. The kraken is now known to be the giant squid; the sea-serpent has achieved a good measure of scientific acceptance: so only the mermaid remains outside the pale of accepted fact today.

Pontoppidan was not so credulous as to believe everything he heard about merfolk (none of us is). Yet after the merely fabulous had been eliminated there remained a substantial amount of

47

evidence that something did exist. He produced the evidence of several hundred witnesses from Bergin and elsewhere in Norway.

He also includes evidence about the marmaele, which he thought were the offspring of mermen and mermaids. These creatures varied in size. Some were 'the bignesse of an infant of half a year old' to a child of three. The lower half was like a fish, the upper part human. When they caught them, the local fishermen would throw them back into the sea; though some had been brought ashore and fed on milk! 'They tell us that these creatures then roll their eyes about strangely, as if out of curiosity, or surprise, to see what they had not seen before.' People hoped to foretell the future by them, but in any case returned them to the sea within a day.

It is curious that as the reports of mermaids become more recent, they become more detailed and circumstantial. If mermaids were entirely fabulous we would expect the reverse. Some of the reports from the last century or so exude an air of authenticity which may shake even the most hardened scepticism.

One such was given in a letter to *The Times* of London by William Munro, a teacher at Thurso in Caithness in Scotland. He saw his mermaid in 1797 at Sandside Bay, near Reay.

My attention was arrested by the appearance of a figure resembling an unclothed human female, sitting upon a rock extending into the sea, and apparently in the action of combing its hair, which flowed around its shoulders, and of a light brown colour . . . The head was covered with hair of the colour above mentioned and shaded on the crown, the forehead round, the face plump, the cheeks ruddy, the eyes blue, the mouth and lips of a natural form, resembling those of a man; the teeth I could not discover, as the mouth was shut; the breasts and abdomen, the arms and fingers the size of a full-grown body of the human species; the fingers, from the action in which the hands were employed, did not appear to be webbed, but as to this I am not positive.

The creature, whatever it may have been, remained on the rock three or four minutes, and then dropped off into the sea. Mr Munro had heard of previous sightings of such a creature, but had not believed them, until his own eyes in the broad daylight convinced him of the truth.

Two years later, in October 1811, at Campbelltown in Scotland, two witnesses, a farmer named John M'Isaac and Katherine Loynachan, then a young girl, swore affidavits before the Sheriff-substitute concerning a mermaid they had seen. And in 1814, two fishermen saw a merman and what might have been his mate in the sea off Port Gordan.

And from Scotland also comes what must be one of the most remarkable tales about the mermaid ever recounted. It was told to Alexander Carmichael, the great gaelic scholar of the last century. Once again the report has a strange air of authenticity far removed from mere folklore. Carmichael heard the story from 'persons still living who saw and touched this curious creature'.

Sometime about 1830 some crofters on Benbecula in the Outer Hebrides were cutting seaweed. One of the women went down to the shore to wash her feet. There she was surprised to see a creature 'in the form of a woman in miniature' only a few feet away from her. Some of the men tried to catch the creature as she plunged away, but failed. Then a boy threw a stone which struck her in the back.

A few days later the unfortunate little creature was washed up two miles down the coast from where she had first been seen and attacked. She was dead. A detailed examination was now made.

The upper part of the creature was about the size of a well-fed child of three or four years of age, with an abnormally developed breast. The hair was long, dark and glossy, while the skin was white, soft, and tender. The lower part of the body was like a salmon, but without scales.

The lifeless corpse attracted a crowd down to the beach where it was stranded. All were convinced that it was a mermaid, and therefore partly human. Indeed the factor for Clanranald, who was also baillie and sheriff for the island, ordered that a coffin be made, and had the creature buried on the shore above the beach. As Gwen Benwell and Sir Arthur Waugh point out, this action is eloquent testimony in itself. That he ordered a burial 'suggested that he thought that she was at least partly human'.

This burial on Benbecula would seem to provide an opportunity for clinical research, for it should not be too difficult to find the place, exhume the corpse and conduct an autopsy. A mermaid would make a curious change of work for the local state pathologist.

In 1833 there was another encounter in Scotland with a mermaid, which was reported to Dr Robert Hamilton, professor of Natural History at Edinburgh University, by a Mr Edmonston, 'a well-known and intelligent observer'.

He claimed that six fishermen from Shetland discovered a mermaid entangled in their lines off the island of Yell. They took her into the boat and removed the fishhook on which she was caught. They had her in the boat for three hours, and so were able to give a good description of her appearance. She was about three feet long. The upper part was shaped, as always, like a woman, though the face was like a monkey's. She kept her small arms folded over her chest. The fingers were not webbed. 'A few stiff bristles were on the top of the head, extending down to the shoulders, and these it could erect and depress at pleasure, something like a crest.' No fins or gills were visible, and the body was without hair or scales. The lower part of the body was fish-like, the tail resembling that of a dog-fish (that is, smooth and thin). At the end of the three hours, during which the creature uttered plaintive little moans, they released her.

Mr Edmonston discussed the capture of the creature with the captain of the boat and with one of his men. He did not think that six experienced fishermen could have mistaken a seal or any other common creature for what seemed to be a mermaid.

Indeed, as Benwell and Waugh again observe, these unembroidered narratives from Scotland, which mention few of the traditional trappings of the mermaid, leave one with a difficult question : What *manner* of sea-creature was so closely observed, and so faithfully reported ? That is still the question.

Fraud plays a small part (so I believe) in the reports I have quoted; though, naturally enough, fake mermaids have a very long history from the triton at Tanagra onwards. There are many records of 'real mermaids' being exhibited, but like the one owned by P. T. Barnum, all were patent fakes. Many of these objects seem to have originated from Japan. Their manufacture was described by Andrew Steinmetz in his book *Japan and Her People*, on his return from a visit in 1859. Fishermen made them out of part of a large fish and half a monkey. They would put the mermaid on display, claiming they had caught it alive in their nets, but that it had soon died. Then they would announce that before she died the mermaid had foretold a plague, and that the only way to avert disaster was to possess a picture of her own self. A large supply of these would already be to hand, and became another source of income for the impoverished fishermen.

Sailors brought many of these mermaids home with them to Europe, and museums in France and Britain hold examples of them. Sir Alister Hardy, the well-known marine biologist, was given one by a family who had owned it for several generations and were convinced it was 'real'. But when he X-rayed the corpse, Hardy revealed the tell-tale wires which held the otherwise convincing object together. In 1961 this little mermaid joined the Piltdown skull in an exhibition of famous fakes and frauds at the British Museum.

Sir Alister Hardy, however, had by then suggested that there might indeed be a connection between mermaids and the early history of man.

In 1960 he outlined a new theory about man's past. He suggested that the ape-like ancestors of man might have passed some of their evolutionary history in the sea. These aquatic apes would have foraged along the shore of temperate African seas in search of shell-fish, seaweed and other sources of food. This would have given them a more varied and interesting diet than was to be had on the open plains.

From groping around in the rocks these apes would have moved out gradually to greater depths. They would have been following the evolutionary adaptation of whales and seals; and like them would have lost their original hairy coat. Only their heads, needing protection from the heat of the sun, would have retained a cap of hair.

Tools would have been developed to open shells, and these would eventually have allowed the water-apes to spread away from the shores back into the open plains, with a decided advantage over their rivals.

Hardy suggested that this theory would perhaps explain why

man alone of the primates enjoys swimming. True, human children have to be taught to swim, but as he pointed out, so do baby otters. His theory also explains man's upright posture, which came from wading about in deep waters. Also it explains man's streamlined body, and the way in which the body-hair tracts flow back along the body from the crown. These tracts run in

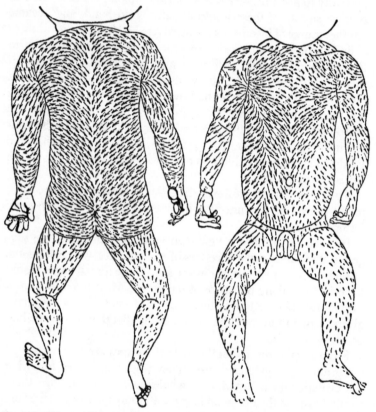

fig. 1 Evidence of man's aquatic past : hair tracts on the human foetus
(from F. W. Jones, *Man's Place Among the Mammals*)

a quite different way to other primates, and he suggests this would have been an adaptation to swimming, as the same streamlining can be seen in seals. Also man has a layer of fat under the skin, as do the seals and whales; other apes do not. This aquatic life would also have encouraged the evolution of the hand as it would have to be more sensitive for feeling out food underwater.

There is, however, no fossil evidence for Hardy's theory; but then the fossil record of man's evolution is as yet very patchy. We could imagine that some of these apes surviving in the seas to this day might give rise to stories of mermaids. By now, after several million years, other evolutionary adaptations would have taken place, and aquatic man – if he existed – would be a very strange creature indeed – perhaps almost as strange as the Creature from the Black Lagoon that haunted our childhoods.

One aspect of this mystery is just how well man does adapt to water. Divers without breathing gear can only stay down for short periods, as is well known. But there is evidence that some individuals can do very much better. The record for staying under water is 13 minutes 42.5 seconds, set up by Robert Foster, an electronics technician, on 15 March 1959. But he had hyperventilated his blood with oxygen for half an hour before diving.

And there are older, and more astonishing claims. There is, for instance, the almost legendary character Nicolas the Fish. Bernard Heuvelmans has described his career in his book *Dans le Sillage des Monstres Marins*, but the passage is not included in the English version of the book.

Nicolas was a Sicilian diver of the twelfth century whose extraordinary swimming abilities earned him the nickname of Nicolas the Fish. He must have been very famous in his day, as many authors of the later Middle Ages speak of him. Walter Mapes, an Englishman who lived in Italy for a long time towards the end of the twelfth century, says Nicolas lived so habitually in the sea that he finally unveiled all its secrets and was able to predict storms. He is said to have died after being taken away from the sea he loved to the court of the King of the Two Sicilies, then William I, who reigned from 1154 to 1166.

Other accounts vary in their details, some of which must be highly-coloured, if not imaginary. He was said for instance to have been able to stay under water for three quarters of an hour. In the seventeenth century, Fr. Athanasius Kircher claimed that he had been able to live in the sea for four or five days, and that he could stay under water for a whole day without breathing. Kircher claimed also that Nicolas had eventually acquired webbed feet and hands; Jovianus Pontanus that he grew fish scales.

Kircher said that he had been tempted to dive into the famous whirlpool of Charybdis by Frederick II (who reigned from 1355 to 1377); clearly there is some error here. Gervase of Tilbury, writing earlier, reported that it was done at the order of Roger of Sicily (probably Roger II, who reigned from 1101 to 1154). Heuvelmans concludes :

If the feats of this celebrated diver have been assigned to very different ages, it is nevertheless probable that a very spectacular sports record is the origin of all these legends.

Remarkable as Nicolas the Fish may have been, even stranger things have been reported. Ivan Sanderson has instanced the curious 'Walkers for Water' of West Africa. He was told in 1932 by a British official in Nigeria about a whole village that was able to 'sleep' underwater while hiding out from the police. Sanderson could not believe him; and if we had only Sanderson to go on, neither would I. But there is other evidence.

The reputable British anthropologist, Geoffrey Gorer, travelled through much of West Africa with his friend the Negro dancer Feral Benga in 1934. He too heard that some fishermen could stay underwater indefinitely, and his curiosity was aroused.

This power is confined to a few members of certain families; the greater number live near Saint Louis [in Senegal]. I was sceptical of this claim and one of the divers appeared to demonstrate. I chose the place where he was to dive where the water was particularly limpid and asked him to stop at the bottom for twenty minutes. He stopped there for three quarters of an hour; I had him continuously in view and he had no apparatus of any kind; occasionally he would send up an air bubble to the surface. At the end of the period he came up to ask if he had stayed down long enough. To all my inquiries as to how he did it he replied that 'he breathed like a fish' which didn't advance matters much. No importance is attached to this hereditary gift; it needs training to be developed. I only heard of these people by chance; for the Wolof they are completely ordinary.

So we can see how the myth of the mermaid might well have

arisen from figures like Nicolas the Fish, or from strange powers such as the Wolof divers possess. They are not unique.

Ludwig Tieck in his work on mermen investigated the strange story of Francesco de la Vega. Born in the village of Lierjanes near Santandar in 1657, Francesco loved the sea and swimming from his earliest years. Then one day he disappeared and was thought to have drowned.

In 1679 some fishermen at Cadiz saw a merman at sea. Captured after three days, he was taken to the Franciscan monastery in Cadiz. There the 'merman' was found to be indeed a man. His flesh was colourless and flabby. There were no nails on his feet or hands. His reddish hair was short. There even seemed to be scales along his spine. All he could say was 'Lierjanes'. The monks made inquiries and discovered this was the name of a small village on the coast.

One of the monks took him back to the place, where the merman entered the village and went at once to his old home, where his mother and brothers welcomed him with delight. 'But he showed no sign of affection or recollection, staring at them with chill fishy eyes, and receiving their embraces with cold indifference.'

The boy remained with his people, but he never settled down. He never spoke, and was indifferent to food, and disliked clothes. After nine years he disappeared once more, and was never seen again at Lierjanes.

But a little later fishermen reported that they had seen a person like Francesco playing in the water of the Bay of Asturias. He escaped capture. The sea-man had returned to the sea.

Sabine Baring-Gould, who quotes this story in his book *Iceland, its Scenes and Sagas* (1863), was very impressed with it, and thought it authentic. He concluded that 'it is quite possible that there may be a foundation of truth to the world-wide fable of the existence of merfolk'.

But on the whole, remarkable as these 'authentic tales' of water folk may seem, I feel a more acceptable explanation of the myth may be found in the reports given earlier in this chapter. And in the almost clinical detail, which reads like a coroner's report, such as we may some day yet receive from Benbecula. Here is one such.

On his visit to Iceland, Baring-Gould collected the following account of a mermaid. It is in the words of Wernhard Guthmund's son, a priest of Ottrár dale :

The lower part of the animal was entirely eaten away, whilst the upper part, from the epigastric and hypogastric region, was in some places partially eaten, in others completely devoured. The sternum, or breast bone, was perfect. This animal appeared to be about the size of a boy of eight or nine years old, and its head was formed like that of a man. The anterior surface of the occiput was very protuberant, and the nape of the neck had a considerable indentation or sinking. The alae of the ears were very large, and extended a good way back. It had front teeth, which were long and pointed, as were also the larger teeth. The eyes were lustreless, and resembled those of a cod fish. It had on its head long, black, coarse hair, very similar to the Fucus filiformis; this hair hung over the shoulders. Its forehead was large and round. The skin above the eyelids was much wrinkled, scanty, and of a bright olive colour, which was indeed the tint of the whole body. The chin was cloven, the shoulders were high, and the neck uncommonly short. The arms were of their natural size, and each hand had a thumb and forefingers covered with flesh. Its breast was formed exactly like that of a man, and there were to be seen on it something like nipples. The back was also like that of a man; the ribs were very cartilaginous. In places where the skin had been rubbed off, a black coarse flesh was seen, very similar to that of the seal. The animal, after having been exposed about a week on the shore, was again thrown back into the sea.

In this report and those quoted earlier, we can detect some seal-like mammal, with a mane, mammary glands, and fore-limbs more developed than in any known species. I am unimpressed with the theory that mermaids are mistaken reports of seals and dugongs. The mermaid reports come from the same seas as the seals – that is certainly true. But only some unknown species will explain all the details such as the long hair, or mossy cap in some reports.

We can still hope, with P. H. Gosse, that mermaids do exist, even if they are not 'green-haired maidens with oary tails [who] lurk in the ocean caves, and keep mirrors and combs upon their rocky shelves'. Perhaps when we do discover them at last, we may not even recognise them for what they are.

Many of the animals in this book, though they can be traced back to some original animal, have only a literary existence. This is not the case with the mermaid. Though she is thousands of years old, mermaids are still reported today. This alone should give pause for thought that there may be something in the legend.

Beryle de Zoete has given an account of one modern mermaid, which appeared in Cochin State on the Malabar coast of southern India in 1937. In April 1938 Miss de Zoete was told by the wife of a Parsee store-keeper that the year before some fishermen had discovered a young man in the sea. No ship was in sight from which he might have come. Aged about twenty, he was 'very fair and beautiful'. They laid him on the beach, where he writhed about, and brought an official down to look at him. But the youth said nothing. He only looked wildly at them all, and coiled his limbs about in the sand. Then as the crowd increased, he wound his way towards the brink of the sea and with one bound slipped into the water and disappeared. He was never seen again.

This, Miss de Zoete and her friend agreed together, must have been a merman.

Another modern account of a mermaid comes from Eric de Bisschop, who was sailing across the Pacific on a raft from Tahiti to Chile. On 3 January 1957, a call of nature brought him on deck. The sailor on watch was missing, but a moment later staggered back from the bow of the raft. He was angry and abusive. It seemed he had heard a loud plop and had gone forward to see what was the matter, for it might have meant a large fish or a dolphin had jumped aboard. But it was neither. He found some creature 'standing up on its tail'. On its head was what appeared to be fine seaweed. Though frightened, he moved towards it. The creature gave a great leap, and knocked him over in escaping to the sea. The sailor was certain what he had seen was a mermaid. His captain was not. But then he noticed that the sailor's arms were glittering with fish scales. De Bisschop went back to his bed, but was compelled to come up again. The sailor was there at the helm – but now there were no scales on his arm.

Was this a hoax intended to enliven a dull part of the voyage? We will never know. De Bisschop died of injuries when another raft he had built was wrecked on Cook Island. But he did add that the mermaid 'smelt'!

In March 1961 there was a series of sightings of mermaids off the Isle of Man, a traditional haunt of these creatures since Celtic times. Among the witnesses was the Lady Mayoress of Peel. Inspired by this, in August 1961, the Manx Tourist Board offered a prize for the capture of a mermaid. Only nets could be used, and the creature had to be brought alive to the office of the Board. An advertisement appeared in a London paper from an enthusiast looking for a diver to join him on a mermaid-hunting expedition into the Irish Sea.

They might have fared better by going on to Ireland itself. For in August 1962, two farmers from Ashdee in County Kerry claimed they had seen a mermaid. They were certain it was not a seal. And in 1967, there were other reports from Victoria in British Columbia, and from South Borneo. So the old legend is far from dead, even in this sceptical age.

CHAPTER SEVEN

SIRENS, CENTAURS AND SATYRS

In Western culture the myths and legends of Greece have permeated our learning and culture for many centuries. The imaginary creatures of the Greeks, and those reported from distant lands by Greek travellers, have become our imaginary monsters as well. Among the more unusual are the sirens, the centaurs and the satyrs.

For the Greeks, the sirens were not mermaids with fish-tails, but human-headed birds, usually women of enticing form. Originally, however, they seem to have been *men*, as the earliest sirens are bearded. Sometimes they hold musical instruments in their arms, the lure of the siren being musical. They became especially common during the sixth century BC.

The sirens are among the menaces of the sea against which Circe warns Ulysses in the *Odyssey*. 'First of all you will come to the sirens, they who bewitch men,' she tells him.

Who ever sails near them unaware shall never again see his wife and children once he has heard the Siren voices. They enchant him with their clear song, as they sit in a meadow that is heaped with the bones of dead men, bones on which still hangs their shrivelled skin. Drive your ship past the place, and so that your men do not hear their song, soften some beeswax and with it stop their ears. But if you yourself wish to listen to the Sirens, get your men to bind you hand and foot with ropes against the mast-step. In this way you may listen in rapture to the voices of the two Sirens. But should you begin to beg your comrades to unloose you, you must make sure that they bind you even more tightly.

The Siren Islands were said to be the Galli Islands at the entrance to the Gulf of Salerno, south of Naples. The sirens themselves appear on many vases, including a famous one in the British Museum, showing Ulysses passing them in safety. It may seem strange to find the sirens among the creatures in the magic zoo, but as a siren graces the pages of the bestiary, something should be said about their natural history.

In the bestiary, the siren is shown with a fish-tail and wings, but there is no doubt that they were birds originally, though in the course of time they turned into, and were confused with, mermaids. Mythically they were birds with marvellous alluring voices that preyed upon the unfortunates of the sea.

Ernle Bradford, the British writer and sailor, has recounted how he heard the sirens singing off the Galli Islands during September 1943. He, and only he, heard what sounded like singing, 'a natural kind of singing one might call it, reminiscent of the waves and the wind. Yet it was certainly neither of these, for there was about it a human quality, disturbing and evocative.' They searched for possible survivors, but found none; and no one else aboard the ship heard anything at all. Nor on a return visit with his wife years later, aboard his own boat, did Bradford hear anything. The sirens never sing to women. There is, it seems, nothing they desire from their own kind.

The centaurs also appear in the medieval bestiaries, and here too, the facts of nature which lie behind the legend are difficult to discover.

The centaurs lived in central Greece, in Magnesia between Mount Ossa and Mount Pelion. They were perhaps originally a primitive mountain tribe like their enemies the Lapiths, whom the Greeks set against each other. A frieze showing the Battle of the Centaurs and Lapiths decorated the Parthenon in Athens; what remains of it is now safely installed in the British Museum. The king of the centaurs, a wild and unruly lot, was the wise and civilised Cheiron. Hercules accidentally wounded Cheiron in the leg with a poisoned arrow, which eventually led to his death.

Robert Graves has suggested that the original centaurs may have been hobby-horse dancers in some forgotten ritual, but it is far more likely that the centaurs were a personification of the wild mountain tribes. When the Spanish invaded Mexico their appearance on horseback bewildered the Indians, who thought that man and horse were one animal. A horseman easily becomes a horse-man. Surprisingly J. C. Lawson discovered at the turn of the century that the myth of the ancient centaurs (along with several other pagan deities) still survived in the folklore of modern Greece. But by now the classical creatures as we find them shown on the frieze of the Parthenon have dwindled down into mere fearsome bogies. So the old gods die, entertaining infants.

The Greek philosopher Lucretius took the centaurs at their face value, and declared them to be impossible. For, he said, men and horses live to different ages, and the horse part of the centaur would die while the man was still in his prime.

The centaur appears in at least one bestiary (Bodleian 602), made in the late twelfth century, and it features as one of the fabulous tribes shown on the Hereford Mappa Mundi. Pliny records that a baby centaur preserved in honey was brought to the Emperor Claudius – an unhappy omen as he was murdered shortly afterwards. And Plutarch describes another which was brought by one of his grooms to Pereander, the ruler of Corinth, which amused the sage Thales very much. His advice was not to employ such men to look after horses, or if one did, to provide wives for them. These objects, like the triton at Tanagra, were relics for the credulous common in any age.

If the sirens represented the perils of the sea, and the centaurs the dangers of the mountains, so the satyrs warned of the mysteries of the wilderness. They were the attendants of Dionysius, the god of wine and revelry, but must have made an earlier history. They were, as H. J. Rose says, 'a sort of mythological feature of the uncultivated lands, as the Tritons are of the sea'.

In appearance they are quasi-human and grotesque. Usually they have goat-legs and pricked ears, and they are always sexually aroused. The Silenoi and Pan himself, 'the simple sheperd's awe-inspiring god', are very similar. Originally spirits of the woods and the wilds, they later became associated with the imported foreign cult of Dionysius, the god of wine. They helped in his conquest of India, but this saga has more to do with Greek politics than with mythology.

Medieval writers associated the satyrs with the wood sprites of Northern Europe such as Puck and Robin Goodfellow, and their counterparts in France, Germany and Scandinavia. Thus by association with the older faiths of Europe, the satyrs became diabolical creatures for all good Christians.

However, lurking somewhere in the myth of the satyrs, there is a hazy idea of semi-human creatures of shaggy appearance haunting the deep woods of ancient Europe. These are more familiar as the Greenmen, or Wodehouses of medieval art. Not unnaturally, more recent reports of the Yeti and his kin have given these ancient legends a new look.

During Roman times some soldiers surprised a satyr in his cave den in the mountains of Thessaly. They brought him to Sulla, the Roman general. The satyr was so hideous and incapable of articulate speech, that Sulla had him returned to the wilderness.

What, one wonders now, could this creature have been? Another fake such as the centaur brought to Claudius, or the triton at Tanagra? As it seems to have been alive, it is tempting to suppose that it may have been a real creature, some as yet unknown denizen of the wilderness. But this is mere speculation, and we have more than enough monsters to investigate for the moment.

The monsters which Socrates mentions with disdain in the passage which I have used as an epigraph for this book – the chimaera, the gorgons and Pegasus – were philosophical creations. The chimaera was derived from an early calendar symbol (so Robert Graves suggests); the gorgons were suggested by the weird masks used in religious rituals; and Pegasus was an appropriate symbol for a poetic flight of fancy. They never appeared in the bestiary, and so have no place in the magic zoo. As I say, we have more than enough monsters without them.

CHAPTER EIGHT

THE PHOENIX

With many fabulous creatures the exact origins of the myth cannot be found. This is not so with the phoenix. The first reference to the legend occurs in the account of Egyptian religious customs in the histories of Herodotus. This is what he says :

> Another sacred bird is the phoenix; I have not seen a phoenix myself, except in paintings, for it is very rare and visits the country (so at least they say at Heliopolis) only at intervals of 500 years, on the occasion of the death of the parent-bird. To judge by the paintings, its plumage is partly golden, partly red, and in shape and size it is exactly like an eagle.

This account seems straightforward enough. Herodotus then proceeds to recount the legend about the bird.

> There is a story about the phoenix : it brings its parent in a lump of myrrh all the way from Arabia and buries the body in the temple of the Sun. To perform this feat, the bird first shapes some myrrh into a sort of egg as big as it finds, by testing, that it can carry; then it hollows the lump out, puts its father inside and smears some myrrh over the whole. The egg-shaped lump is then just of the same weight as it was originally. Finally it is carried by the bird to the temple of the Sun in Egypt. I give the story as it was told to me – but I don't believe it.

There seem to be two parts to this account : one about a real bird found in paintings, and perhaps in real life, about which we are given a few details as to colour and size.

The second part comes, clearly enough, from the Egyptian priests in the Temple of the Sun at Heliopolis. The elaborate detail about the ball of myrrh suggests some sort of ritual performance on their part.

Herodotus is not our only source however. Herodotus died in 415 or 424 BC. Pliny the Elder, who died on the slopes of Vesuvius in 79 AD during an eruption of the volcano, also added to the legend. Like Herodotus, Pliny had doubts about the bird, but this did not prevent him recording the following details.

Arabia has one [bird] that is famous before all others (though perhaps it is fabulous), the phoenix, the only one in the whole world and hardly ever seen.

The story is that it is as big as an eagle, and has a gleam of gold around its neck and all the rest of it is purple, but the tail which is blue picked out with rose-coloured feathers and the throat picked out with tufts, and a feathered crest adorning its head.

The description is now more detailed, perhaps because Pliny is drawing on different paintings of the bird. Works of art, rather than living animals, are often the source of such exact reports in classical authors.

According to Pliny 'the first and most exact account' of the phoenix was given by Manilius, an eminent Roman senator who was largely self-educated, and, so he implies, therefore more credulous (though it is hard to imagine anyone more credulous than Pliny himself).

He stated that nobody has ever existed who has seen one feeding, that it lives 540 years, that when it is growing old it constructs a nest with sprigs of wild cinnamon and frankincense, fills it with scents and lies on it till it dies; that subsequently from its bones and marrow is born a sort of maggot, and this grows into a chicken, and that this begins by paying due funeral rites to the former bird and carrying the whole nest down to the City of the Sun near Panchaia and depositing it on the altar there.

From Manilius, Pliny also quotes the connection with the Sothic Great Year. The year of this period had been 215 AVC, that is 97 BC.

Cornelius Valerianus reports that a phoenix flew down into Egypt in the consulship of Quintus Platius and Sextus Papinius

[AD 36]; it was even brought to Rome in the Censorship of Emperor Claudius, AVC 800 [AD 47] and displayed in the Comitium, a fact attested to by the records, although nobody would doubt that this phoenix was a fabrication.

The date of this phoenix is also given by Dio in his Roman history as 36 AD, though Tacitus in his *Annals* puts it back a couple of years :

In the consulship of Paulus Fabius and Lucius Vitellius, after a long period of ages, the bird known as the phoenix visited Egypt, and supplied the learned of that country and of Greece with the materials for long disquisitions on the miracle.

Tacitus goes on to sort out whatever details he feels to be not too unlikely in these accounts.

That the creature is sacred to the sun and distinguished from the other birds by its head and the variegation of its plumage, is agreed by all who have depicted its form : as to the term of years, the tradition varies.

Five hundred years was a generally accepted period, though some said there was an interval of 1461 years between the appearances of the phoenix. There had been three earlier appearances within memory : first in the reign of Sesoris; second in the reign of Amasis (569–526 BC), and finally in the reign of Ptolemy III (247–222 BC). 'The three earlier phoenixes flew to the city called Heliopolis with a great escort of common birds amazed at the novelty of their appearance.' The question of the dates puzzled Tacitus.

For while antiquity is obscure, between Ptolemy and Tiberius, there were less than 250 years : whence the belief has been held that this was a spurious phoenix, not originating on the soil of Arabia, and following none of the practises affirmed by ancient tradition.

Tacitus then recounts the ancient legend of the phoenix building a nest on which it dies and a young one is born, and how the young phoenix brings the ashes of its father to the altar of the sun. 'The details are uncertain and heightened by fable; but that the bird occasionally appears in Egypt is unquestioned.'

Such is the classical evidence for the existence of the phoenix. All three writers express some doubts about the story, and yet it seems fairly certain that in 36 AD some strange bird appeared in Egypt which caused great surprise and comment.

Our modern idea of the phoenix – that it burns itself up on its nest and is reborn from the ashes – does not comply with the earliest account of the bird given by Herodotus. Indeed it is not until the fourth century AD that the notion of the fiery death of the phoenix is recorded, in two long poems on the bird by Claudian and Lactantius.

Claudian (who lived around 400 AD) was court poet to the weak emperor Honorius and was patronised by the Vandal general, Stilicho. In an overwhelmingly Christian era he remained staunchly pagan, looking back to the glories of the old Roman world. His poem on the phoenix breathes the atmosphere of an earlier age:

> He shakes his locks, and from his golden head
> Shoots one bright beam, which smites with vital fire
> The willing bird, to burn is his desire,
> That he may live again; he's proud in death,
> And goes in haste to gain a better breath.

The *Carmen de Ave Phoenice* attributed to Lactantius contains an even more elaborate treatment of the myth. Lactantius was born a pagan, but later converted to the new religion and was appointed tutor to the Emperor Constantine's son. Famous as a defender of Christianity, we can perhaps see in his poem the adoption of the phoenix as symbol of the hoped-for resurrection promised by Christ. Written in the fourth century, the poem was paraphrased by the English author of *The Phoenix*, one of the early poems in the *Book of Exeter*. It was also well known throughout Europe.

The phoenix appears, naturally enough, in the bestiary, where the legend has attributed to it this new symbolic meaning. 'Now Our Lord Jesus Christ exhibits the character of this bird, who says: "I have the power to lay down my life and to take it up again" . . . The symbolism of this bird therefore teaches us to believe in the Resurrection.'

If this all implied a belief in the existence of the phoenix, it did not last long. There is only a brief reference to the bird in the *Hortus Sanitatis*, the standard natural history work of the late Middle Ages. By the time of Gesner and Aldrovandus, the phoenix had become a literary puzzle rather than a fact of avian biology. The fathers of the Church, among them St Cyril, St Ambrose, Tertullian, Origines Adamantius, connect the phoenix with the Resurrection, if 'the account be truthful' as Tertullian observes.

Sir John Mandeville (whoever he may have been) also mentions the phoenix and the City of the Sun in his *Travels*, but then the author of that spurious work manages to mention nearly every known wonder of the world.

Shakespeare has several references to the phoenix, but unlike Sebastian in *The Tempest* he shows no inclination to believe

> That there are unicorns : that in Arabia
> There is one tree, the Phoenix throne; one Phoenix
> At this time reigning there.

But as T. H. White observes, Shakespeare was not a student of the medieval bestiaries, and he has few enough references to their wonders : no manticora, or aspidochelone, or amphisbaena. This indeed is an argument that Shakespeare is not the real author of *The Phoenix and the Turtle*, the long poem often attributed to him.

The phoenix was a badge of royalty from the days of the Romans. It was the badge of Jane Seymour, and a favourite image for Queen Elizabeth I, and for James I, who was seen as a phoenix sprung from the ashes of his unfortunate mother, Mary Queen of Scots.

Fynes Moryson alleges that in 1599 the Pope sent the Earl of Tyrone, whom he was supporting against Elizabeth, a gift of a crown of phoenix feathers, 'perhaps in imitation of Pope Urban III, who sent John, the son of King Henry the Second, then made lord of Ireland, a little crown woven of peacock's feathers.' Where these precious items came from does not seem to be recorded.

Sir Thomas Browne rightly baulked at the evidence for the phoenix, ancient though it was.

All which, not withstanding, we cannot presume the existence of this Animall, nor dare we affirm there is any Phoenix in Nature. For, first, there wants herein the definite test of things uncertain – that is, the sense of man. For though many writers have much enlarged hereon, there is not any ocular describer, or such as presumeth to confirm it upon aspection.

The New Science demanded definite tests of things uncertain, and the phoenix failed such tests. And though the phoenix lingered on as a sign over chemists' shops through its association with alchemy, it was of more interest to a Paracelsus than a Thomas Pennant.

The focus now changed from whether the bird existed to discovering how the legend had arisen in the first place. The phoenix became the property of archaeologists and curious biologists.

Baron Georges Cuvier seems to have been impressed by the testimony of Pliny and Tacitus that a phoenix had appeared in Egypt in 34 AD. He suggested that at remote intervals a golden pheasant from China might have strayed across Asia as far as Arabia or Egypt, and so given rise to the legend. The appearance of such a bird would indeed cause a sensation. But Maurice Burton feels 'such an event is most unlikely', even though the theory has appealed to many other writers. But even this idea, to which I will return, does little to explain the whole of the legend.

As Herodotus mentions seeing a painting of the Egyptian phoenix, it might be thought that Egyptologists would by now have cleared up the mystery. But on the whole they cast more darkness on the subject, and are in danger of obscuring it completely. Originally it was thought by archaeologists that the phoenix was a bird 'represented on the monuments with human hands and feet, in an attitude of prayer'. But then in 1851 Stuart Poole suggested that the phoenix was identical with the *bn.w*, or *benu*, the sacred bird of Osiris, and that the other was the 'pure soul' of the king.

Now the benu is clearly enough represented on the monuments as a stork, heron, or egret. This represented the sun – which died in its own flames at night only to rise again in the morning in the east out of Arabia. The Greek word phoenix also means 'palm tree' – hence Phoenicia, the land of the palms; and also 'purple'. Hence it has been further suggested that the benu was in fact the Purple Heron (*Ardea purpurea*).

As herons build their nests on the tops of tall trees, it is not unlikely that they might have nested in the palms around the sanctuary of the sun at Heliopolis. And indeed a blue heron does appear in Egyptian tomb paintings, such as that of the architect Ankerhan at Thebes, built in the xxth dynasty.

Attractive as this theory is, the purple heron cannot possibly fit the description of the phoenix given by Herodotus, and confirmed by Pliny and Tacitus. They describe a bird the size of an eagle, with a variegated plumage mainly gold, red, and blue. And this is a description which fits only such classes of tropical birds as parrots, pheasants and birds of paradise.

All of these come from Eastern Asia and Indonesia. It would be unlikely that they could fly as far as Egypt, but it is not impossible that they could have been *brought* (however rarely) by traders or travellers.

There is some confirmation of this theory in the Feng-Whang, the so-called 'phoenix' of China. This bird is one of the four sacred animals of Chinese mythology (the others are the dragon, the unicorn and the tortoise). And as with the original phoenix there is no tradition of self-immolation. M. V. Hachisuka suggests that the traditional description of the Feng-Whang, cock's head, snake's neck, swallow's chin, tortoise back and fish's tail, fits one particular bird, the ocellated pheasant, Rheinart's Crested Argus (*Rheinarta ocellata*), which is found in Central Vietnam and the Malayan peninsula. Strange, mysterious birds, the American zoologist William Beebe says that in 'appearance they recall some Chinese phoenix'.

None of this, however, provides an explanation of some of the essential features of the phoenix myth : the fiery nest and the perfumes and incense. What have these to do with birds, or with bird behaviour?

It was only in 1957 that Maurice Burton, fresh from his investigations of other animal legends, stumbled on the answer. He has described his researches in one of the most remarkable books about animal behaviour in recent decades, appropriately entitled *Phoenix Reborn*.

In May, 1957, a tame rook named Niger, living in an aviary in my garden at East Horsley, in Surrey, disported himself on a heap of burning straw. With flames enveloping the lower part of his body and smoke drifting all around him, he flapped his wings, snatched at burning embers with his beak and appeared to be trying to put them under his wings. The sight of this was breath-taking, but there was more still to come. Every now and then he would pose amid the flames with his wings outstretched and his head turned to one side, looking exactly like the traditional picture of the phoenix.

Burton had been investigating at that time a peculiar piece of bird behaviour called 'anting'. Though it had been observed for over a century, this behaviour pattern was first named by Professor Erwin Stresemann of Berlin in 1935. It was found that some birds would pick up ants and rub them over their wings and plumes. In 1938 Roy Ivor, a Canadian, undertook an extensive study of the mystery. It has since been found that the behaviour is limited (with a few exceptions) to perching birds.

The birds, it would seem, derive some sort of pleasure from the action of the formic acid on their bodies. They get high on it. Burton, however, discovered first that aromatics were equally effective, and then that smoke was also. Then he discovered a pattern of association between birds and fires, which led in the end to his experiments with his modern phoenix.

So it would seem that far from being either bizarre or fantastic, the details of the phoenix myth of ancient times conform to known bird behaviour, in nearly every way. Certainly 'anting' with fire would be rarely observed, but often enough to give rise in Egypt, where the Temple of the Sun would have been filled with fires and aromatics, to the myth of the death and resurrection of the phoenix.

CHAPTER NINE

THE GRIFFIN

Alice was wandering through the mazes of Wonderland with the irritable Queen of Hearts.

They soon came upon a Gryphon, lying fast asleep in the sun. (If you don't know what a gryphon is, look at the picture) . . . Alice didn't like the look of the creature, but on the whole she thought it would be quite as safe to stay with it as to go after that savage Queen : so she waited.

Alice was wise to be cautious, for the gryphon, or griffin as it is also known, had a reputation as a fearsome predatory beast. Hers turned out to be a maudlin academic, but Sir John Tenniel's drawing does indeed give an excellent idea of the traditional griffin.

The griffin is a composite creature, with the body of a lion, and the head and wings of an eagle. The creature has a long and complicated history, both in art and legend. Even today many experts are puzzled about its identity.

The name is derived from the Greek word *gryps*, in Latin *gryphus*, which means to seize. The animal was a popular image in Near Eastern and Classical countries for many centuries. It seems to have originated (so far as we know) in the Levant before 2000 BC. By 1500 BC it is found on seals and ivories all over western Asia, and also on the island of Crete. By 1400 BC it had spread to Greece.

The typical Asiatic griffin has a crested head; those in Minoan and Greek art have a mane with spiral curls.

In earlier art the griffin is often shown lying down, or on its haunches. It appears as both victim and predator, and also fighting with warriors.

Throughout the Iron Age the griffin continued to be used in Asia and Greece. At Carchemish on the Euphrates (which T. E.

fig. 2 Griffin from an Assyrian ivory, 8th century BC

Lawrence helped to excavate before World War I), a griffin is carved on the tenth-century palace wall. Griffins are also found on Assyrian carvings during the following centuries.

In the eighth century BC they are found on cast bronzes and westward through Anatolia into Greece. During the next two centuries the griffin was popular in Greek art. The Greek version showed an open mouth with large ears and a knob on top of the head. A very similar type is found in Etruscan art after 600 BC. Greek traders carried silverware decorated with griffins into the country of the Scythians, where it established itself in the local art.

Over the next two thousand years the griffin spread westwards, until finally, at the end of the Middle Ages, a pair of griffins are to be found carved on the walls of Cashel Cathedral in Ireland in the far west of Europe. These date from around 1500 AD. For some three millennia and longer the griffin image pervaded Western cultures.

What did the griffin mean to all these different peoples? The large griffins painted on the wall of the Throne Room of the Minoan palace at Knossos on Crete, uncovered by Sir Arthur Evans, suggested to classical scholars a protective function for the beast. But what it was remained a mystery, as Ann Perkins admits:

> Apparently the griffin was in some sense sacred, appearing in sanctuary and tomb furnishings, but its precise meaning is unknown. The few references in the ancient authors give no clear idea of the creature or its role in cult or legend.

But the griffin of ancient legend is nevertheless a strange creature.

The first literary reference to griffins was made by Aristeas of Proconnesus. But he is himself such a mysterious person that this does little to enlighten us. The British classical scholar J. D. P. Bolton has, however, convincingly pieced together both the life of Aristeas and the story of the griffins.

Aristeas of Proconnesus (an island with a Greek colony in the sea of Marmara) flourished about the third quarter of the seventh century BC. Inspired by his devotion to the cult of Apollo, he set out on a journey to visit the Hyperboreans (the Back-of-the-North-Wind People), among whom that god was also worshipped. From somewhere about the Sea of Azov he headed inland into Central Asia. He passed from tribe to tribe along the corridor of the steppes. At the head waters of the Ishim he came upon the Issedonians, with whom he stayed awhile. They told him that beyond them 'to the north' were lofty, storm-wrapped mountains – the western outliers of the Central Asiatic highlands – which they called by a name which Aristeas took to be 'Caucusus', whence a furious wind issued from a cavern. This he took to be Boreas, and beyond that were the Hyperboreans. He was told something about the settled life of the Chinese, who were looked upon as vegetarians because they ate cereals.

The Issedonians also told him about a tribe of men with only one eye, the Arimaspoi, who had driven them away from the mountains. These may well have been nomad Mongols, who were indeed forcing the peoples of the steppes to move further west at about this time. These people lived beside a gold-bearing river, and stole their stocks of gold from the guardianship of swift and fierce monsters.

Aristeas called these monsters 'griffins', after the composite creatures familiar to him in his native art. What the Issedonians called them, however, we do not know. He was also told about hideous and monstrous 'swan-maidens' who could lay aside their feathers and become hags. These he thought might be the Gorgons and Graeae of Greek myth. He also heard of cannibals, and how falling 'feathers' (snow) hampered sight in those parts.

Aristeas eventually returned home, and wrote a long poem describing his adventures and what he had learned about those distant regions. He had in fact travelled much further than any Greek was to venture for many centuries to come. Then he disappeared. He was never seen again. Bolton concludes that 'it is pleasing to fancy that this time his persistence was rewarded, and that he ended his days in China'.

It was from his poem the *Arimaspea* that later writers derived not only a great deal of confused lore about Inner Asia, but also their references to the one-eyed Arimaspians and their enemies the griffins. There seems little doubt that the poem, now lost except for a few passages preserved in the works of other writers, contained not only a genuine account of travel among strange peoples but also some actual Central Asian folklore.

The gold-guarding griffins easily became confused with the gold-guarding ants, but originally they were different. References to both have been traced in Indian and Chinese sources. The Chinese sources are two works *Ch'u Tz'u* and *Shan Hai Ching*, which incorporate the shamanistic lore of the Yangtze Valley culture. We shall deal with the giant ants in a later chapter, but for the present we should note that the *Shan Hai Ching* also says:

> The land of the Kuei is to the north of the body of Erh Fu. These people have the faces of men but only one eye . . . The Ch'iung-ch'i is like a tiger with wings . . . To the east of the Ch'iung-ch'i are the giant wasps which look like wasps and the giant ants which look like ants.

Chinese ideas about the barbarian tribes of Central Asia were often the products of their imaginations, but some of them at least seem to be derived from the geninue folklore of Inner Asia. The 'tiger with wings' certainly seems to be related to the griffin of Aristeas, especially as both are placed in proximity to a one-eyed race.

So it would seem that the *Arimaspea* comprised the observations of someone, whom we may as well call Aristeas, of the Eurasian hinterland, including items of Asiatic folklore. But these things were interpreted in terms which his Greek audience would understand.

Herodotus tells us about Aristeas and the griffins. Also Aeschylus seems to have used the poem as a source for his play *Prometheus Bound*. The setting of that play is in the Caucasus, not the mountains we know by that name, but the range which Aristeas had described. Prometheus warns Io about the dangers of that country, which include

'the silent hounds of Zeus,
the sharp-beaked griffins . . .'

Milton, over two thousand years later, found room for them in the panoramic horrors of *Paradise Lost*:

As when a gryfon through the Wilderness
With winged course ore Hill or moarie Dale
Pursues the *Arimaspian* who by stelth

75

> Had from his wakeful custody purloined
> The guarded gold.

Much of what Herodotus has to tell us about the tribes of Inner Asia has been shown by recent research to be quite accurate. Only some of his information came from Aristeas. More he gathered himself when he visited Olbia, a Greek city at the confluence of the Bug and Ingul Rivers (now the modern Russian city of Niko-layev). The smallest details are often right. So what then were the griffins? Were they merely a myth, a mistake based on confusion, or was there some real creature behind the legend?

Modern theories about the griffins of Aristeas have been numerous. Tournier thought that the Arimaspians might have been a real tribe whose other eye had become atrophied from being squinted up while aiming a bow. Or they could have been miners whose 'eye' was a lamp on their foreheads.

Minns and Hennig thought that the 'griffins' had been confused with the 'giant ants'. But this seems unlikely, as that legend has a distinct source of its own. Adolf Erman thought that the fossil bones which are found in such abundance on the banks of Siberian rivers, and which are in fact thought to be the bones of a giant bird by the Samoyed, was the source of the legend. But Siberia is a long way from the Altai Mountains, and the Turco-Tartars that Aristeas was describing.

The real crux of the problem is that we do not know how the Issedonians themselves described the creature, as Bolton points out. 'Actually as half-lion and half-eagle? Or rather as monsters with the characteristics of speed, ferocity and vigilance, whose physical appearance was not clear to Aristeas, so leading him to make his own identification with a monster he already knew?'

Ctesias gives us an account of the griffins (which has been partly preserved by Bishop Photius in his *Myriobiblion*). He says that the gold was to be found in certain 'high towering mountains which are inhabited by the griffins, a race of four-footed birds, almost as large as wolves, having legs and claws like those of a lion, and covered all over the body with black feathers, except only on the breast, where they are red. On account of these birds the gold, with which the mountains abound, is difficult to get.'

As often with Ctesias, and the monsters he describes, one wonders whether he is describing a real animal, repeating something he has been told, or remembering one of the bizarre composite creatures which were such a feature of Persepolis when he lived there. One of these did indeed show a creature much like the griffin fighting with a warrior. Clearly enough these creatures he describes were intended to deter the Greeks and Persians from seeking out the sources of the gold in Central Asia. But where were the vivid colours he describes obtained from?

Aelian, writing several centuries later, adds that the wings of the griffins are white, the neck variegated with blue feathers, and the beak was like an eagle's. The Bactrians said the griffins built their nests of gold, but this was denied by the Indians. The gold district where the griffins lived was a frightful desert – perhaps in the old sense of being an uninhabited place.

That basically was the classical lore about the griffins. Pliny refers to their ears and hooked beaks, but thought that they were actually fabulous creatures. There are, of course, many references to griffins in later times. The *Romance of Alexander*, which was popular in the Middle Ages, contained the story of how he flew in an iron cage harnessed to a team of griffins. This was a subject which often appeared in the art of the period.

Marco Polo, who thought that the reports of the Roc bird from the island of Madagascar might refer to griffins, may have had in mind the twelfth-century relief of Alexander's aerial journey carved on the front of San Marco in Venice, which he would have known in his childhood.

Another famous account of the griffins was contained in Sir John Mandeville's *Travels*. The bestiary account of these creatures inspired many carvings of them in churches and cathedrals across Europe. In medieval times the griffin had various and contradictory meanings. Dante made the griffin a symbol of Christ, and in the *Purgatio* he describes a solemn procession in which the griffin draws a chariot symbolising the Church. He had in mind the comparision often made of Christ with both the lion and the eagle that make up the griffin. Isidore of Seville noted in his *Etymologies* 'Christ is a lion because he reigns and has strength; and an eagle because, after the Resurrection, he ascended to heaven.'

But for others the griffin was a type of demon swooping down to carry off unfortunate sinners. The passion of the griffins for gold later made them an emblem of Scientia or Knowledge. But in the Renaissance their gold hoarding suggested usury instead, though Sir Thomas Browne was of the opinion that the griffin was a creature symbolising guardianship. All of these various ideas, though they bore little resemblance to their origins, can be traced back to the text of Aristeas quoted by Herodotus. These passages have naturally enough been the focus of much learned comment in modern times.

Valentine Ball, writing in 1884, had an original solution to the mystery of the griffins :

> Taking Photios's account alone, and excluding from it the word birds, and for feathers reading hair, we have a tolerably accurate description of the hairy black-and-tan coloured Thibetan mastiffs, which are now, as they were doubtless formerly, the custodians of the dwellings of the Thibetans, their gold miners as well as others. They attracted the special attention of Marco Polo, as well as of many other travellers in Thibet; and for a recent account of them reference may be made to Captain Gill's *River of Golden Sand*.

And indeed Marco Polo had mentioned 'dogs the size of asses' in Tibet. These mastiffs are called *gyake*, or royal dogs, on account of their size and ferocity. But this does not seem to have anything to do with the origin of the word griffin, which Ball admits comes from 'the Persian *giriften* (to grip, or seize)'. Hindustani contains several words derived thence, such as *giriftan*, a captive; *girift*, seizure, and so on.

One wishes that all mysteries could be so easily resolved as by assuming what has been thought of as a *bird* for four thousand years is in fact a *dog*. Given the long history of the griffin in art and legend, there can be no doubt that it was assumed to be some sort of flying creature. Exactly what, remains to be discovered.

Herodotus claimed that the tales of the griffins came to the Scythians around the Black Sea from the Issedonians, a race who lived beyond the Ural Mountains. Gold mines in this region of Russia, which at one time had not been very productive, were in 1860 yielding four to five million pounds sterling worth of the metal a year. Today this would be even more. So even if Herodotus himself was not inclined to believe in the one-eyed Arimaspians, their gold was real enough. Since 1860 archaeologists have recovered evidence of the high standard of gold-working among the tribes of this region.

Other writers have however looked elsewhere for the gold. Horace Wilson, writing in 1836, pointed to the Himalayas, to the country of the Kafirs and to Tibet as the sources of the gold. In Tibet, he said, there was a superstition about collecting the precious metal (on which the natives themselves set little value), for it was regarded as the property of the spirits and demons of the god of wealth. Unless these were appeased it would have been fatal to take the gold away. 'These superstitions,' he concludes, 'may have formed the basis of the stories of the griffins and ants as large as dogs.'

Wilson goes on to suggest that the griffins may be related in some way to Garuda, the monster bird of Hindu myth – but we shall leave that for another chapter. But he draws attention to another myth which may be more relevant. There is also a bird in Indian myth called in Mena *Hema-kara*, or Gold-Maker. According to Wilford this was commonly said to be of vast size and to live in the mountains to the north-east of India. This bird's dung, mixed with the sand of that country, converted it to gold. A bird that voids gold is also mentioned in the Hindu sacred book the *Panchatantra*.

Here, though at a long remove, we have another from Central Asia. What seems to have happened is that the earlier image of the griffin, which was traditional in art, became confused with the creatures reported by Aristeas from the fifth century onwards.

The danger of obtaining gold from Central Asia also lies somewhere behind the legend. As with the strange story of the giant ants, with which I will deal in another chapter, there were real facts behind the story.

The Arimaspi do seem to have been a nomadic tribe of Central Asia, who obtained their gold from other territories, either in the Eastern Altai (as seems most likely) or from the Tein-Shan or the Gobi. The name means either 'dwellers in the desert', 'having docile horses', or 'owners of wild horses' : which makes one have doubts about the etymology of names.

As for the griffins, they too became an established part of the Central Asian scene for the Greeks. Greek traders had their wares decorated with griffins specially for sale in Asia. In 1904 a silver mirror was discovered in a barrow at Kelermes, near the river Kuban in the north-western foothills of the Caucasus. In one of the eight segments on the back is engraved a picture of two 'wild men' fighting a griffin. It was made in a Greek colony of South Russia about 575 BC. Instead of the more traditional design of two warriors the artist substituted two savages : it is attractive to think of them as Arimaspians fighting their famous foe.

A gold medallion which was part of the famous Treasure of the Oxus, found and rescued by chance in 1877, shows a griffin by itself. Such items are common enough in the art of South Russia, but there is no literary evidence extant to explain their significance to those who wore them and made them. Could the 'griffins' have been a common feature of their lives?

As mentioned above, the griffin appears in *Prometheus Bound*, by Aeschylus. He seems to have thought of it as some sort of large eagle, similar to the vultures that picked on the liver of the en-chained hero. One bird does exist which is intermediate between the eagles and vultures. This is the Lämmergeier, or Bearded Vul-ture (*Gypaetus Barbatus Aureus*). It has a tuft of long bristly hairs on the chin and stiff bristles hide the nostrils. It is blackish grey above, otherwise pale tawny. The white cap is bordered by black; the iris of the eye is light orange, and the white of the eye is scarlet. The common variety, which is forty to forty-six inches long, has a wingspread of nearly ten feet. The Lämmergeier is spread over the high mountains of Southern Europe, Central Asia and parts of Africa.

The details of the Lämmergeier fit in well enough with the griffin of Aristeas. The hairy mane around the head of the bird would recall to some the mane of a lion, as would the light tawny colour. These birds are so called because they are said in the Alps to carry away lambs, though this is disputed by zoologists. A fierce and impressive bird, the Lämmergeier is a worthy original of the griffin of legend.

And the griffin of art? Is that too based on the Lämmergeier? Or are the more romantic notions that it might be an attempt to represent the pterodactyl justified? For my part I am content with the Lämmergeier.

It would be romantic to think that the griffin of legend might be a garbled account of some early flying reptile such as Pterodon, or early bird such as archaeopteryx. Indeed the first specimen of that oldest bird was called 'the griffin lizard' by Andreas Wagner after its discovery in 1861. The curious combination of features in the griffin does indeed suggest some prehistoric monster. As I say, it would be romantic, but unscientific. I am afraid that the fearsome enough Lämmergeier will have to fill the role of 'the real griffin'.

Ironically it was a Lämmergeier that mistook the bald head of Aeschylus for a stone and dropped a tortoise on it, so killing him. Doubtless the pious folk of ancient Athens saw in this the revenge of Zeus on the champion of Prometheus.

Behind the classical legend of the griffin there lie other, less familiar creatures of Middle Eastern and Hindu mythology. One of these is the Indian myth of garuda. The garuda is the great sacred bird of India, associated with Vishnu, the second-ranking god of Hindu mythology. Garuda was the symbol of strength and swiftness. In the temples dedicated to Vishnu images of the garuda were set up and worshipped as well. It seems that the garuda was an older god than Vishnu, perhaps one of the aboriginal animistic gods which were taken over by the invading Hindus.

Garuda naturally evolved, becoming in time partly human. But did the original deity have a natural origin? Richard Carrington has pointed out that early man was impressed with the larger birds of prey, and that these would naturally have become the objects of sacred awe and worship.

Yet the bird with which the garuda is associated today in India is not one of the larger eagles or vultures, but the much smaller bird, the Brahminy Kite (*Haliastur indus*), which is also called Haliaëtus garuda by the scientists.

The kite is regarded by the Hindus as a sacred bird. In Madras, at Chingleput near Madras city, the Hill of the Sacred Kites, it is believed two of the birds are reincarnations of sages who have been living there since time out of mind. Garuda is traditionally said to have a white face, red wings and a golden body: the

Brahminy Kite is golden red, with a white head and breast feathers. Like the sacred cows, the kites of India are ubiquitous and unharassed by the native Hindus.

Another mythological bird related to both the griffin and the garuda is the simurgh of Persian mythology, a creature now very familiar since its adoption as the emblem of Iranian Airways. Nothing better demonstrates the connections between the cultures of the Middle East. Traces of these myths can be found even among the Jews.

Rabbinical writings have many references to the ziz bird. He is so called because of the peculiarly varied flavours of his flesh, tasting of this (zeh) and that (zeh). Some real bird may have originally been behind the legend, as the bird was a clean fowl, fit for food. He was created by God to protect the lesser birds against predators.

Many of the legends current about the ziz are similar to those among the Arabs about the roc (which is discussed in the following chapter): he is said to be the largest bird in creation, his outspread wings darken the sun and prevent the hot south wind from parching the earth. A rabbi named Bar-Hana reports that on a sea-voyage he saw a ziz standing in the middle of the ocean, which yet reached only to its ankles. The sea there must be shallow, he thought; but a voice from above warned him that 'seven years before a ship's carpenter dropped his axe at this spot and it has not yet touched bottom'.

The hen-ziz was said to lay a huge egg, far away in some distant range of mountains. An addled egg broke once, and the stinking yolk drowned sixty settlements and swept away three hundred cedar trees. At the millennium, when God will judge mankind, the ziz will be slaughtered with Leviathan and Behemoth, and be served up as food for the righteous.

CHAPTER TEN

THE ROC BIRD

In medieval Europe the griffin was as familiar as the garuda in India, or the simurgh among the Persians. Among the medieval Arabs the giant bird of mythology was called the roc, or rukh. Though it shares some of the legendary features of the other birds, the roc seems to have quite a different natural history, so to speak, to the other birds in our fabulous mythology. It has become familiar in the West, however, through the description of Marco Polo, and the famously popular *Arabian Nights' Entertainment*.

In his travels Marco Polo describes the island of Madagascar, a place he had not visited himself, but of which he had heard tales from other travellers and traders. The natives there reported the appearance at 'a certain season' of a giant bird. This extraordinary creature, which they called the rukh, 'makes its appearance from the southern ocean'.

In form it is said to resemble the eagle, but it is incomparably greater in size; being so large and strong as to seize an elephant with its talons, and to lift it into the air, from when it lets it fall to the ground, in order that when dead it may prey upon the carcase. Persons who have seen this bird assert that when the wings are spread they measure sixteen paces in extent, from point to point; and that the feathers are eight paces in length, and thick in proportion.

Reports of this bird reached China when Marco Polo was living there. He thought they might be griffins, similar to those fabulous creatures which were shown on a relief on the church of San Marco in his native Venice. But they did not fit the traditional description.

The Great Khan Kublai sent special messengers to the island, ostensibly to obtain the release of one of his subjects, but in fact to find out what they could about this prodigy of nature. When they returned they brought with them a feather from a rukh, which Polo heard 'measured ninety spans, and the quill part . . . two palms in circumference'. The Khan was very pleased with this judicious, if unusual, gift.

This 'feather' was probably a palm frond, or so Sir Henry Yule, the great British authority on Polo, thought. Though the French explorer of Madagascar, Alfred Grandidier, says that it was a bamboo stalk, for in the Yemen these are made into water vases called *plumes de rukh*, roc's feathers.

The size of the 'feather' would indeed have represented a very large bird, if from a real creature. But the actual sizes of the bird given him by eyewitnesses are not really so large as to be incredible. The Khan's messengers may well have been Arabs (though the Chinese themselves had reached the east coast of Africa already by this date), and to them the roc was a familiar monster. Their tales about it were to become well known in Europe from 'The Tale of Sinbad the Sailor' in *The Thousand and One Nights*.

On his second voyage Sinbad is left on a desert island, where he comes upon a strange, white, domed object. While he is trying to find some way into this object, the sun is suddenly darkened and a giant bird flies in from the sea and settles down on it. Then he realises it is a giant egg and that the bird is the famous roc of which he had heard tales. He ties himself to the leg of the bird, and so is carried off the island to the mainland.

A little later, on his fifth voyage, he and his companions reach another island, where again they find a marvellous white dome. They strike it with stones and it breaks open, for to their astonishment it is the egg of a roc. They pull out the roc chick and kill it for meat. When Sinbad, who was not with them, heard about this he warned them of the great danger they were all in. And sure enough, when the roc parents returned to find their nest pillaged, they flew over the ship and, dropping rocks on it from the air, sank it with all hands, except for Sinbad.

Stories of the roc are also found in Arabic scientific works, such as the geography of Al Kazwini in the thirteenth century, and the natural history of Ibn Al Wardi. In the middle of the fourteenth century the Arab traveller Ibn Battuta saw a roc in the China seas. At first they thought it was a distant mountain, but then: 'What we took for a mountain is the rukh! If it sees us it will send us to destruction . . . but God . . . sent us a fair wind which turned us from the direction in which the rukh was.' Pigafetta, the historian of Magellan's voyage around the world, also said the China seas were the haunt of the bird. And one appears in Johannes Stradanus' engraving of Magellan's *Discovery of the Straits* done about 1590. He shows it carrying away an elephant, and his model may have been a Persian miniature such as Lane used to illustrate the story of the roc. (The Rabbi Benjamin of Tudela who travelled in the Orient in 1160–73 reported that sailors in the China seas wrapped themselves in ox-hides and were seized as a consequence by griffins from shipwreck.) Other travellers also compared the roc with the griffin, but the Venetian Fra Mauro, on his map of the world made in 1459, says that in 1420 some sailors found near the Cape of Good Hope the eggs of the roc 'which they say carries away an elephant or any other great animal'.

Stradanus seems to have based his design on a Persian miniature such as could be found in Florence at that time in Oriental manuscripts. His picture made its way into the ornithology of Ulisse Aldrovandi in 1599. He, however, classed the roc among the birds of fable, though without actually denying completely its possible existence.

What seemed to be a solution to the mystery of the roc came half a century later. In 1658 Admiral Etienne de Flacourt published his *History of the Great Island of Madagascar* after a long stay in the country. He refers to the

> *Vouroupatra*, a large bird which haunts the Ampatres and lays eggs like the ostrich's; so that the people of these places may not take it, it seeks the most lonely place.

Later travellers added to the legends about the eggs being large enough to use as water tanks. No one believed this. If the eggs were larger than an ostrich's, which stands eight feet high, a bird that could lay these eggs would be a veritable monster. Or, indeed, the roc itself.

But in 1832 the French naturalist Victor Sganzin saw an enormous half eggshell on the island; but his sketch of this strange discovery disappeared. Another traveller named Goudot also found parts of similar eggs. He showed them to Professor Paul Gervais, who attributed them to an ostrich of some sort.

Then in October 1848 John Joliffe, the surgeon on HMS *Geyser*, met a French merchant named Dumarele who told him about an enormous egg which held thirteen wine quart bottles of fluid, as he had measured for himself. The egg was then in the possession of some islanders who refused to sell it to him. 'The natives said the egg was found in the jungle, and observed that such eggs were *very very rarely* met with, and that the bird which produces them is still more rarely met with.'

Not much attention was given to this fantastic tale. But in 1851 a merchant captain named Abadie found three eggs and some fragments of bone on the south-west coast of the island. Each egg would have held six ostrich eggs, or 148 hen's eggs.

On the basis of these remains, Isidore Geoffroy-Saint-Hilaire named the bird *aepyornis maximus*, 'the tallest of the tall birds'. He thought the bird they came from stood sixteen feet high – actually it only came to ten feet, being bulky rather than tall.

In 1866 Alfred Grandidier recovered from pools at Ambolisatra other huge bones, perfectly preserved. At first it was thought they belonged to a pachyderm of some kind, but on re-examination it was seen that they belonged to the huge bird, whose whole skeleton was soon reconstructed.

There is no doubt that this bird was de Flacourt's vouroupatra, but was it the original of the roc? The aepyornis was, after all, a flightless bird. And though they may have been aepyornis eggs which the sailors of 1420, and the Arabs before them, thought were roc's eggs, doubts remained. Going back to Marco Polo, can his description, partly based on eyewitness reports, and the early Arab traditions, refer to a flightless bird? Are there any other birds that might have given rise to the legend?

The only eagle local to Madagascar is the Sea-Eagle, *Concuma vociferoides*, but that is only two feet long. Polo tells us that the Arabs speak of the roc as 'resorting to Madagascar from the southern ocean' which suggests that the legend (in this instance) might have been based on brief sightings of some large rare bird.

Sir Richard Burton, writing in 1886, thought that all these legends of giant birds might be based on memories of the ptero-dactyls of remote ages past. He refers naturally enough to the discovery of the aepyornis, and says that a Herr Hildebrand had discovered traces of another large bird on the African coast facing Madagascar. I have not been able to track down this elusive savant, but in any case there is no need in my opinion to resort to either surviving pterodactyls or unknown birds to explain the legend of the roc. There are other candidates.

One might be the South African Condor, another the Wandering Albatross. Some of the condors measure no less than fifteen feet between wing-tips (and there are rumours of even larger birds in the Andes), and to those who see them for the first time they must seem extraordinary.

Sir John Barrow (who, like Sir Richard Burton, believed in the unicorn) writes in his *Travels into the Interior of South Africa*, about these birds.

Crows, kites and vultures, are almost the only kinds of birds that are met with [in the Roggeveld]. Of the last, I broke the wing of one of that species called by the ornithologists the condor, of an amazingly large size. The spread of its wings was ten feet one inch. It kept three dogs for some time completely at bay, and having at length seized one of them with its claws, and torn away a large piece of flesh from its thigh, they all immediately retreated.

Even more likely to my mind is the identity of the roc with the albatross. This weird sea-wanderer is familiar from Coleridge's *Rime of the Ancient Mariner*. Actually he seems to have had in

fig. 3 Wandering Albatross

mind the smaller version, the Sooty Albatross, and not, as many readers and his illustrator Gustave Doré thought, the larger Wandering Albatross.

Flying out of the Southern Oceans only rarely into the latitude of Madagascar, it is easy to imagine the effect on Arab sailors whose imaginations were already stocked with Oriental myths about a bird so large its wings covered the sun. Even today the sight of the Wandering Albatross flying over a ship far from land is an amazing sight.

The average wing span of *Diomeda exulans* is about eleven feet. W. B. Alexander says, however, that specimens have been found up to fourteen feet. The wing span of a bird in flight is very hard to judge, but C. Parkinson mentions 'a gigantic specimen in the Sydney Museum extends over seventeen feet six inches, with a bill six inches long'. This is coming close to Marco Polo's 'sixteen paces' for the size of the roc's wing span. And the albatross is the only giant bird which could make its appearance from the Southern Oceans at certain seasons of the year.

So though the great eggs of the aepyornis have contributed something to the legend, the roc is actually a slightly exaggerated report of the Wandering Albatross.

CHAPTER ELEVEN

THE GIANT ANTS OF INDIA

The Persian conquests of the fifth century brought the Greeks more in contact with the Orient. From the Persians they began hearing wonderful tales of India, which meant for them that part of the sub-continent north of the Indus into Tibet and Central Asia. Among the first wonders of India were tales about giant gold-digging ants.

This legend was first recorded by the Greek historian Herodotus, who died in 415, or perhaps 424. Herodotus reports that the Indians annually paid 360 talents of gold-dust in tribute to the Persians. The Indians obtained this vast amount of gold from the desert regions beyond their own country.

There is found in this desert a kind of ant of great size – bigger than a fox, though not so big as a dog. Some specimens which were caught are kept in the palace of the Persian king. As they burrow underground these animals throw up the sand in heaps, just as our own ants throw up the earth, and are very like ours in shape. The sand has a rich content of gold, and it is that the Indians are after when they make their expeditions into the desert.

The Indians, Herodotus continues, get the gold in the midday heat when the sun keeps the 'ants' underground. They fill up their bags and start for home as fast as they can for fear of being caught by the creatures. Indian animals, Herodotus claimed, are bigger than elsewhere – but these giant ants were an incredible wonder even by Indian standards, and they caught the Western imagination for centuries.

Other details about them can be gathered from later writers. The Greek traveller Megasthenes, quoted by the geographer Strabo, placed the source of the gold on the tableland among the Derdae in the high ranges of Kafiristan and Tibet. Nearchus, the admiral of Alexander the Great, saw the skins of some of these giant ants – which suggests that they were animals of some kind, albeit unusual. Pliny, who died in 79 AD, noted that a pair of feelers from a giant ant were to be seen on display at Erythae. And the Ottoman emperor Soliman received at Istanbul in the sixteenth century a pair of the actual ants.

These creatures featured in European works of natural history and travel lore until at least 1536. They were also mentioned in the curious forgery which purported to be a letter from the legendary Prester John, a Christian king in Central Asia somewhere, to the Emperor of Byzantium. Inevitably they were soon dismissed as utterly fabulous, until further researches in the last hundred years have begun to throw a new light on these mythical monsters.

The gold is real enough. Herodotus was right about that. In Sanskrit this gold from Central Asia was called 'Pipilika', or 'ant-gold'. This was because it came down from the mountains of Turkestan as gold dust rather than nuggets. Some of this gold would have been washed out of streams, but some of it may well have been grubbed up by pangolins or marmots digging their burrows.

The Red Marmot (*Marmota caudata*) is much larger than the European species with which the Greeks would have been familiar, and has a longer tail. The animals live in open country in colony burrows, which may have suggested to some travellers that they were a kind of ant. This would have then been confirmed for them by the name given to the gold dust recovered from their diggings.

Valentine Ball, writing in 1884, thought that these 'ants' were more likely to have been the fierce Tibetan mastiffs, which were still a source of surprise – and fear – to modern travellers. A few years before, Captain William Gill, on a journey from the head-waters of the Yellow River, encountered not only Tibetan gold-diggers, but also the ferocity of the Tibetan guard dogs.

This theory seems unlikely to me. But Ball also suggests that the 'feelers' mentioned by Pliny could have been the horn picks with which the Tibetan gold-miners still worked in his day. The skins seen by Nearchus, and the 'ants' kept at the Persian king's palace, and those sent to Soliman, might well have been dogs. But they are more likely to have been the large marmots. Note that Herodotus mentioned that they are like foxes – which is to say, they are red-haired – as the Red Marmots are.

It may seem strange that so ordinary an animal as the marmot should have been turned through the course of the centuries into a bizarre and extraordinary monster. But as we shall see, this has happened over and over again. The marmots had the disadvantage of being merely mammals: monsters from remoter India would have to be monsters.

There is more to the 'giant ants' than it seemed before. They are almost certainly a genuine piece of Central Asian folklore. Laufer conjectures that the story arose from a confusion between the name of a Mongolian tribe (*Shiraighol*) and the Mongolian word for ant (*shirgol*). But he also notes that there are references to giant ants in the Mongolian region in Chinese sources. These occur in two works which I mentioned earlier in the chapter on the griffin : they are *Ch'u Tz* and *Shan Hai Ching*, which include magical material from the Yangtze Valley.

A poem from the first of these, *Chao Hun*, dates from about the third century BC.

Oh soul come back ! for the west holds many perils :
The Shifting Sands stretch on for a thousand leagues.
You will be swept into the Thunder's Chasm, and
dashed into pieces, unable to help yourself;
And even should you chance to escape from that, beyond is the
    empty desert,
And red ants as large as elephants, and wasps as big as gourds.

The second book dates from the first century AD, though it incorporates material from much earlier. A passage in *Hai Nei Pei Ching* ('Within the Sea, North') mentions that 'To the east of the Ch'iung-ch'i are the giant wasps which look like wasps and the giant ants which look like ants.'

This new information gives one pause to think. Are these monsters merely fabulous, or can there in fact be 'giant ants' or similar insects in the Mongolian region? The red-marmot theory may explain the classical references familiar in European literature, but they do not very easily explain these Chinese legends. The search for the giant ants continues.

CHAPTER TWELVE

THE UNICORN

The unicorn is among the most familiar of all fabulous beasts. As one of the supporters of the British royal arms, it has become known the world over, and in appearance seems almost as natural as the lion which faces it across the shield.

Indeed for a very long time it seemed so natural that very few were sceptical about its reality. Rumours of its existence in Asia or Africa were still coming in during the nineteenth century. And not so long before that, unicorn horns – or alicorns as they were dubbed by Odell Shepard – fetched a good price in Europe. Now a belief in the value of powdered horn as an aphrodisiac seems restricted to Chinese quacks, and the unicorn has finally been relegated to the realm of the imaginary. Or so it is often thought.

The origins of the unicorn legend are lost in antiquity. The strange creature in the main cavern at Lascaux has often been described as a 'unicorn'. It is not, of course, but it does suggest that even in the Old Stone Age there may have been some legend of a long-horned, elusive quadruped. But the first real reference to the unicorn comes much later. The legend as we know it comes from three sources: a Greek traveller, the Bible, and the Physiologus.

The Greek was our old friend Ctesias, the historian and traveller, who lived for many years around 400 BC at the court of the Persian king, Darius II, at Persepolis. (Persepolis is now an extensive and impressive ruin in the Luristan region of Persia: its shattered decorations include immense reliefs of mythological scenes and fabulous monsters.) When Ctesias returned home about 398 he wrote a book about India, based upon what he had heard about that country while in Persia. Though this book is now lost, fragments of it are preserved in many later writers, particularly in an abstract made in the ninth century AD by Photius, Patriarch of Constantinople.

It was from Ctesias that the Greeks, and later much of educated Europe, derived their ideas about the marvels of the East: such as the pygmies, the sciapods, men with their faces in their chests, giants, men with tails, giant ants, griffins. And the unicorn. The origin of the unicorn legend is the following passage from Ctesias:

There are in India certain wild asses which are as large as horses, and larger. Their bodies are white, their heads dark red, and their eyes dark blue. They have a horn on the forehead which is about a foot and a half long. The dust filed from this horn is administered in a potion as a protection against drugs. The base of this horn, for some two hands-breadth above the brow, is pure white; the upper part is sharp and of a vivid crimson; and the remainder, or middle portion, is black. Those who drink out of these horns, made into drinking vessels, are not subject, they say, to convulsions or to the holy disease [epilepsy]. Indeed, they are immune even to poisons if, either before or after swallowing such, they drink wine, water, or anything else from these beakers. Other asses, both the tame and the wild, and in fact all animals with solid hoofs, are without the ankle-bone and have no gall in the liver, but these have both the ankle-bone and the gall. This ankle-bone, the most beautiful I have ever seen, is like that of an ox in general appearance and size, but it is as heavy as lead and its colour is that of cinnibar through and through. The animal is exceedingly swift and powerful, so that no creature, neither horse nor any other, can overtake it.

These sentences have been the source of endless speculation and controversy. What exactly Ctesias had in mind is uncertain even today. But it was from Ctesias that much of the later lore about the unicorn derives, certainly much of what was written about it by the Greeks and Romans.

For them the unicorn was not a fabulous beast, but a real animal of India. Aristotle clearly took it for granted:

> We have never seen an animal with a solid hoof and with two horns, and there are only a few that have a solid hoof and one horn, as the Indian Ass and the Oryx. Of all animals with a solid hoof, the Indian ass alone has a talus.

But now he has introduced us to *two* types of unicorn. The Arabian Oryx (now almost extinct in the wild) has in fact got two horns, but when seen in profile or after the loss of a horn in a fight, it has the appearance of a unicorn. And it is white, as would be expected of a desert-dwelling animal. Ctesias, however, in his account seems to have conflated rumours of the Onager, or Wild Ass, with the Indian one-horned rhinoceros. The natural history of the unicorn is, as one can see, a very complicated affair.

Further references to the wild-ass unicorn occur in Pliny, Aelian, Oppian, even in Julius Caesar. These passages were to be of enormous interest to scholars at a later date, but only for a special reason: the unicorn was thought to have behind it the force of Sacred Scripture.

When the seventy-two Hebrew scholars of Alexandria prepared their translation of the Hebrew Bible into Greek in the third century BC, they were faced with many difficulties about finding the right words for many references. When they came to the word *re'em* they had a special problem. The seven references in the text to the creature suggested some strange powerful beast. They were not to know that it meant the aurochs (*bos primigenius*), which by then was extinct in the Middle East. So they put down *mono-ceros*, and so the unicorn came into the Bible. In the Latin Vulgate prepared by St Jerome the name became *unicornis*.

It was from these two sources that the medieval legend of the unicorn derived, and from that our modern ideas. But also of great influence was the third source I mentioned above, the Physiologus or the *Book of Beasts*. The unicorn of the *Bestiary* was yet another kind, a small goat-like creature, which it was said could be captured only with the aid of a virgin. The unicorn would come up to her and lay its head trustingly on her lap, and the hunters would seize the creature. Originally this seems to have come from hunters' stories about how monkeys were used to arouse rhinoceroses in Africa. However, in a far more refined form the theme of the Holy Hunt and the Virgin Capture was one which engrossed medieval Europe and was the subject of count-less paintings, sculptures and tapestries. The legend was given a religious gloss, with the unicorn being Christ and the virgin his Mother; but only by overlooking the obvious sexual overtones of the story.

The unicorn in art and legend is a complicated subject, and has been discussed at length in recent books by Rüdiger Robert Beer and Margaret Freeman. Odell Shepard in his earlier book has laid out with great clarity the permutations of the legend itself through the centuries. His book was published as long ago as 1930 : but it was to have a curious sequel which has a direct bearing on the origins of the unicorn myth.

One thing we can be certain about, and that is the origin of the unicorn's horn. The long, white spiral horn is now an established part of the unicorn's make-up. This was not always so. Some time before 900 AD there began to circulate in Europe numbers of horns, with a peculiar right-hand twist. These were said to be unicorn horns, and as such made their way into many collections : Elizabeth I had a famous one at Windsor, and there was another almost as famous at St Denis (it is now in the Cluny Museum). For many centuries these horns were a mystery. Then in 1638 Ole Wurm, university professor, zoologist and antiquarian, gave a public reading in Copenhagen of his Latin dissertation on the true origin and nature of unicorn horns. He demonstrated conclusively that they came from a type of small whale peculiar to the cold northern seas called the Narwhale. These were only found around the Arctic waters off Iceland and Greenland, and as Iceland was only settled by the Norse towards the end of the ninth century, the horns must have arrived in Europe later than that.

At first his revelation had little effect on the trade in these horns, or on the belief in the existence of the unicorn. The horns were still used to ward off the effect of poisons. Only slowly did such beliefs wane. Indeed, though the properties of the horn were discounted, a belief in the reality of the unicorn was as strong in 1886 as it had been three centuries earlier.

There were those who claimed to have seen a living unicorn (though not as many as have claimed to have seen mermaids). Marco Polo was disappointed when he saw the Indian one-horned rhino – as it was nothing like the unicorns known in Europe. In 1503 Ludovico Barthema, from Bologna, travelled through the countries of the Near East. In his *Itinerary* he says that he saw at the city of Zeila some cattle which had single horns about a palm and a half long rising from their heads and bending backwards. Also he said there existed (though he did not claim to have seen them) two unicorns in the temple at Mecca in Arabia. These had come from Ethiopia.

The connection between these 'unicorns' and the cattle at Zeila

fig. 3a Kaffirs manipulating cattlehorns

98

was not clear for a long time. However, at the end of the eighteenth century the French traveller Le Vaillant described how the Kaffirs manipulate the horns of their cattle into all kinds of curious shapes, making some of them into unicorns. This is also done by tribes along the White Nile to the north, and by the Nandi in Kenya.

Not surprisingly there were constant rumours of unicorns in Africa during the nineteenth century. These reports are in themselves a unique chapter in the history of the unicorn. In 1827 Georges Cuvier had stated that the unicorn was a physical impossibility : no horn could grow on the cleft skull of a cloven-hoofed animal, such as the unicorn was supposed to be. Yet the French geographer Malte-Brun in 1817 had been very impressed with the reports emanating from all parts of Africa. He felt that though the existence of the animal had not been proved, it had not been proved impossible. These reports have the advantage of being close to the present day in time, and so open to better critical appraisal than ancient or medieval legends.

Towards the end of the previous century there were reports from South Africa. Andreas Sparrman, Baron von Wurmb and Cornelius de Jong all recount rumours of the unicorn from that part of the continent. Sir John Barrow on his travels into the interior was eager to discover evidence about the unicorn. In several caves he found what he thought was indeed Bushman drawings of unicorns, and a picture of one appears in his book redrawn by the artist Daniell.

In 1845 Charles Hamilton Smith claimed that similar drawings were frequently seen, 'and we remember to have seen among the papers of the same artist, in the hands of his late brother, another drawing, likewise copied from a cave in the interior of South Africa, and representing with exceedingly characteristic fidelity, a group of Elands, Boselaphas Oreas, Hartebeest, Acronotus caama, and Spring Bock, Antilope Euchore; among which is placed, with head and shoulders towering over the rest, a *Rhinocertine* animal in form lighter than a wild bull, having an arched neck and a long nasal horn protruding in the form of a sabre.' Smith thought that a horn which he had seen in the British Museum might belong to this unknown form of rhinoceros from which the legend of the unicorn derived.

99

Indeed, at Mashowa in 1820 the missionary John Campbell saw a dead rhino of a new kind which he illustrated in his book about his experiences as 'a unicorn'. Campbell is thus unique in being the only man in modern times to bring home from the field what he claimed to be a 'real unicorn'. It was, needless to say, a species of rhinoceros, possibly a large White Rhinoceros. There were also reports of the unicorn from further north in Africa, from Ethiopia, Darfur and Kordofan : these were not so easily explained away.

Eduard Rüppell in 1829 quoted some of these reports but was himself sceptical about the matter. Von Katte in 1836 also heard rumours of a unicorn in Ethiopia, as did Joseph Russeger. Fulgence Fresnel in the 1840s was convinced about the existence of some kind of unicorn-like animal in Darfur. Indeed the Arab traveller Mohammed Ibn Omar from Tunisia was taken to task by French scholars for not mentioning one in his account of that country in 1845.

The English explorer William Baikie heard rumours of the unicorn somewhere in Northern Nigeria. David Livingstone was convinced it existed, and also in South Africa the Reverend Freeman was told about an animal called the *Nzoo-dzoo* which was said to be a unicorn and common about Makona. These constant reports might carry greater weight were it not that some confusion is clearly evident in some reports. Baikie quotes a series of native names for the unicorn, among them *mariri* in Hausa. But in fact this is their name for the Oryx.

And yet some doubt remains. Francis Galton, one of the best minds of the age, was convinced about the existence of the unicorn after his travels in South Africa in 1852.

The Bushmen, without any leading question or previous talk upon the subject, mentioned the unicorn. I cross questioned them thoroughly, but they persisted in describing a one-horned animal, something like a gemsbok in shape and size, whose horn was in the middle of its forehead, and pointed forwards. The spoor of the animal was, they said, like that of a zebra. The horn was in shape like a gemsbok, but shorter. They spoke of the animal as though they knew of it, but were not familiar with it. It will indeed be strange if, after all, the creature has a real existence. There are recent travellers in the north of tropical

Africa who have heard of it there, and believe in it, and there is surely room to find something new in the vast belt of *terra incognita* that lies in this continent.

Another British traveller writing in 1862, after his return from Africa, Winwood Reade (author of the now unread classic *The Martyrdom of Man*) was also convinced about the existence of the unicorn in the unknown heart of Africa. After quoting several earlier reports, he goes on :

> That such an animal has existed, there can, I think, be little doubt : it is possible he is extinct; but more probable that, flying from fire-arms (which, it must always be remembered, are used by tribes whom no white men have visited), he has concealed himself in those vast forest-wastes of Central Africa which are uninhabited and unexplored.

This seemed reasonable enough in 1862, but the unicorn in the wild proved elusive, and the rest of the century produced no evidence about it. But it did uncover the existence of other strange animals in those forests of central Africa where Reade had travelled at the early age of twenty-three.

Among these animals was Cotton's White Rhinoceros. The White Rhinoceros (so called from the Dutch *weid*, referring to the width of its muzzle) was familiar from south of the Zambezi River. The Reverend Campbell's unicorn would have been one of these then little-known animals, in which the long front horn can stand five feet from the ground. However a white rhino skull was brought back from Lado on the Upper Nile, and soon Major Cotton-Powell collected other specimens. The new race (*Cerato-therium simum cottoni*) was formally described by Richard Lydekker in 1901. The animal was found to cover a wide range of territory from Uele to Zaire. As Bernard Heuvelmans comments, 'that such a huge beast could have remained unnoticed in a country generally thought to be well-explored seemed almost a joke'.

But the greatest discovery of all was the appearance of the okapi. Much earlier, H. M. Stanley had referred to a 'donkey' called the atti, known to the Wambutti pygmies. But asses were unknown in the Congo. In 1899 Sir Harry Johnson confirmed the existence of the okapi in eastern Zaire – the donkey was not a legend after all. It turned out, when he obtained a skin of the creature, that it was really a relative of the giraffe. It had two small horns under the skin on its head, which made a bump on its forehead. Could the okapi after all be the animal with 'the horn on its forehead' which had been long sought?

Meanwhile the rumours of unicorns in the wild were to be found coming from their original source, the India of Ctesias: the mountains of Central Asia.

Richard Lydekker in 1911 described a set of unicorn rams which had been brought to England from Nepal; and some years later W. R. Dawson also reported on 'the supposed discovery of unicorns in Tibet'.

These animals formed part of a large collection of Nepalese animals which were presented to the Prince of Wales (later George V) and which were exhibited at the London zoo in 1906. There was some mystery about the creatures, for though the rams were unicorns, underneath the horn sheath were found two horn buds. Further inquiries revealed that they were not natural, nor were they freaks, but artificial creations. The male lambs were branded with irons to make the horn buds grow together after being healed with oil and soot. Great sums of money were paid for these animals in Nepal. But this did not seem to explain the whole process, which remained shrouded in Himalayan mystery.

Odell Shepard referred to these rams and to other 'real' unicorns such as the African cattle in his book *The Lore of the Unicorn* in 1930. Some years later, after reading the book, an American biologist made some experiments which cast a flood of light upon the mystery. He was Dr William Franklin Dove, then in charge of an experimental biology station at the University of Maine. In 1934 he created a unicorn out of a day-old bull calf.

He transplanted both horn buds, or rather the little knots of tissue that normally produce a pair of horns, to a side-by-side position on the centre of the calf's brow-ridge. When the horn buds were cut loose from the skull, a strip of skin and underlying flesh was left attached to each one to carry the normal blood supply until the transplanted beginnings of the horns could take hold on the new site to which they were transferred. Since the horn buds were round, Dr Dove cut the edges flat so that he could set them close together, and so encourage the growth of a single horn.

In this way Dr Dove induced the growth of a massive single horn that proved to be a very efficient weapon. The one horn was so much more successful than two horns that it gave the young calf undisputed dominance over the rest of the herd. The animal developed much of the proud yet unaggressive bearing and disposition of the unicorn of legend.

The unicorn was two and a half years old before Dr Dove published his report of his work. His Ayrshire unicorn was then strong, fearless, well able to fight though seldom doing so. His marked docility was due, Dr Dove thought, to a knowledge of his own unique power and the superiority in combat that his single weapon gave him : complete confidence had done away with his truculence.

Moreover, Dr Dove had proved Cuvier was quite mistaken when he said it was impossible for a horn to grow over the cleft skull bone of a cloven-hoofed animal. A key objection to the natural existence of the unicorn had collapsed. Dr Dove was well aware of the earlier lore of the unicorn, including references to horn manipulation by Pliny and reports of this from Nepal and Africa. Plutarch had also recorded that his farm-hands had sent Pericles in Athens the skull of a unicorn ram : this would have been their herd leader, and a potent symbol of leadership and power.

So the confused history of the unicorn seems to have arisen in the first instance from unique sports of nature, which were then imitated by herdsmen to produce herd-leaders. The animal reported by Ctesias may well have been the Indian rhinoceros, but behind it and for many centuries afterwards the strange idea of the unicorn drew on more ancient sources. Though its nature was simple enough, at the end of three thousand years the legend had become something else again. But Dr Dove brought life to that legend, leaving us to wonder once again about what may lie behind the lore of other, stranger monsters.

CHAPTER THIRTEEN

THE MANTICORA

The manticora is another of those animals, originally classical, that passed into the bestiaries, and from them into the works of the early naturalists. Eventually it became part of European folk-lore, as an embodiment of evil. But the final idea of the creature bore little resemblance to its original.

Once again we have that credulous medical man Ctesias to thank. In his lost work on India he makes the first reference to the manticora in chapter seven. He says that he himself had seen this creature at the Persian court. The creature had been brought to Persepolis from India. Ctesias' account of the manticora is preserved by the Roman writer Aelian:

> An animal said to have the face of a man and the bulk of a lion; to be of red-colour, having three rows of teeth in each jaw, with human ears but larger, and grey eyes; equipped with a tail above a cubit long, pointed with a sting like that of a scorpion,

and armed with upright and transverse spines, a wound from any one of which is fatal. When assailed by a distant foe, the Martichora (*sic*) turns its tail in that direction, and darts its spines from it like arrows from a bow. It can cast these spines to the distance of a plethron (about 10 feet), and they kill any animal except an elephant. The spines are a foot long, and the thickness of a slender cord. The meaning of martichora is *man-eater*, as it devours many of those whom it has slain; it also preys upon animals. It fights with its talons as well as its spines; and when any of the latter have been shot away, others grow in their place. India abounds with these animals, and they are often killed with darts by men who hunt them on elephants.

fig. 4 Manticora from bestiary

This description was taken up also by Aristotle, Pausanias and Pliny. Ctesias called the animal the *martikhora*; a corrupt reading in Aristotle changed this into *mantichora*, and it was as *manticora* that it became widely known.

An attractive picture of the creature, with a man's head wearing a Phrygian cap, was added to the account in the bestiary. Gesner, writing in 1551, elaborated on the legend; his English translator Edward Topsell added a fine elaborate picture of the monster. It was this utterly fantastic picture of the monster which convinced many later writers that the manticora was a creature of the imagination and not a real animal.

Some thought otherwise. Pausanias commented that the manticora was the Indian tiger. 'The false reports were circulated by the Indians owing to their excessive fear of the beast.'

Colonel Jim Corbett in his book *Man-Eaters of Kumaon* gives vivid impressions of the very real terror in which man-eating tigers are held by Indian villagers. His area of India, in the foothills of the Himalayas, would have been part of the classical India of Ctesias.

However in his account Ctesias has clearly got the porcupine mixed up with the tiger. It was indeed thought that porcupines could shoot their darts like arrows, as Ctesias describes. This is not true to nature, but Ctesias seems to have been fond of oddities. And we should also allow for some confusion on the part of those quoting him.

Corbett says that one of the common reasons for tigers becoming man-eaters is incapacity; another is old age. One of the animals he had to shoot had several porcupine quills in one leg which were suppurating and causing it great pain. This prevented her from taking her usual prey, and so she took to man-eating. Villagers were easy to kill.

But on the whole the description of the manticora suggests a were-tiger. The French traveller Jules de Thevenot described an encounter in 1666: 'I arrived at Debca (now Dewa) which lies on the side of a Wood seven leagues from Sourban. The Inhabitants of the town were formerly such as are called *Merdi-Coura* or *Anthrophagi*, man-eaters, and it is not very many years since mans-flesh was there publickly sold in the Markets. This place seems to be a nest of robbers; the Inhabitants are for the most part armed with swords.'

James Tod, who travelled in the same region of India in the 1830s, also encountered the sect of Aghori, 'who, among other unspeakable viands, fed on dead bodies'. He mentions a fanatic cannibal named Futteh Poori, who disembowelled whomever came his way, and had himself walled up in a cave in the end.

Seal in mermaid pose

Man-headed monster from Persepolis

Centaur from Parthenon

Modern phoenix: Niger advances towards the fire

Niger rises phoenix-like from the flames

Origin of the griffin: monster from Persepolis

Pair of griffins from Cashel Cathedral

Forehead of Dr Dove's unicorn (*photo: Dr F.W. Dove*)

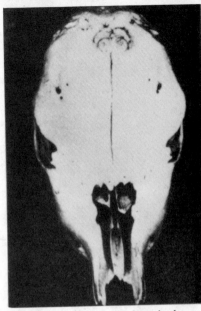

Skull of unicorn showing horn buds fused (*photo: Dr F.W. Dove*)

Modern unicorn at 2 years old (*photo: Dr F.W. Dove*)

The gnu, the origin of the Catoblepas

A triumph for cryptozoology: *Homo pongoides,* a surviving Neanderthaler, photographed in ice

Reconstruction by Alika Watteau

(*Left*) Dr Bernard Heuvelmans, 'the father of cryptozoology'

(*Below*) The ultimate monster - the Boojum Snark surprises his victim

Such aspects of India, what Leigh Hunt refers to as 'the outrageous tendency to excess on the side of superstition, and of brute contradictions to humanity, characteristic of the lowest form of Indian degradation', disgusted many early visitors.

The resort to superstition as an explanation of the manticora did not satisfy the Irish scholar Valentine Ball. He worked for many years as a geologist in India and later became director of the new National Museum in Dublin. His researches had convinced him that many of the critics of Ctesias were ignorant of the real India, and that nearly everything that the Greek author had reported could be traced to real facts. The manticora was the subject of a paper he published in 1884. Pausanias and others had suggested that the manticora was the Indian tiger, but no one had explained how the description given by Ctesias, which seems quite fantastic, fitted such a well-known animal.

It was true that tigers are common in India (or were then) and were hunted by local princes from hodahs on the backs of elephants. Ball showed first of all that the name manticora did indeed mean man-eater, and was *mard-khor* in archaic Persian. (This derivation had been pointed out first by Adrian Reland, an early etymologist.) So far so good.

Ball also pointed out that the 'triple row of teeth' had its origin in the distinctive three lobes of the carnivorous molar, 'which is of such a different type from the molars of ruminants and horses'. But what of the stinging tail?

Among facts not generally known, though mentioned in some works of zoology, is one which I can state from my own personal knowledge is familiar to Indian shikaris – it is that at the extremity of the tail of the tiger, as well as other felidae, there is a little horny-dermal structure like a claw or nail, which I doubt not, the natives regard as analagous to the sting of the scorpion.

Moreover, Indians believed that the tiger's whiskers were poisonous quills, and hunters, unless they were careful, often found they had been plucked out by their shikaris to prevent accidents. And, Ball concludes, 'it would not be difficult to present an account of the tiger derived from the attributes and characteristics ascribed to the animal at the present day by the natives, which would have far less substantial basis in fact than has the one given to us by Ctesias'.

Indeed the Indians themselves did have strange ideas about the tiger. Megasthenes, as quoted by Strabo, claimed that the largest tigers were to be found among the Prasii (that is Easterners, from the Sanskrit *Prachyas*), being twice the size of a lion, and so strong that a tame tiger, led by four men, having seized a mule by one of the hind legs, overpowered it and dragged it away despite their efforts to resist him. Such an incident, Ball remarks, would not surprise Indian sportsmen; and Colonel Corbett's stories a generation later bear him out.

Ball had no doubt that the Indian tiger lay behind the legend of the manticora. Ctesias had probably seen one at the Persian court at Persepolis about 400 BC, as he claimed. But his highly coloured account, derived from what he picked up from the Persians, was to have a long history.

From the pictures in the bestiary and the early zoologists, the manticora passed over into European art and architecture. Representations of manticoras were common enough in the Middle Ages. There is one on the Hereford World Map drawn in the thirteenth century. An early example appears on a column of Souvigny Abbey (illustrated in Mâle), and another in the cathedral of Aosta (illustrated in Aus'm Weerth). Appearing among the heraldic creatures and monsters of medieval churches, the manticora passed with some authority into folklore.

The English poet John Skelton (who died himself in 1529), lamenting the death of poor pet Philip Sparrow, cursed the cat who had slain him : 'The mantycors of the montaynes Might fede upon thy braynes.'

There was something peculiarly terrifying about this man-faced monster. Leigh Hunt recalls in his autobiography how his childhood in the 1790s was terrorised by his elder brother with tales of the manticora. He had a horror of dreadful faces, even in books. The picture of the manticora 'unspeakably shocked me'. It always seemed to be in profile (the picture was from Topsell, of course), and would he thought have scared an army. 'Even fully grown dictionary makers have been frightened out of their propriety at the thought of him. "Mantichora", says old Morell – "bestia horrenda" – a brute fit to give one the horrors.'

In vain my brother played me repeated tricks with this frightful anomaly. I was always ready to be frightened again. At one time he would grin like the Mantichora; then he would rore like him; then call about him in the dark. I remember him asking me to come up to him one night at the top of the house. I ascended, and found the door shut. Suddenly a voice came through the key-hole, saying, in its hollowest tones, 'The Mantichora's coming.' Down I rushed to the parlour, fancying the terror at my heels.

The manticora, Hunt confesses, 'cost me many a bitter night', and in his childhood terror we can catch something of the terror the beast must have inspired in medieval Europe. For not only he has confessed to being frightened by it. That the man-eater was a man-tiger, or were-tiger, was an easy conclusion. As T. H. White points out, there is some resemblance between the manticora and the *Cigouave* that haunts the jungles and imaginations of Haiti. In their novel *The Beast of the Haitian Hills,* the native authors Philippe Thoby-Marcelin and Pierre Marcelin give a strange account of how even the most rational of minds can collapse in the face of such primeval terrors.

Until recently the manticora, or the fear of it, survived in Spain. David Garnett informed T. H. White that his friend Mr Richard Strachey was mistaken for a manticora in the village of Ugijar, Andalusia, in 1930, and was mobbed on that hypothesis. David Garnett has himself disclosed more details about this curious event.

Strachey was staying with his friend the British writer Gerald Brennan when he was attacked by sedentary gypsies who took him for the sinister beast because of his beard. That, as I say, was in 1930.

In 1964 Garnett was informed by an old friend of a mutual acquaintance that while travelling in Spain she had stopped in Granada near the Alhambra in a little inn with a long garden. Next day, however, their hostess came to her :

'My servants are all leaving today because of the dark bearded gentleman. They will not serve him. They say he is a Mantiquera and will steal their babies at night and cut them up and eat them.' The good lady protested that her kind friend would not eat babies.

'Yes I'm sure, but our peasants from the hills still believe the Mantiquera exists and nothing I can say about you will help.'

That evening the English lady arranged to dine in the garden, and while the hidden peasants watched (their babies safely out of harm's way), went up to her friend Caurino, kissed him lovingly, petted him, and said how gentle he was. Her ruse worked, and they were left to enjoy their holiday, the strange fears of the peasants banished, for a while at least.

How strange that what had entered literature as a vague and distorted account of the man-eating Indian tiger twenty-three centuries ago, should still survive in European folklore as a beast of ill-omen.

André Thévet, writing in 1571, described the manticora from personal experience. 'When I travelled on the Red Sea, some Indians arrived from the mainland . . . and they brought along a monster of the size and proportions of a tiger without a tail, but the face was that of a well-formed man.' The picture in his text shows a manticora without a tail, drawn by his artist from European tradition. But what Thévet saw was probably one of the anthropoid apes of Africa, or perhaps a Lemur or Indris from Madagascar. Mild enough creatures, but easily turned into a monster by the mere force of artistic tradition. Which is a thought more terrible than the manticora itself.

CHAPTER FOURTEEN

THE CATOBLEPAS

At the end of his strange drama *The Temptation of Saint Anthony*, published in 1874, Flaubert introduces among the many monsters that beset the hermit, the strange Catoblepas. This he describes as a

> black buffalo with the head of a hog, hanging close to the ground, joined to its body by a thin neck, long and loose as an emptied intestine.
>
> It wallows in the mud, and its legs are smothered under the huge mane of stiff bristles that hide its face.
>
> 'Obese, downhearted, wary, I do nothing but feel under my belly the warm mud. My head is so heavy that I cannot bear its weight. I wind it slowly around my body; with half-open jaws, I pull up with my tongue poisonous plants dampened by my breath. Once, I ate up my forelegs unawares.
>
> 'No one, Anthony, has ever seen my eyes; or else, those who

have seen them have died. If I were to lift my eyelids – my pink and swollen eyelids – you would die on the spot.'

This passage marks the final appearance in literature of the Catoblepas, though this pathetic monster is far removed from the original, less gothic version of the creature.

Pliny, an invaluable source of monsters, is the first to describe the Catoblepas, in his *Natural History*. To the south of Egypt on the borders of Ethiopia, he writes, near the sources of the Nile.

> there is found a wild beast called the Catoblepas; an animal of moderate size, and in other respects sluggish in the movement of the rest of its limbs; its head is remarkably heavy, and it only carries it with great difficulty, being always bent down towards the earth. Were it not for this circumstance, it would prove the destruction of the human race; for all who behold its eyes, fall dead upon the spot.

As the deadly basilisk follows at once in his text, some confusion may have arisen in Pliny's mind over the deadly gaze of these creatures. Two centuries later Aelian also mentions the Catoblepas, adding that it was like a bull. This makes it sound like a real animal. But by the time it emerged in Gesner it had become a fully fledged monster. In Topsell it has become confused with the Gorgon :

> It is a beast all set over with scales like a dragon, having no haire except on his head, great teeth like swine, having wings to flie, and hands to handle, in stature betwixt a bull and a calfe.

This version was figured by Topsell in an alarming illustration of a bull with scales. Whatever the catoblepas may have been for Pliny, this Renaissance Gorgon was a composite monster. 'And this much may serve for a discription of this beast, untill by god's providence, more can be knowne thereof.' So Edward Topsell in 1607.

In 1652 the Dutch landed at the Cape of Good Hope to establish a colony there. And in the mountains of South Africa they soon after discovered the wildebeest, or gnu, the original of the catoblepas.

The gnu was first described for science by George Buffon in 1777. The existence of the animals was brought to his attention by Lord Bute, but he was also sent a sketch by Viscomte de Ouerhoënt. Both referred to an animal brought to the Cape from the interior in 1773. The animal was called *feva heda* or *nou* by the Kaffirs.

When publishing a new edition of his *Natural History*, Buffon included an account of the gnu which had been included by his translator Professor Allemand in the Dutch edition of the book. Another gnu had been sent to the menagerie of the Prince of Orange in Holland, which Allemand had examined. Allemand wrote of the creature :

> The ancients have told us that Africa was fertile with monsters; by this they meant that it held more unknown animals than other parts of the world. This has been confirmed in our own day, when this vast region has been penetrated.

He admitted that when he received a sketch of the gnu from South Africa, he did not publish it because he thought it might be a drawing of a fabulous animal. Only after he heard a report of the creature from a Captain Gordan did he use it in his Dutch version of Buffon. Captain Gordan presented him with a head of this 'chimerical animal'.

The discovery of the gnu sent naturalists back to look again at some of those monsters that Africa was so fertile with. Among these was Pliny's catoblepas.

Cuvier, writing in 1817, thought the gnu was an 'extraordinary animal', which 'at first glance seems to be a monster composed of different animals'. Indeed it does. Lightly built in the rump, the gnu has a heavy horned head covered by a long hairy mane. It also carries its head cast down because its shoulders are high. Among the animals of Africa it is distinctive and peculiar, one of the few indeed that everyone knows by name today. Thus it fills very well all the details of Pliny's description of the catoblepas.

But what Cuvier and the others did not explain is how an author who died in 79 AD knew about an animal from the high plains of Southern and Eastern Africa. The solution to this mystery lies in an almost forgotten feat of early exploration.

Outside of Egypt, Africa was largely unknown to the Greeks

and Romans. Herodotus tells how the continent was circumnavigated by a party of Carthaginians, but the interior was a mystery. And the great mystery of Africa was the source of the Nile, over which the ancients made many conjectures. The true source was only discovered by nineteenth-century explorers. But the ancients had made some brave attempts.

The Emperor Nero, for instance, sent an expedition down the Nile which seems to have got as far as the great marshes in southern Sudan. They may have heard rumours of the strange animals to be found further south, and Pliny may have got his information this way. But there is another possibility.

For one ancient explorer did reach central Africa. Sometime after the reign of Nero, a Greek named Diogenes was blown by accident down the east African coast for twenty-five days to a place called Rhapta (probably the modern Dar-es-Salaam). There he landed and travelled inland. He is said to have reached the neighbourhood of two great lakes, and a range of snow-covered mountains, where the Nile had its source. These were the Mountains of the Moon. Or perhaps he may only have been told all of this by Arab traders (or rather slavers) in Rhapta.

We can no longer be certain of this. Diogenes wrote an account of his journey, with a map. These have now vanished, though they were quoted in a lost work by Marinus of Tyre and by his follower Ptolemy. From what Ptolemy says, the mountains may have been either Mount Kenya and Mount Kilimanjaro, or the Ruwenzori further west.

In this part of Africa herds of gnu are a feature of the landscape. And so it was most probably from the account of Diogenes (or from some now unknown traveller) that Pliny derived his description of the catoblepas. So this unlikely monster, as it later became, is an echo of a great but almost forgotten adventure.

CHAPTER FIFTEEN

LEVIATHAN AND BEHEMOTH

When Christianity at last became the established religion of the Western world, it exerted an influence over people's ideas about many other things besides faith and morals. Natural history also took on a Christian aspect.

The version of the Bible familiar throughout Europe before the Reformation was that translated into Greek, derived from the Septuagint version of the Old Testament (which was so called after the seventy scholars of Alexandria who had produced it). The Vulgate or Latin version of the Bible appeared in 392 AD.

As I mentioned earlier, in seeking a term to translate the Hebrew word *re'em*, the Septuagint had selected the Greek word monoceros, and so added the authority of the Divine Word (so it seemed to many) to the existence of the unicorn.

Other puzzling references appeared in the Bible as well, to dragons and satyrs for example. But by reference to the text of the original Hebrew it became clear that these were meant to be ordinary creatures such as jackals and owls, and not the monsters of classical antiquity.

But the identity of two great Biblical creatures continued to puzzle many scholars, remote in time and place from the Middle Eastern scene. These were Leviathan and Behemoth.

The name Leviathan (from the Hebrew *Livyatan*) appears in the Old Testament. Derived from the words *livyah* and *tan*, the name means something like 'tortuous monster'. *Tan*, in various contexts, means anything from a snake, whale, or dragon to a great fish. From the passage in Psalm 104, 26 : 'There go the ships; there is that leviathan, whom thou hast made to play therein', some sort of whale seems to be the creature intended. But the more detailed description in the book of Job suggests quite a different creature :

> Canst thou draw out leviathan with a hook? or his tongue with a cord which thou lettest down?
>
> Canst thou put an hook into his nose? or bore his jaw through with a thorn?
>
> . . . Canst thou fill his skin with barbed irons, or his head with spears . . .
>
> I will not conceal his parts, nor his power, nor his comely proportion . . .
>
> Who can open the doors of his face? his teeth are terrible round about.
>
> His scales are his pride, shut up together as with a close seal.
>
> One is so near to another, that no air can come between them.
>
> They are joined one to another, they stick together, that they cannot be sundered . . .
>
> The flakes of his flesh are joined together : they are firm in themselves; they cannot be moved.

And so on through thirty-four verses of poetic description. Picking out the various details, it is clear that the poet refers to some large, savage, scaly animal with fierce-looking teeth and an impregnable hide.

Mixed up in the description are whales and earlier ideas of the Great Dragon but for the most part the creature is a crocodile.

Crocodiles were common in the Nile, and the ancient Egyptians worshipped them at Crocodopolis, Ombos, Athribis, Thebes and Ciptos. Their mummies have been found in many of these places, as carefully preserved as the bodies of kings and princes. According to Plutarch, crocodiles had the useful habit of laying their eggs just above the level of the seasonal flood of the Nile, which was a great help to farmers. The crocodile was sacred and had no natural enemies – except a mysterious creature called the Ichneumon, which ate its eggs. They were seldom hunted, but when they were they were caught on hooks baited with meat and killed with forks, just as the Bible says.

The crocodile would not have been familiar to the Jews, even though they were once native to Palestine, and Robert Graves says they survived there in the River Zarka until the beginning of this century. So they were easily turned into monsters.

Paired with Leviathan in the book of Job is Behemoth. This too has seemed a mysterious creature to many people. Some even thought it might have been the elephant, but it is clearly enough the hippopotamus, another denizen of the Nile.

The description given in the Bible fits quite well. 'Behold now behemoth, which I made with thee; he eateth grass like an ox ... he lieth under the shady trees, in the covert of the reed, and the fens. The shady trees cover him with their shadow; the willows of the brook compass him about.'

This almost exactly describes the habits of the hippopotamus, as does the drinking capacity of the creature!

Among the Egyptians, the hippopotamus was even more sacred than the crocodile. She was Taurat, the goddess of the Nile itself. As such she was the special deity of childbirth. Also in ancient Egyptian mythology Seth took the shape of a hippopotamus and was killed by Horus.

During the First Dynasty priests of Horus at Solfu would row out into the middle of the sacred lake there and dismember a hippo-shaped cake. There is also some evidence that ritual hippo hunts took place on the Nile; these would have been analagous to the sacrifices of crocodiles. Also among the most popular toys of ancient Egypt were little faience hippos in various colours, which still retain their great charm today.

Inevitably in later Rabbinical tradition, these ordinary animals became more mysterious, monstrous and menacing. However, these Jewish traditions seem to have been exclusive, and not to have influenced the mythical monsters of Europe in general.

In Isaiah (XXXIV, 16) there is a reference to a long-lost book of lore entitled *The Book of Yahweh*, which seems to have been a mythological bestiary according to Robert Graves and Raphael Patai. It may well be that some of the strange creatures it contained re-emerged to the light of day in the text of the Physiologus, and so in that way Jewish traditions joined the mainstream of intellectual history.

CHAPTER SIXTEEN

THE DRAGON

The Dragon as we know it is a medieval creation. Earlier eras had their monsters, but they have been called dragons only because they resemble the great beasts of medieval legend.

To the Greeks, for instance, *dracones* (from which the word dragon is derived) were merely large snakes, usually those found around tombs, which were, so they believed, the spirits of departed heroes. The monsters slain by some of these heroes, such as Perseus when he rescued Andromeda, seem to have been thought of as something quite different.

In Europe the dragon is associated with St George. After the Crusades, he became the patron saint of England. But in recent years some doubt has been expressed about his historical reality. The trouble is not that there was no St George, but that there are too many of them: the choice of Gibbon was an Arian heretic.

The story of St George and the dragon first appears in the *Golden Legend* of Jacob of Voraigne. His version begins, in the translation of Sabine Baring-Gould : 'George, a tribune, was born in Cappadocia and came to Libya, to the town called Silene, near which was a pond infested by a monster.' The story goes on : we are told of the creature's poisonous breath, and how the citizens sacrificed from their herds to keep it away from the city walls. When there were no more animals, they began to choose by lot from among their sons and daughters. At last it was the turn of the princess. But she was saved by St George (as was Andromeda in the earlier legend).

Another version has the princess rescued from a castle in which the people are shut up and dying from lack of water. Their only source was a well at the foot of the hill guarded by the dragon.

Gwyn Williams, the Welsh writer, familiar with Libya, was impressed by the verisimilitude of this story. 'Such a version, to anyone familiar with the typical Roman fort or township or forti-fied farm in the Jebel Akbar part of Cyrenaica, with well and cisterns lower down the slope and the fort or farm perched on a rock above the cultivable land, is perhaps the more realistically Cyrenaican form of the story.'

Where then was the 'town of Silene'? At first he thought it might have been Slonta or Slunt, a very small village, on the road between Barce and Cyrene. The situation of the town, a fortified place on a hill top, fitted, and there were wells below and a de-pression which might once have been a swamp in an earlier and wetter era.

I wondered whether the mysterious rock-carvings at Slonta, vaguely referred to as primitive Libyan by the archaeologists, could represent sacrifices to the monster, particularly since the grotesque figure cut in the mound at the entrance to the shrine reminds me strongly of the Egyptian monster-god Bes, who is closely associated with the Dragon.

(Bes was, in fact, the god of the underworld).

Another possibility lay in the territory of the Seti, along the Syrtic coast. Two towns belonged to them in ancient times, and Oric Bates suggests that the snake may have been their totem. Pliny and Lucan report that they had a peculiar way with snakes, and at birth exposed their children to snake bites. But then he found a far more likely place.

Then, one day, as I was planning an excursion into the Jebel, my eye fell on the name Gasr Silina on the map. Gasr means fort or castle, and Gasr Silina is marked on the Society of Antiquarians' map of the Roman province of Cyrene on a minor road. Looking at a modern map of the area I found no sign of Gasr Silina, but marked at about the same spot the words El Aggar u-Silina. A student who comes from the Jebel Akbdar tells me that *aggarah* is a local word for a pool of water left by a flood – just the thing to make a swamp and keep a holy crocodile in.

More than likely any such cult would have been derived from the ancient Egyptians. 'Whatever beast the Cyrenaican dragon was, the sacrifices associated with him suggest ritual practices, so that the story of this killing may be that of the end of paganism and the christianising of Cyrenaica.' This, I suppose, would have been in the third century AD.

Would that all dragon legends were so easily explained. In Provence, for instance, there is the legend of the Tarasque and St Martha. She is said to have brought Christianity to Provence and to have overcome the monster which haunted the Rhône between Arles and Avignon. The creature was said to have lived in a wood but then to have retreated to an underwater cave on the river beneath the citadel of Tarascon. This amphibious monster appears on several carvings and pictures, but these are all based on a processional monster which is carried round the town on the saint's feast day. This sort of monster was once common all over Europe – St George and the dragon were the usual actors, but the one at Tarascon is the only one that now survives.

But what sort of amphibious creature originally haunted the Rhône marshes? A crocodile or an alligator seems the most likely, and the connection of St Martha with Eygpt (the home of the crocodile cult) is suggestive.

These perambulating monsters were one source of people's ideas about dragons. Another source was, oddly enough, primitive kites called *dracones*. These were really windsock banners. They seem to have originated in Central Asia, spread westward and lasted until the late Middle Ages. These banners were used by the Scythians, Persians and Dacians. Adopted by the Rome legions, they spread all over the Empire, and are the origins of the flying dragons of Welsh mythology – dracones were the banners of the Celtic chiefs.

These banners were often very realistic, and, not unnaturally, some people thought they were really alive. In the early Middle Ages, the practice arose of placing a lighted torch in the mouth of the banner, hence the fiery flying dragons which feature in many other northern legends. The red dragon of Merlin may well have been such a device. A passage from a Polish history describing the battle of Wahlstatt (in April 1241) reports that such banners were carried by the Tartars. The flares and fumes overawed the Polish soldiers and they were defeated.

These banners, like the processional monsters, kept alive the idea of the dragon. But the origin of the myth must be sought much further back in history.

Whatever they may have become, dragons are clearly enough reptiles of some kind, as their scales show. And the larger lizards and snakes played a major role in the development of the idea of what they were like.

The dragon of the *Bestiary* is clearly enough based on the large pythons of India, which may often exceed thirty feet.

Draco, the Dragon, is the biggest of all serpents, in fact of all living things on earth. The Greeks call it *draconta* and hence it has turned into Latin under the name 'draco'.

When this dragon has come out of its cave, it is often carried into the sky, and the air becomes ardent. It has a crest, a small mouth and a narrow gullet through which it draws breath or puts out its tongue. Moreover, its strength is not in its teeth but in its tail, and it inflicts injury by blows rather than by stinging. So it is harmless as regards poison. But they point out that poisons are not necessary to it for killing, since if it winds round anyone it kills him like that. Even the elephant is not protected from it by the size of its body; for the dragon, lying in wait near the paths along which the elephants usually saunter, lassos their legs in a knot with its tail and destroys them by suffocation.

Much of this was derived from the usual classical sources such as Pliny, but there is little in it which gives the impression of a dragon as we know it.

Clearly the dragon is here conceived as a large snake of some kind, and much of what is said about its habits applies to the pythons – though a python would not take on an elephant. The dragon carried into the sky and making the air ardent refers to the firedrake or meteor, such as the one seen before the Battle of Hastings in 1066. The modern idea of the dragon came from further east again, from the legends of the Extreme Orient.

The Chinese dragon, the Lung, was one of the four sacred animals of Chinese mythology. (The others are the phoenix, the kylin and the tortoise.) It is one of the commonest motifs in Chinese art. It is usually represented with a bearded scowling head, open jaws, straight horns, a scaly serpentine body, with four sharp-clawed feet. The traditional form is said to have the 'nine resemblances'. That is a camel's head, a deer's horns, a rabbit's eyes, a cow's ears, a snake's neck, a frog's belly, a carp's scales, a hawk's claws and a tiger's palms. In actual form this exotic assemblage was much simplified. More often than not, eastern dragons have no wings.

The Chinese dragon is always associated with water, a benign rain god with the power to send the rain needed by the crops, as well as storms and floods when angry. When angry, the dragon had to be appeased, but essentially it was a gentle creature representing the principles of Yang, the Earth and Light.

Much of this is in contrast to the malign and evil monster of Western tradition. In China the dragon was the special symbol of the Emperor, the son of Heaven. The imperial dragon had five claws; ordinary ones four or three. The earliest ones have only three. The five-clawed dragon was called lung; the four-clawed was called mang, which also means python – from which it may have developed. Other forms of dragons developed over the centuries, such as the Buddhist dragon (*fa lung*) or the flying-fish dragon (*fei-yu*) and the *chi'ih* dragon which had no horns.

In Chinese apothecary shops dragon bones are still found on

sale. These are usually the fossil bones of huge prehistoric saurians. Dragons' eggs are the eggs of an extinct ostrich from the Gobi desert (*Struthiolithus chersonensis*). As in Europe, these relics tended to reinforce the legend.

Does the Chinese dragon have a different origin from the European; is our dragon derived from the Oriental one?

As we have seen, the python has contributed something to the natural history of the dragon but for the ultimate source we must look elsewhere. As Richard Carrington points out 'the final form of all eastern dragons is strongly reminiscent of one well-known creature – the Chinese alligator of the lower Yangtze Kiang'.

This creature is the only Old World representative of the alligators, which adds to its distinction. There is evidence that within historical times this alligator was widely distributed in eastern China. The connection between the dragon and the alligator is confirmed by Chinese legends and by Chinese pharmacies which sell parts of dried alligators as magical and medical remedies derived from dragons.

The discovery of the various dinosaurs and other prehistoric reptiles in the nineteenth century made some critics think again about the almost universal legend of dragons and other primeval monsters. For here in the iguanadon, the pterodactyl and the others were the very monsters of the old legends.

This was the belief of N. B. Dennys, an authority on Chinese folklore writing in 1893. He had 'little doubt' that the dragon was derived from a creature which once really existed as the 'most fearful embodiment of animal ferocity to be found'.

A little earlier Charles Gould in *Mythical Monsters* had waxed eloquent on the possibility, even going so far as to describe the creature and its habitat.

We may infer that it was a long terrestrial lizard, hibernating and carnivorous with the power of constricting with its snake-like body and tail; possibly furnished with wing-like expansions of its integuement, after the fashion of *draco volans* and capable of occasional progress on its hind legs alone when excited in attack ... Probably it preferred sandy open country to forest land ... Although terrestrial, it probably, in common with most reptiles, enjoyed frequent bathing, and when not so engaged, or basking in the sun, secluded itself under some over-hanging bank or cavern.

In 1886, that might have seemed fantasy, but discoveries in the Indonesian island of Komodo have proved Gould right in some ways.

In 1912 an airman who had force-landed on the island of Komodo returned with a strange tale of fierce dragons twelve feet long. The only people on the island were convicts exiled by the Rajah of Dumbawa and they had told him the creatures ate pigs, goats, deer, even horses. No one believed him.

But confirmation soon followed. Major P. A. Ouwens, the curator of the Botanical Gardens at Buitenzorg, had been corresponding with the civil administrator of Flores, J. K. H. Van Steyn van Hensbroeck, about these monsters since the end of 1910. The natives had told van Steyn about 'a land crocodile' on Komodo, and when he had occasion to visit the island in the course of his duties, he looked into the matter. From two Euro-peans living on the island he heard that the creatures grew to be twenty feet long.

But a specimen which van Steyn obtained was only seven feet long. He sent this and a photograph to Major Ouwens, saying he would try and capture a living specimen. Ouwens sent out a Malay animal catcher, who caught four of the creatures alive. The largest were nine feet six inches and seven feet eight inches. Van Steyn reported, however, that soon after a twelve-foot speci-men was shot by a sergeant named Becker.

When he examined the creatures, Major Ouwens saw at once that they were a giant species of monitor lizard. He called it *Varanus Komodoensis*. It turned out that though the fierce-some creature was indeed carnivorous, it was not dangerous to man.

The Komodo dragon belongs to a group called the Varanoida. The largest of the group was *Varanus priscus* of Australia which was over thirty feet long. It became extinct only in historical times after man invaded that southern continent. And today there are persistent rumours of a giant lizard over twenty feet long in the jungles of New Guinea.

The Komodo dragon, with its lithe yellow tongue which flashes like a fork of flame, might well make a better original for the fire-breathing dragon legend. But looking over the evidence, many have felt that perhaps there is something in the dinosaur theory.

Dr Edgard Dacqué, sometime professor of geology at Munich University, suggested at the turn of the century that man might have a 'racial memory' of the carnivorous dinosaurs of the Mesozoic. As the last of these creatures are thought to have become extinct seventy million years ago, Dacqué suggested that some 'memory' of these creatures comes down to us from the lemur-like ancestors of modern man which then existed.

This idea has more recently been espoused by Carl Sagan, the American astronomer and exobiologist. In *The Dragons of Eden* he suggests that a collective memory of the scaly winged creatures between the dinosaurs and birds may be preserved in legends about dragons. These monsters would have been the chief predators of man's earliest ancestors. The deep structures of the mind of modern man are ancient organisms, and carry still the fear of these creatures.

It may be that this is true, and that these primal fears were later attached to other animals such as the larger lizards and reptiles. The myths have elaborated the original fears, but behind the magnificent creatures of Oriental art, or indeed of Renaissance painting, lie the brute facts of evolutionary history.

CHAPTER SEVENTEEN

BASILISK AND SALAMANDER

The basilisk and the salamander might well be described as minor dragons. Both are reptiles with histories almost as long and as complicated as that of the dragon itself. We will take the basilisk first, and try to untangle a little of its knotted evolution.

The basilisk began as an ordinary snake. In Greek the name comes from the diminutive of basileus, meaning a king. So the snake may have been thought of as the little king of the serpents.

Pliny in his *Natural History* says the basilisk was a snake bearing a livid spot in the shape of a crown on its forehead. This is at least within the bounds of zoological possibility: and in 1813, the name was applied to a small South American lizard with a hollow crest which it can inflate at will. But what Pliny's original snake may have been we have no way of knowing, for between times the basilisk turned into a fully fledged monster.

In the *Bestiary* the basilisk is still regarded as the king of snakes, 'so much so, that people who see it run for their lives, because it can kill them merely by its smell'. The basilisk was also thought to be able to kill at a glance. Birds flying over it would be overwhelmed by its venom and fall dead out of the sky. 'Nevertheless, basilisks are conquered by weasels.' These were put down into the snake's nest and killed them. 'God never makes anything without a remedy,' the Physiologus comments. He also adds that the basilisk 'is striped lengthwise with white marks six inches in size'.

This is little help in identifying the creature. But the story of the weasel derives from the use of the mongoose in India and elsewhere for catching snakes. The basilisk may have been the King Cobra originally, for that does have a peculiar marking on its head, and was used as an emblem of royalty in Egypt.

In classical times the basilisk was thought of as peculiar to Libya and the other parts of Africa near by. Lucan describes the fierce encounter between the monsters of the desert and Roman legionaries. The story of its baleful glance lingered on for a very long time. It was thought at one time that the only way to kill a basilisk was to show it its own reflection in a mirror. One was found in Rome during the reign of Pope Leo X, though its foul breath had already begun a plague. At Halle in Saxony there is a monument to a basilisk, and in 1202 another was found in a well in Vienna after many people had been overcome by the poisonous fumes it emitted. Another was killed in Warsaw in 1587, though here again we can be sure that escaping sulphur fumes are a more likely source of the stupefaction than a basilisk.

Pepys, writing in his diary for 4 February 1662, records a very similar story about the huge snakes said to be found in Lancashire. Sir Thomas Browne, who was not much given to a belief in marvels, thought the basilisk a likely enough creature, though he did not believe that it was born of a cock's egg which was incubated by a toad. However he thought it might indeed kill with a glance, for after all were not 'plagues and pestilential atoms' airborne?

Raymond Ditmars, a leading modern authority on snakes, confirms this in writing about the King Cobra. 'It seems that in striking, the snake simultaneously compresses the poison glands by a contraction of the jaw and muscles and ejects the poison, though quite accidentally, in the direction of its annoyance. If the fluid should enter the eyes, blindness or death are probable consequences.'

Pliny had originally reported the deadly glance of the basilisk, but it was the English naturalist Alexander Neckham (about 1180) who added the story that the creature was born from the egg of an aged cock.

Now it is a fact of biology that old roosters do indeed develop such an egg in their bodies. This had been observed by Aristotle : 'substances resembling an egg . . . have been found in the cock when cut open, underneath the midriff where the hen has her eggs, and these are entirely yellow in appearance and of the same size as ordinary eggs'.

It was thought in the Middle Ages that these 'cock's eggs' were incubated by toads and that the basilisk was hatched from them. For this reason it was sometimes called the Cockatrice as well. The picture of the basilisk in the *Bestiary* shows a creature with a snake's body and the head and wings of a cock. In due course the name made its way into the Bible, where once established it seemed to confirm any doubts about the real existence of such a bizarre creature.

Further complications arose from confusions, mainly of an etymological rather than zoological nature, between the Ichneumon, Enhydris, Hydrus, Cocatris, Crocodile and Basilisk. The *Oxford English Dictionary* made some effort to cast darkness on the topic, which was finally resolved into some sort of order by Dr Ansell Robin in his book *Animal Lore in English Literature* (1932). But this was on the basis that the creature was entirely fabulous.

P. H. Gosse had doubts about this. While he was staying in Jamaica he heard reports about a curious snake of some size which had wattles on its head similar to those on a cock. Various strange stories were told about this little-seen creature, which made him think he had stumbled across the original of the Cockatrice. There is little doubt that the snake did exist. Moreover when he returned to London, he discovered in Seba's *Thesarus* some old illustrations of snakes which seemed very similar. They were not of course recognised by zoologists as having any real existence. But Gosse was satisfied. Nor were they only found in the New World, for Francis Galton found similar reports in South Africa when he travelled there. But for us it is enough to know that the creature does have some claim to being a real animal, even if only as the King Cobra, a snake which still arouses great fear in many people.

The salamander had an even stranger history than the basilisk.

For us the salamander is a small, tailed amphibian which lives in damp places. It is common enough in Southern Europe. To

fig. 5 The salamander of medieval legend, from Gesner

this small, harmless creature has become attached a remarkable legend. Benvenuto Cellini, the Renaissance artist and silversmith, records in his autobiography a curious incident from his childhood; the year, he recalls, was 1505:

When I was about five years old, my father being in our small cellar, in which they had been washing clothes and where there was still a good fire of oak boughs, Giovanni with his viol in his arms played and sang to himself beside the fire. By chance he saw in the midst of the hottest flames a little animal like a lizard, which was sporting about in midst of the most scorching blaze. Having immediately perceived what it was he caused my sister and me to be summoned and pointing it out to us children, he gave me a violent box on the ear, at which I began to cry most excessively. He comforting me kindly, spoke to me thus: 'My dear little son, I did not give you that blow on account of anything you have done wrong, but only that you may remember that the lizard you saw in the fire is a salamander, a creature that has never been seen by anyone else of whom we have reliable information.'

I have begun with this quite late account of the salamander simply because it is, as Cellini's father claimed, a unique story. Cellini seems to be the only man who ever claimed to have seen a salamander actually in a fire, but the idea that it could survive there was, however, a very old one.

Aristotle recorded that the salamander 'not only walks through fire, but puts it out in doing so'. That is indeed quite likely, but it was not enough for Pliny. He exaggerated the story, and it was from him that it passed to other later writers and so into popular legend. He writes (in the charming words of Philemon Holland):

He is of so cold a complexion, that if he do but touch fire, he will quench it as presently as if ice were put into it. The Salamander casteth up at the mouth a certain venomous matter like milk, let it but once touch any bare part of a man or woman's body, all their hair will fall off, and the part so touched will change the colour of the skin to a white morphew.

This is altogether a more sinister creature. Pliny adds that the salamander can poison whole nations, infecting trees, fruit and water. If one touched the wood for a baker's fire, or even the bread itself, those who ate it would be poisoned.

In this version of the legend has been seen a reference to the horrendous effects of rye-ergot, which in past centuries was the cause of many plagues. In 922 in France alone, 40,000 died of the 'ignis sacer', the Holy Fire. In Paris in 1128 14,000 died. It was easy to blame a salamander found among the sacks of flour for an outbreak of the disease.

But there may be another explanation for Pliny's account of the hair falling out and the skin withering up. Pliny elsewhere mentions (XIX, 4) indestructible garments which could be cleaned by fire. These curious clothes were said to be made from 'salamander's wool'. As salamanders were clearly neither woolly nor hairy, it was thought that they made themselves up into cocoons (rather like silk worms), and it was from this that the wool, so-called, was derived.

At the Vatican there was said to be kept the sudarium, the face-napkin from the tomb of Christ, which was preserved in a cloth woven from salamander's wool. This had been presented to the Pope by a Tartar prince. Marco Polo, while on his travels, discovered the real source of this strange product. In western China at a town called Chinchitalas, on the edge of the Gobi Desert, he arrived at the place where it was actually mined.

A substance is likewise found of the nature of the salamander, for when woven into cloth, and thrown into the fire, it remains incombustible. The following mode of preparing it I learned from one of my travelling companions, named Curficar, a very intelligent Turkoman, who had the direction of the mining operations of the province for three years. The fossil substance procured from the mountain consists of fibres not unlike those of wool. This, after being exposed to the sun to dry, is pounded in a brass mortar, and is then worked until all the earthy particles are separated. The fibres thus cleansed and detached from each other they then spin into thread and weave into cloth. In order to render the texture white, they put it into the fire, and suffer it to remain there about an hour, when they draw it out uninjured by the flames and become as white as snow. By the same process they afterwards cleanse it, when it happens to contract spots, no other absergent lotion than an igneous one being ever applied to it.

However, he was unable to discover any trace of the salamander as a reptile 'supposed to exist in fire'.

This substance was clearly asbestos. Recently it has become known that asbestos is a cancer-causing agent. The baleful effects of Pliny's account – hair falling out, a change in the skin – sound as if they might be caused by cancer. Asbestos *is* dangerous : so another legend is found to have substance.

There seems to have been a small trade in garments made of 'salamander's wool' in the Middle Ages. In the letter to the Byzantine Emperor Manuel Comnenus (1120–1180) from Prester John, that mythical ruler of Central Asia claimed : 'Our realm yields the worm known as salamander. Salamanders live in fire and make cocoons, which our court ladies spin and use to weave cloth and garments. To wash and clean these fabrics, they throw them into flames.' Here again there is a conflation of silk and asbestos.

Legend had it that the Emperor of India had a suit made from a thousand salamander skins. Pope Alexander III also had a tunic of salamander's wool, which was highly valued by him. The belief in the 'wool' lasted until the middle of the seventeenth century. But by that time critical minds were taking stock of the salamander.

Jerome Cardan, the sixteenth-century Italian, carefully searched in vain for any signs of hair on the body of the little reptile. Sir Thomas Browne was well aware that 'Nor is this salamander's wool desumed from any animal, but a mineral substance, metaphorically so called for this received opinion'. Gesner was also aware of the distinction : in his work there is a fine little cut of the real *Salamandra maculata* common in Germany, and another of the hairy, starry-spined salamander of legend.

However the legend of the salamander's other virtues lingered on a little longer, even into the era of experimental science. The following appeared in the *Philosophical Transactions of the Royal Society* in 1716 :

> A salamander on being thrown into the fire the animal thereupon swelled presently and then vomited store of thick slimey matter, which did put out the neighbouring coals, to which the salamander retired immediately, putting them out again in the same manner, as soon as they rekindled; and by those means saving himself from the force of the fire for the space of two hours; That afterwards lived for nine months.

But in 1842 the Reverend Charles Owen conducted another trial. 'The common report is that the salamander is able to live in the fire which is a vulgar error. The Hieroglyphic Historian observes that upon trial made it was so far from quenching it that it consumed immediately.'

So vanished the salamander of legend. It does seem, however, that the little amphibians do exude a substance when frightened, and that if placed on a weak fire, they might well put it out. The observation of this strange behaviour in antiquity would have been enough to give rise to the legend.

Nor should we forget that the survival of life at extreme temperatures can have strange effects. Many people have made their living as performers defying the effects of fire. There was Signora Josephine Giraldelli, who flourished about 1819, who called herself 'The Original Salamander'. She was said to be able to survive the heat of furnaces, to pass red-hot irons over her body, arms and legs, tongue and hair. All this must have seemed very impressive indeed, but doubtless she used Wood's Metal, an alloy which melts at 155 degrees for the 'melted lead' which she also swallowed as part of her act.

Then there was Chamouni, 'the Russian Salamander', who died in an oven in 1828, while being roasted with a leg of lamb. This had been part of his act as 'the Incombustible' for a good while. But his luck ran out. And there have been many others who have combined trickery and skill in equal measure in the century since. However at a series of tests with Indian fire-walkers at the Alexandra Palace in 1937, Harry Price discovered that trickery was not involved in what they did. The secret of fire-walking lay in having the feet quite dry, and in taking no more than four steps over the coals (which reached 1472 degrees).

These human feats are more than equalled in the animal world. There is a fish *Barbus callensis* which is found in Algeria mainly, which lives in hot water springs at a temperature of 180 degrees Fahrenheit. As John Vinden notes, 'at this temperature it would be possible to cook an egg'. There is also the beetle *Trogoderma granarium* which lives on stored grain, and can eat malt at a temperature of 120 degrees. And the Fire Brat, *Thermobia domestica*, which imitates the salamander of legend by flourishing in the vicinity of furnaces.

But not to be outdone, it is recorded that Sir Joseph Banks stayed in a room at a temperature of 211 degrees, though his internal temperature did not rise at all. And in 1895, at a meeting of the Association of American Physicians, a New York doctor, Dr Jacobi, reported on a male patient whose temperature reached 148 degrees at one point, and averaged 122 degrees for five days. A fever of 108 is rare and usually fatal.

In the course of my research I am afraid that I could not bring myself to conduct any experiments on salamanders to see just how they do react. There are some things one cannot do merely to satisfy one's curiosity!

CHAPTER EIGHTEEN

THE BARNACLE GOOSE

In modern colloquial French, the phrase 'l'histoire d'un canard', or simply 'un canard', is an echo of the medieval myth that the Barnacle Goose grew from the familiar ship's barnacles found on the hulls of boats or on pieces of timber floating in the sea. In France, where the Barnacle Goose was not to be found, the myth became attached to a species of wild duck called the Macreuse. Once the myth was discredited, the Barnacle Goose became a synonym for any fabulous story, hoax, or false report.

Both the barnacles and the geese, a common variety along the north-western coast of the British Isles, were well known. However the Barnacle Goose did not nest there, and as its breeding grounds were unknown, its eggs and young were never seen. It was from this small mystery that the myth derived.

The myth of the Barnacle Goose is one of the few zoological fantasies that can be dated almost exactly. It originated (so far as we know) in 1186, the year that Gerald de Barri, who was known as Giraldus Cambrensis, read his description of Ireland to the scholars of the University of Oxford.

Ireland had been invaded by Anglo-Norman knights and their Welsh followers in 1167, and twenty years later Henry II was trying to assert his royal rights there as overlord. He sent over his son Prince John to tour the conquered parts and receive submissions. The prince was accompanied by Gerald, who wrote both an account of the conquest and a description of the country, partly to support the king's claims, and partly to show what a benighted lot the native Irish were. His *Topography of Ireland* includes many colourful stories, among them a report on the real origin of the geese found on the west coast of Ireland.

There are in this place many birds which are called Bernacae : Nature produces them against Nature in the most extraordinary way. They are like marsh geese but somewhat smaller. They are produced from fir timber tossed along the sea, and are at first like gum. Afterwards they hang down by their beaks as if they were a sea-weed attached to the timber, and are surrounded by shells in order to grow more freely. Having thus in the process of time been clothed with a strong coat of feathers, they either fall into the water or fly freely away in the air. They derive their food and growth from the sap of the wood or from the sea, by a secret and most wonderful process of alimentation. I have frequently seen, with my own eyes, more than a thousand of these small bodies of birds, hanging down on the sea-shore from one piece of timber, enclosed in their shells, and already formed. They do not breed and lay eggs, nor do they seem to build nests in any corner of the earth. Hence bishops and men of religion in some parts of Ireland do not scruple to dine off these birds at the time of fasting, because they are not flesh nor born of flesh.

These Irish clerics (doubtless those beyond the reach of the English) are beneath his contempt. For in eating these birds 'they are led into sin. For if anyone were to eat of the leg of our first parent although he were not born of flesh, that person would not be adjudged innocent of eating meat.'

Two points to observe about this account : Gerald does not mention a tree from which the geese grew, but clearly describes the barnacles often found on floating timbers. He calls them Bernacae, which is the Celtic name for the shell-fish. Also this story leads into a diatribe against the Jews, about whose conversion he had an obsession.

This then is the earliest written account of the mythical origin of the Barnacle Goose – or perhaps the Brent Goose, as these early writers made little distinction between the two, and modern science has also confused the issue by calling the Brent Goose *Branta bernicla*.

Though Gerald's description of Ireland was not printed until 1603 in Frankfurt, his account of the Barnacle Geese passed rapidly among the literate men of Europe. To have lectured at Oxford on the genesis of the birds was then enough to ensure that every learned community in Europe was soon aware of the myth.

The next reference to the myth is in the work of Alexander Neckham, a near contemporary of the Welshman. Neckham was the earliest of the true English naturalists, and his book *The Nature of Things* contains many echoes of the old classical learning which was returning to Europe through contact with the Arabs in Spain and Sicily. Neckham's account of the origin of the Barnacle Goose fellows Gerald, but is less detailed and less definite about the locale.

As Neckham was associated with Oxford (he was to teach theology there from about 1190), he may have heard the legend there, or indeed, even heard Gerald himself. But Neckham is not convinced, for elsewhere in an elegiac on divine wisdom, he returns to the Barnacle Goose. 'Rumour has it that by a process of Nature pinewood steeped in the sea gives forth young birds. This is done by a viscous humour : what public opinion asserts, philosophy indignantly denies.'

One kind of stalked barnacle (*Lepas fascicularis*) produces a mucus bubble which hardens into a whitish, spongy float to which they attach themselves. This may be the origin of the 'gum' and the 'viscous humour' mentioned by Gerald and Neckham.

Another sceptic was the Emperor Frederick II of Hohenstaufen, at whose court in Sicily the new learning of the Arabs was much in vogue. In his vast work on falconry he discusses other birds, among them the Barnacle Goose. He relates the popular tradition that they spring from worms born in rotting timber which develop into little geese. (This derives from an observation of the marine boring worm *Teredo*).

We have made prolonged research into the origin and truth of this legend and even sent special envoys to the North with orders to bring back specimens of these mythical timbers for our inspection. When we examined them we did observe shell-like formations clinging to the rotten wood, but these bore no resemblance to any avian body. We therefore doubt the truth of this legend in the absence of corroborating evidence. In our opinion this superstition arose from the fact the barnacle goose breed in such remote latitudes that men, in ignorance of their real nesting place, invented this explanation.

This verdict, written before 1248, or within half a century of the appearance of the myth, was correct. But the emperor was a little too exact in saying that the Barnacles clinging to the wood 'bore no resemblance to any avian body'. The real trouble was that they did, as we shall see.

However, once the myth of the Barnacle Goose became the property of the learned men of Europe, it began a long literary life which was to last down to the nineteenth century. A few sceptics were not going to keep a splendid legend down, and their voices made little noise beside this chorus of learned opinion.

Edward Heron-Allen, a biologist with such varied interests as violins, the history of rings and the poetry of Omar Khayyám, devoted a whole book to the ramifications of the myth over more than four hundred years. He quotes from nearly three hundred authors – a catalogue of the leading intellectuals of Western Europe. Even a resumé of all of this material would be quite beyond the brief scope of this chapter.

And perhaps unnecessary. For aside from Gerald de Barri, the authors who added to the myth, or in some way influenced its development, are few enough.

Inevitably variations on the original myth soon emerged. Most of these arose from careless renderings of Gerald or from elaborations of what he had said.

Soon it was believed that the geese were produced, not from fir trunks floating on the sea, but from actual trees growing on the sea shore. Those birds which fell on the land died; those that fell in the sea lived and grew into adult geese. The myth of the arboreal origin of the geese was, as Heron-Allen, observes, 'in wide repute in the twelfth and thirteenth centuries'. It appeared in the medieval encyclopedia of Vincent of Beauvais (c.1190–c.1264), which was a widely read and copied work.

A sceptical note was struck in the work of Albertus Magnus, writing in 1478. He had noted that he and his friends had seen the geese lay and hatch in the ordinary way. Belon, the pioneer zoologist, also noted this in 1555, as did some Dutch sailors in 1596, who actually observed the birds nesting in Novaya Zemlya. (These would have been Brent Geese rather than true Barnacle Geese.) But the significance of these records did not destroy the myth.

It was of course convenient in Lent if one could treat as fish birds which lived on the water. The custom of so defining waterbirds was common in the Middle Ages, and not only in Ireland. In England and Wales, beavers, because of their scaly tails, were thought of as fish and so eaten – which may well have contributed to their extinction in those countries. The fourth general Lateran Council of the Church in 1215 dealt with this abuse, and Pope Innocent III issued a Papal Bull forbidding the use of the Barnacle Goose in Lent. (There was also some controversy, Max Müller observes, among Jewish rabbis about this same problem.)

The Barnacle Goose was too famous a wonder for the author of the travels of Sir John Mandeville to leave out of that work, a much loved medieval compendium of marvels and wonders.

But Aeneas Sylvius Piccolomini, afterwards Pope Pius II, while on a visit to James I of Scotland in 1435, made inquiries about the. Barnacle Goose. He learnt nothing, except that it might be found in the Orkneys. He complained that such 'miracles flee further and further' as one searches, like a will-o'-the-wisp.

Traces of the myth are said to be found among the Arabs, but even the diligent Heron-Allen did not have the energy to explore this aspect of the matter. Professor Max Müller and Edward Armstrong have also tried to show that the myth is of Jewish origin : but the sources they have traced antedate Gerald de Barri, and seem to me to have depended on his original report.

The myth appeared in the *Hortus Sanitatis*, one of the earliest of printed books. The first pictures of the Barnacle Goose tree appear in the edition of 1491. These pictures later underwent their own evolution, adding a spurious authenticity to the myth.

Many of the later accounts of the Barnacle Goose myth were not taken from Gerald, but from the description by Hector Boece in his quite credulous *History of Scotland*, where he also gives one of the earliest accounts of a Scottish lake monster. Boece claimed to have seen at Petsligo, where he was a priest, in 1490 a tree washed up on the shore on which there appeared to be 'little featherless birds'. Another such tree appeared on the Firth of Tay near Dundee in 1492. He also quotes the experience of Master Alexander Galloway, Parson of Kinkell, who had been with him when he travelled in the Hebrides. Galloway had found a mass of what seemed to be mussels on the shore. 'Soon after he opened one of the mussel shells, but he was more astonished than before; for he saw no fish in it, but a perfectly shaped fowl, small and great always proportionate to the quantity of the shell.'

The claim to have seen such small birds growing from shells attached to timbers was also made by John Gerard in his famous *Herball* published in 1597. This might well have been wondered at by then, but he claimed 'what our eies have seen, and hands have touched, we shall declare'. His editor Thomas Johnson, who prepared a second edition of the book in 1636, declined to believe him, when he said he had seen shells with little birds inside them on a small island in Lancashire, and elsewhere as well.

In one of the early volumes of the august *Philosophical Transactions of the Royal Society*, Sir Robert Moray described, albeit from memory, in 1677 how he too had seen 'a young bird complete in every detail' inside the shell of a barnacle. His claim was refuted sternly in another paper for the Royal Society a decade later by Dr Tancred Robinson. Of course Sir Robert Moray and all those

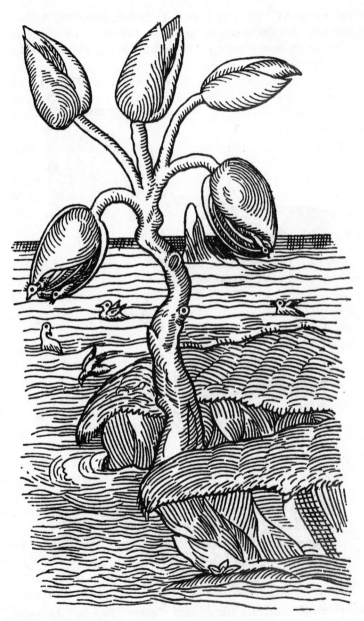

fig. 6 The Barnacle Goose tree, from Gerard's *Herbal*

other 'witnesses' stretching back to Gerald de Barri had not seen a little bird, but something else almost as curious.

The Ship's Barnacle (or Goose-neck Barnacle, as it is called in

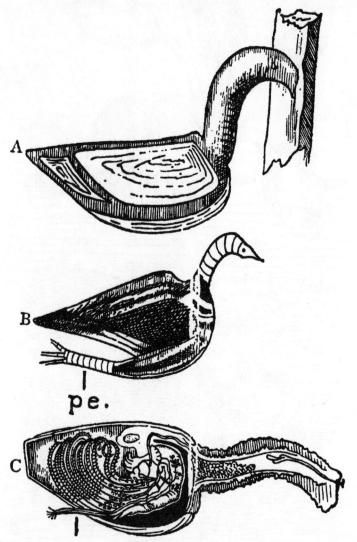

fig. 7 How the barnacle turned into a goose (from Ray Lankester, *Diversions of a Naturalist*)

America), *Lepas anatifera*, attaches itself to the hull of a ship or to floating timbers by its stalk or 'peduncle'. As can be seen in the drawings above (see fig. 7), if we look at the shell as the body, we do seem to have the shape of a 'young bird'. On being opened out, the inside of the shell has a feathery appearance as well as a resemblance to a fetal fowl. It was this casual appearance which suggested to the Irish on the west coast that they might be in fact baby birds. The breeding habits of the Barnacle Goose also being a mystery in the west of Ireland, it was thought that these might be the young of the 'Barnacle Goose'.

The absolute absurdity of the myth was demonstrated by Fabius Colonna in 1592, and finally by J. F. Guettard in 1787. But a full explanation of how the myth arose in the first place had to wait until Sir Ray Lankester, writing in 1918. It was his account of the Barnacle Goose in his *Diversions of a Naturalist* which inspired Edward Heron-Allen to undertake his lengthy investigation of the myth a decade later.

Explanations of the myth had been numerous enough. Max Müller, for instance, suggested a philological origin. But this did not cover the facts of the matter. For the legend clearly arose from the striking resemblance to the feathers of a bird of the barnacle's cirri, the plume-like appendages to the cirripede crustacean. Incidentally the barnacles are not related to the mussels and oysters at all, but to the lobsters, crabs and crayfish, strange as it may seem.

The real explanation seems to have been first propounded by John Hill in 1751 and 1752. But where had the myth orginated? Sir Edwin Ray Lankester was told that in Java there was, according to a 'native' story, a shellfish-like animal, part of which becomes transformed into a bird – said to be a kind of snip – and flies free of the shell. He was shown the shell by a Dutch lady, and identified it as a large freshwater mussel, one of the Unionidae.

But Java is too far to seek the origin of the myth – especially as it may well have been taken there by Muslims or Europeans. Some source nearer home is needed.

The most curious aspect of the Barnacle myth was only developed at the end of the last century, when the French scholar Frédéric Houssay noticed 'lepas anserisé', or what Ray Lankester later called 'a barnaculised goose' on some of the objects excavated by Schliemann at Mycenae and elsewhere in the 1870s.

For example, on an ossuary from Crete several geese are shown in association with a floral or arboreal motif. They are all somewhat different as if the artist were trying to achieve a particular effect, rather than delineate a type of real bird. On the handle of

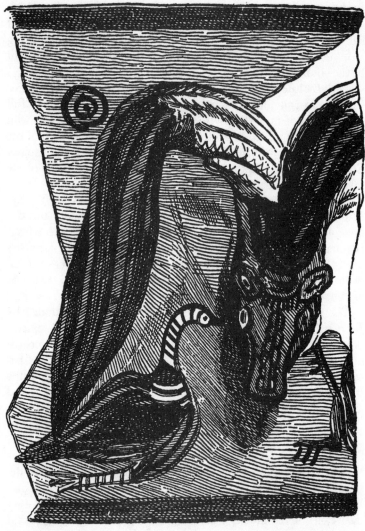

fig. 8 Barnaculised goose from Mycenean pot (from Schliemann)

a wine-cup, which Schliemann himself discovered at Mycenae, there is shown a stylised bird like a goose. Its connection with the Barnacle Goose myth becomes clear when it is compared with an opened barnacle. The creature on the cup is a fantastic blend of goose and barnacle : the stalk becoming the head and neck with the addition of an eye; the body resembling the shell in shape and markings; and the seminal duct of the barnacle becoming a strange single limb.

Other examples of such tree-birds, or Barnacle Geese, also exist. They may have been common to Mycenae, Crete and Troy, and date from around the second millennium BC.

Behind these strange designs there may have lain some vague early theory about the origin of life and its evolution and change. Or so Frédéric Houssay believed. The geese may, however, have evolved simply enough from an earlier floral pattern of a formal kind. But, as Ray Lankester pointed out, they do seem to show the peculiar stalk and seminal duct of the barnacle. So there seems to be little doubt that in some way they are related to the strange story Gerald heard from the West of Ireland, and which still survives along the west coast today. Father Patrick Dineen in his dictionary of the Irish language notes the use of the same word *giúgann* for both the barnacle and the Barnacle Goose. Edward Armstrong, himself from Ulster, notes other modern reports from Donegal and Kerry.

Writing at the end of the nineteenth century, when sweeping theories were much in vogue, Count Goblet d'Alviella studied the migration of symbols across Eurasia. The swastika, then without sinister associations, was found as a life symbol across a whole range of cultures. He drew up the following chart to show how it had spread out from its point of origin :

This chart, as more recent researches have shown, indicates not so much the course of conquests, so much as the ancient routes along which travelled traders and missionaries. The migration of the swastika, and the Barnaculised Goose, from Troy to Ireland need not surprise us today. On one of the upright stones at Stonehenge there has been discovered the incised shape of a Mycenean dagger.

Is it not permitted to us [concludes Heron-Allen] to postulate that, like the Swastika, the 'barnaculised goose' which Houssay has, I think rightly, regarded in the light of a symbol, reached Europe in the same way and, by reason of its evident antiquity, found itself collated with the mystery already surrounding *Lepas anatifera*, and sooner or later, with the inclinations of the clergy of the Early Christian Church?

The myth of the Barnacle Goose is often held out as a famous example of medieval credulity. But as we have seen there was at least some basis in observation for the bizarre idea, and in any case, at the height of its fame, the myth was the property, not of hard-headed countrymen, but of over-credulous academics.

Though it may appear to be only an outmoded piece of natural history, the myth of the Barnacle Goose actually preserves the last traces of the prehistoric trade routes along the sea-board of Western Europe by which their ancient cultures reached Ireland and Britain.

There is one final mystery about the Barnacle Goose : an enigma wrapped in a riddle. The riddle in this case is Riddle X in *The Exeter Book*, a collection of Anglo-Saxon poems, dating from sometime about 800 AD. The riddle has recently been translated by the English poet Kevin Crossley-Holland from the obscure Old English :

> My beak was bound and I was immersed,
> the current swept round me as I lay covered
> by mountain streams; I matured in the sea,
> above the milling waves, my body
> locked to a stray, floating spar.
> When, in black garments, I left the waves

146

and the wood, I was full of life;
some of my clothing was white
when the tides of air lifted me,
the wind from the wave, then carried me far
over the seal's bath. Say what I am called.

The accepted answer is 'Barnacle Goose'. If this is correct it does not seem to have struck any Old English scholars that this pushes the date for the origin of the legend back another four hundred years, and takes it from Ireland to the shores of the North Sea. But whereas the account of the legend given by Gerald de Barri is clear enough, and was the source of the European acceptance of the story, this riddle might well have a different answer. But what it might be I cannot suggest.

CHAPTER NINETEEN

THE VEGETABLE LAMB

Into medieval Europe came rumours of a bizarre creature which, like the Barnacle Goose, was partly animal and partly plant. This was the Barometz, or Vegetable Lamb of Tartary, which was said to be a plant which grew a gourd-like fruit which ripened and burst open to disclose a little lamb, complete in every detail.

The legend originated in the book of travels ascribed to Sir John Mandeville, who relates it as follows:

Now schalle I seye you semyngly of Countrees and Yles that ben beyonde the Countrees that I have spoken of. Wherefore I seye you in passynge be the Lond of Cathaye toward the high Ynde, and towards Bacharye, men passen by a Kyngdom that men clepen Caldilhe : that is a fair Contree. And there growethe a maner of Fruyt, as though it were Gowrdes : and whan thei ben rype men kutten hem ato, and men fynden with inne a lytylle Best, in Flesche, in Bon and Blode, as though it were a Lytylle Lomb with outen Wolle. And men eten both the Frut and the Best, and that is a great Marveylle. Of that I have eaten; alle though it were wondirfulle, but that I knowe wel that God is marveyllous in his Werkes.

This was written some time before 1356. The man who was Mandeville (and the latest idea is that he may well have been English as he claims) may have made a journey to the Near East, but the rest of the book was concocted out of earlier travellers in the Orient such as Marco Polo and Friar Odoric.

Friar Odoric of Friuli, one of the order of Minorites, had returned from his journey to China before 1331, and wrote his account of what he saw in May of that year. It was from Odoric that 'Sir John Mandeville' derived his account of the Vegetable Lamb.

I heard of another wonder from persons worthy of credit; namely, that in a province of the said Can, in which is the mountains of Capsius (the province is called Kalor), there grow gourds, which when they are ripe, open, and within them is found a little beast like unto a young lamb, even as I myself have heard reported that there stand certain trees upon the shore of the Irish Sea bearing fruits like unto a gourd, which at a certaine time of the year do fall into the water and become birds called Bernacles; and this is true.

The Vegetable Lamb was, in time, to become almost as notorious as the Barnacle Goose. But it was through Mandeville rather than Odoric that it did so, for the fantastic travels of the English knight were to become one of the most popular of all medieval books.

The mountains of Capsius would be Mount Caspius, south of the Caspian Sea, near modern Teheran. This geographic detail is worth remembering, for it bears directly on the solution to the mystery.

Fortunio Liceti, writing in 1518, quotes both accounts of the Vegetable Lamb, adding that Friar Odoric saw the creature himself, and described it as being 'as white as snow'. But this passage has not been traced in any edition of Odoric. In turn Juan Eusebio Nieremberg, writing in 1605, copies the earlier passages from Liceti, but adds nothing new himself.

But something original was reported by Sigismund Baron von Herberstein in his book on Muscovy in 1549. He gives a long account of the Barometz, quoting as his source an informant named Demetrius Danielovich, 'a person in high authority'.

According to this man the Vegetable Lamb was to be found in the neighbourhood of the Caspian Sea, between the Volga and the Jaick. His father had been sent on a mission from Moscow to the Tartar king of the region.

Whilst he was there, he saw and remarked, amongst other things, a certain seed like that of a melon, but rather rounded and longer, from which, when it was set in the earth, grew a plant resembling a lamb, and attaining to a height of about two and a half feet, and which was called in the language of the country 'Borametz', or 'the little lamb'. It had a head, eyes, ears and all other parts of the body, as a newly-born lamb. He also stated that it had an exceedingly soft wool, which was frequently used for the manufacturing of head-coverings. Many persons also affirmed to me that they had seen this wool. Further, he told me that this plant, if plant it should be called, had blood, but not true flesh: that, in place of flesh, it had a substance similar to the flesh of the crab, and that its hoofs were not horny, like those of a lamb, but of hairs brought together into the divided hoof of a living lamb. It was rooted by the navel in the middle of the belly, and devoured the surrounding herbage and grass, and lived as long as it lasted; but when there was no more within its reach the stem withered, and the lamb died. It was of so excellent a flavour that it was the favourite food of wolves and other rapacious animals.

The baron himself adds that he had not believed in the Vegetable Lamb, but as this was not the only account he had heard of it, he thought it only right to describe it.

And this with less hesitation because I was told by Guillaume Postel, a man of much learning, that a person named Michel, interpreter of the Turkish and Arabic languages to the Republic of Venice, assured him that he had seen brought to Chalibontis, on the south-eastern shore of the Caspian Sea, from Samarkand and other districts lying towards the south, the very soft and delicate wool of a certain plant used by the Mussulmans as padding for the small caps which they wear on their shaven heads, and also as a protection for their chests.

But this Michel had not himself seen the plant-animal; however he thought there was more truth in the legend than might be thought at first.

Giralamo Cardano, discussing the mystery in 1557, argued the physical impossibility of such a creature actually existing. He thought it an absurd legend. If it had blood it must have a heart, and the soil in which a plant grows is not fitted to supply a heart with movement. As an embryo also, it would not be nourished or warmed by a plant. Logic was defeating the legend.

Julius Caesar Scaliger made fun of Cardano, but his sarcastic satire was often mistaken for a belief in the Barometz by later writers. Among these was Claude Duret, who did believe it existed. So also did the poet Guillaume du Bartas, who included it among the animals in Eden in his poem on the Creation.

But by the middle of the seventeenth century belief in the Vegetable Lamb had declined among scientists and men of letters, though the mystery was discussed and investigated for another 150 years. Athanasius Kircher, professor of mathematics at Avignon, wrote in 1641 that he believed that the Barometz would, in the end, be found to be a plant. And he was to be proved right, eventually. But not until 1887.

A Dutch traveller named Jans Janszoon Strauss, who travelled in Tartary from 1647 to 1672, next describes the wonderful plant, compounding all the old accounts, and confusing the Barometz with the very fine wool found on the west side of the Volga and

fig. 9 The Scythian Lamb, from Claude Duret

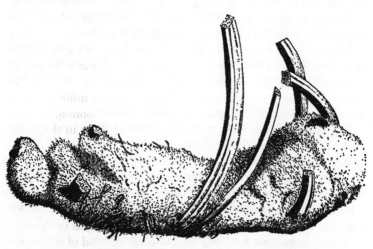

fig. 10 Chinese 'vegetable lamb' described by Hans Sloane

around the Caspian. This is the wool called Astrakhan, which is taken from the skins of unborn lambs. This barbarous product does seem to figure somewhere in the genesis of the legend, or at least in it being located around the Caspian.

However, Jans Strauss reports that in the house of Mr Swammerdam in Amsterdam, he had seen one of these 'fruits', brought to the anatomist Jan Swammerdam (1637–1680), who worked in his father's house for many years, by a sailor who had formerly been a slave in China.

He had found it growing there in a wood, and brought away sufficient of its skin to make an under-waistcoat. The description he gave of it did very much agree with what the inhabitants of Astrachan informed me of it.

What was this new kind of 'Vegetable Lamb' from China, and what was its connection with the original Barometz?

There is little doubt that the Barometz proper had some connection with Astrakhan. Dr Engelbrecht Kaempfer, who went with a mission to Persia in 1683, was certain that this was the case. He pointed out that the earlier the operation to procure the unborn lamb was done, the finer the fetal wool. The pelt is so thin that it is scarcely heavier than a membrane, and when dry loses the shape of a lamb and assumes that of a round gourd. This object might well be palmed off on naïve travellers as a 'Vegetable Lamb'.

But the sailor's souvenir of China was something quite different. Another of these objects appeared soon after in London, where it was examined by Sir Hans Sloane, no less. Writing in the *Philosophical Transactions of the Royal Society*, he reported on the objects from a Chinese cabinet, one of which was very peculiar.

The figure represents what is commonly, but falsely, in India, called 'the Tartarian Lamb', sent down from thence by Mr Buckley. This was more than a foot long, as big as one's wrist, having seven protuberances, and towards the end of some footstalks about three or four inches long, exactly like the footstalks of a lamb, without and within. Most part of this was covered with a down of a dark yellowish snuff colour, some of it a quarter of an inch long. This down is commonly used for spitting of the blood, about six grains going to a dose, and these doses pretended to cure such a haemorrhage. In Jamaica are many scandent and tree ferns which grow to the bigness of trees, and have a kind of *lanugo* (the down on an unborn child) on them, and some of the capillaries have something like it. It seemed to be shaped by art to imitate a lamb, the roots or climbing parts being made to resemble the body, and the extant foot-stalks the legs.

A century later, Juan de Loureiro, a Portuguese botanist and fellow of the Royal Society of Lisbon, who had spent thirty years in Indo-China as a missionary, provided a more exact description of the plant, which was indeed a fern.

The *Polypodium borametz* grows in hilly woods in China and Cochin China. Many authors have written of the Scythian Lamb, or Borametz – most of them fabulously. Ours is not a fruit, but a root, which is easily shaped by the help of a little art into the form of a small rufous dog, by which name, and not by that of a 'lamb', it is called by the Chinese.

In fact these little toy dogs are called Caw-tieh and Kew-tsie in China and Indo-China.

The explanation of the origin of the legend of the Vegetable Lamb – that it was derived from the root of a species of fern found in south-east Asia now called Lyncopodium Barometz – came to be the widely accepted one. It is now enshrined in the *Oxford English Dictionary*, where diligent Victorian scholarship places it under Barometz ! Nevertheless both the dictionary makers and Sir Hans Sloane are wrong.

How could a fern root from South China made up into a toy animal be the source of a legend which was very specifically located, even in the earliest accounts, on the shores of the Caspian ? Clearly the legend came first, and when the toys reached Europe from China they were taken to be the origin of the legend from their appearance alone. In actual fact they had nothing to do with it. Henry Lee in 1887 was able to trace records of four Vegetable Lambs of this kind in European collections, two of which still sur-

fig. 11 Toy dog from South China

vived at that date: one in the British Museum, another in the College of Surgeons. But two centuries earlier there must have been many more in circulation.

What then was the real origin of the Vegetable Lamb? As Henry Lee pointed out, the story was of a plant which grew in Asia, and which produced gourds or pods, inside which was found 'a little lamb', or rather, a fleecy substance of some kind. This could be only one thing: a somewhat distorted account of the cotton plant.

fig. 12 The original Barometz – the cotton plant

By the middle of the nineteenth century cotton was taken for granted as the basis of a great British industry, the vital product of the American South. But once it had been a mysterious substance. It was introduced into Europe through the Arabs – the name comes from *al qut'n*. They used it for caps and padded armour.

However the earliest references to cotton – and a solution to the mystery of the Vegetable Lamb legend – occur in early Greek writers. Herodotus (writing about 445 BC) tells us that in India:

> Certain trees bear for their fruit fleeces surpassing those of sheep in beauty and excellence, and the natives clothe themselves in clothes made therefrom.

Earlier he refers to a corslet sent by Amasis II, King of Egypt to the Spartans which was 'ornamented with gold and *fleeces from trees*' – that is, padded with cotton.

Our old friend Ctesias mentions in his *Indica* (says Bishop Photius), 'tree-garments'; and Varro says that 'Ctesias says that in India there are *trees that bear wool*.'

Two of Alexander the Great's officers, Nearchus and Aristobulus, refer to these wool-bearing trees and the white garments made from the 'wool'. Strabo adds that the Macedonians used it for stuffing saddles and mattresses.

Theophrastus, writing in 306 BC, says that the cotton plant resembles a dog-rose and that when planted in rows they looked like vines. Elsewhere he adds:

> They bear no fruit, but the pod containing the wool is about the size of a spring apple, which is unripe and closed, but when it is ripe it opens: the wool is then gathered from it, and woven into clothes of various qualities – some inferior, but others of great value.

Pliny, in his usual way, gives a very confused account of cotton; he seems to have thought it was flax. Transcribing Theophrastus he says the trees bear 'gourds' the size of a quince. He, it seems, is the ultimate source of the *gourd* part of the Vegetable Lamb legend. Julius Pollux (177 AD) adds the exact detail that the fruit is three-cleft. This exactly observed fact had not been noticed before.

Now the Greek word for fruit used by Theophrastus also means an apple, or a *sheep*. So to a careless reader his 'spring apple' could become a 'vernal sheep' or 'spring lamb'. This linguistic confusion (as well as Pliny's error over the gourd), would easily turn a tree bearing wool into a lamb-bearing plant. So that once the figurative description had been taken literally, the rest of the legend about how it fed and died arose naturally enough.

Cotton came from the uplands of Persia and India. The lamb's wool and astrakhan produced in Tartary, and traded through Samarkand (as noted by Michel to Guillaume Postel), added to the confusion. And so by word of mouth the legend spread westward into Europe, brought back by travellers such as Friar Odoric.

The Vegetable Lamb is an object lesson in fabulous zoology. Those writers who dismissed Sir John Mandeville's story as nonsense were wrong. For behind the confusion and the bizarre details lay a real fact of botany : the curious and wonderful cotton plant, which does indeed produce a 'wolle' of brilliant whiteness.

And in conclusion I can do no better than quote the comments of Henry Lee, who first suggested the real solution to the mystery a century ago.

I have found that all these old myths which I have been able to trace to their source have originated in a perfectly true statement of some curious and interesting fact; which statement has been so garbled and distorted by numerous writers, that in the course of centuries its original meaning has been lost, and a monstrous fiction substituted for it. 'Truth lies at the bottom of the well', says the adage; and in searching for the origin of these old myths and legends, the deeper we can dive down into the past the greater the probability of discovering the truth concerning them.

This may well be true for the monsters of antiquity and the Middle Ages, but monsters continue to appear in new forms, even today. And the explanation of them may be another matter.

CHAPTER TWENTY

THE CARRABUNCLE

The carbuncle is familiar to most of us only as a brilliant, livid gem. But in some parts of South America it is a mysterious animal, which seems to have relatives in Europe.

To the geologist the carbuncle, from the Latin carbunculus, 'a little coal', is a type of ruby. The carbuncle of the ancient and medieval writers is thought to have been a garnet. According to Isidore of Seville, the medieval encyclopedist, the carbuncle was to be found in the head of a snake. In his *Etymologies* he writes:

> It is taken from the dragon's brain but does not harden into a gem unless the head is cut from the living beast; wizards, for this reason, cut the heads from sleeping dragons. Men bold enough to venture into dragons' lairs scatter grain that has been treated to make these beasts sleepy, and when they have fallen asleep their heads are struck off and the gems plucked out.

For Isidore, writing about the year 630 AD, these 'dragons' would have been the larger snakes and reptiles. Shakespeare refers to this idea in *As You Like It*, when he mentions that the toad though 'ugly and venomous, Wears yet a precious jewel in his head...'

Toadstones came to be any stone like a toad in shape or colour, or that was thought to be produced by a toad. These were often worn as jewels or amulets, or as rings. The most valued kind was the kind thought to be from the toad's head. The earliest use of the word given in the *Oxford English Dictionary* is 1558.

By extension carbuncle came to refer to a livid tumour, and also to the spots on the nose due to drinking too much.

But in sixteenth-century South America, carbuncle was the name given by the Spanish conquerors to a mysterious and little-seen animal. It was a mystery because no one had seen it well enough to decide exactly what it was, whether a sort of bird or a mammal.

Gonzalo Fernández de Oviedo thought that two lights which he saw shining out of the darkness as he sailed through the Strait of Magellan, were carbuncles. These he associated with the precious stone in the dragon's brain.

Martín Barco del Centenera, writing in 1602, described a creature which he had seen in Paraguay. 'A smallish animal, with a shining mirror on its head, like a glowing coal . . .' As the precious stone was thought to be of great luck, Barco del Centenera underwent many tribulations searching for the elusive monster in the backlands of Paraguay. He never found it.

But he might have done so if he had taken his search to the south of Ireland. In 1756, Charles Smith in his *History and Present State of Kerry* first reported the presence of the carbuncle in Killarney Lake. 'The common people here-about have a strange, romantic notion of their seeing in fair weather what they call a carrabuncle at the bottom of the lake in a particular part of the lake which they say is more than 60 fathoms deep.' Smith seems to have assumed that by 'carrabuncle' the Kerrymen meant some sort of bright precious stone, and in a footnote he expresses his doubts about its reality.

However it seems that Smith had not heard the whole story. Over a century later, in the early 1880s, the botanist Henry Hart was exploring the Kerry mountains for plants. He describes how a countryman who accompanied him on a visit to Mount Brandon in 1883, told him that in Lough Veagh, one of the lakes below the mountain, the local people often found pearl shells. These, he said, came off an enormous animal called the carrabuncle, 'which was seen glittering like silver in the water at night'. This animal had gold, jewels and precious stones hanging about its carapace. Hart expressed the ironical hope that the carrabuncle might soon be added to the collection of Irish animals in the new National Museum in Dublin.

From another Irish naturalist, Nathaniel Colgan, we learn yet more about the carrabuncle. On a visit to Brandon in 1888, Colgan happened to meet Hart's informant and asked him about the legend. It seemed that the monster actually lived in Lough Geal (and not Lough Veagh), and was a kind of snake which made the lake shine at night, and sloughed off shells with precious stones in them. He had never seen it, but thought that if you could capture it you would make your fortune. If only Barco del Centenera had known!

At Connor's public house in Cloghane, where he was staying, Colgan heard yet more about the carrabuncle from Connor himself. He too had never seen the creature, but had often heard tales of it. It was said to be seen only once every seven years and was 'like a cashk rowlin' about in the wather'.

His wife added that she had always thought that it was a fish, and it was connected in her mind with the pearls which some fishermen had taken from the lake some years before. (These, Colgan thought, would have been freshwater mussels, which sometimes do have small pearls in them.) Next morning the local postman confirmed that the carrabuncle lit up the whole lake, and that it was the animals that produced the pearls. Lough Geal, by the way, is 360 feet up on the slope of Mount Brandon as you come through the Connor Pass to Cloghane.

All of this was strange enough. But Colgan later came across a passage in Alfred Russell Wallace's *Travels on the Amazon and Rio Negro*, where the explorer laments the sad fact that the Amazons from which the river took its name, 'must be placed with those legends of the Curipara, or Demon of the Woods, and the Carbuncle of the Upper Amazon and Peru'.

On reading this, Colgan wrote off at once to the great man Wallace, then very old, asking for more information about the Amazonian legend of the carbuncle. Wallace replied that he could not recall it now at all, but that perhaps Henry Bates, who had been his companion, might do. But Bates, by then also a very eminent man, replied that he no longer wasted his time on such matters. Colgan gave up the hunt.

What then is the connection between the monster in the Kerry lake and the legendary animal of South America? Colgan wondered if some Spanish traveller had not turned up in Kerry and left the name behind him, which is not unlikely, given the long standing, indeed prehistoric, connections between Ireland and Iberia.

But only the name and legend? Why not a real animal, perhaps some species of red and white phosphorescent tropical fish? Or some amphibian with a red warty skin? There is also the possibility that the creature drifted up on the Gulf Stream, as happens with other plants and animals, and was put alive into a lake not far from the sea-shore.

But what sort of fish? And is it still there? I recommend the mystery to some enterprising biology student, or lover of mysteries, in need of a summer project or a change from the Loch Ness monster.

CHAPTER TWENTY-ONE

HERALDIC CREATURES

The use of animals in heraldry, and then in decoration generally, brought about many more changes in traditional creatures of fancy, resulting in even more fantastic creatures.

Heraldic devices developed during the Middle Ages from the early battle badges of the Greeks, Romans and Barbarians. As practised even to this day by such institutions as the Royal College of Heralds in Britain, heraldry became almost an exact science.

Some of the animals used by heralds were familiar monsters such as the dragon, the unicorn and the griffin. These are well known from many badges and devices.

Others were compounded creatures, created often enough by uniting the arms of different families. Such creations as the ass-bittern, ram-eagle, cat-fish, lion-fish, dragon-tiger, falcon-fish were not to be found in nature. The double-headed eagle, the imperial insignia of the Holy Roman Empire, was adopted by several European kingdoms, such as Austria and Prussia. It originated in the eagles of ancient Rome and was also found in Byzantine art. These were simple creations compared with some of the more bizarre creatures of heraldry.

The allerion was an heraldic bird represented as an eaglet without a beak or claws. This may have been derived from the strange bird described in the famous letter from Prester John to the Byzantine Emperor who described the allerion as fiery plumed birds with razor-edged feathers. Only two lived at any one time, yet they lived for sixty years. Then they laid two or three egss which hatched after forty days. The parents then drowned themselves in the sea, watched over by all the other birds. Clearly this story owes much to the legend of the phoenix.

Then there was the enfield, which was used by several Irish families, with a fox's head, the chest of a greyhound, a lion's body, and the legs and tail of a wolf and eagle's talons. This monstrous hound-like creature is a fairly typical heraldic monster.

Another sort of heraldic creature was the alphyn. In shape like a tiger, this animal was derived from *al-fil*, the elephant piece on the Arab chess board, the equivalent to the knight.

The calygreyhound was adopted by the de Veres, the Earls of Oxford, in 1513 : this animal was like an antelope with the fore-legs of an eagle and the rear legs of an ox.

The allocamelus had the body of a camel and the head of an ass. The bagwyn, which appeared only about 1540, had the tail of a horse and the backward-curving horns of a goat.

The falcon-fish, which was half-bird, half-fish, had dog's ears. The lympago, which was half-man, half-lion or -tiger, must have been derived from the manticora. The opinicus was a variant of the griffin which had the body and legs of a lion. The pantheon was an heraldic panther.

These creatures give a small idea of the weird variety of heraldic creatures. But they have little to do with real zoology. The last creatures of the heralds which we will look at are of more interest : these are the wyvern, the yale and the wodehouse.

The wyvern was a flying serpent, a dragon with wings which had only two legs and a barbed tail. Originally they seem to have been symbols of pestilence and plague, but later, perhaps as a precaution to ward off disease, they were adopted by heraldry. In England they figure frequently on the arms of many cities and towns.

The yale too was once a familiar creature. It supports the arms of Christ's College in Cambridge, and is found carved above several arches on the campus. Sir Arthur Shipley, the Cambridge zoologist, who was Master of Christ's College, was inspired to track down the origins of the yale, also known as the eale.

He found it first referred to in Pliny (where else indeed?), who reported that it was a creature that lived in Ethiopia; it was about the size of a horse with a spotted body. An elephant's tail, boar's tusks and movable horns, which could be turned backwards and forwards at will, completed his description. In England the yale became one of the Queen's beasts; and (so Hugh London claims) stood guard in Indian temples against evil spirits. Naturally enough it made its way into the bestiaries, and so into the heraldic menagerie.

In May 1911, a correspondence in *The Times* of London disputed the origins of the creature. Some writers thought that it must have been some sort of antelope, as the long horns suggested. Mr D. C. Druce, one of the greatest authorities on the *Bestiary* of that period, in a very learned paper published that year, thought, however, that the yale could not be identified with any real animals. He suggested that it might merely have been an artistic convention, or an antelope that flicked its ears.

Sir Arthur Shipley would have none of this. He confidently traced the yale back to ancient Egypt. In Hebrew *ya'el* means 'a mountain goat'. This was the source of the name which Pliny would perhaps have got from a Greek writer. The animal itself, Shipley suggests, was a species of cow in which the horns are artificially trained, one forward, one backward. Such cattle have in fact been found in Egyptian paintings. And even today among the Nandi of Kenya, there are cows called 'Kamari cows' in which the horns are trained in the same way. According to G. W. B. Huntingfort, a Nandi warrior who does not own such a cow is only half a man, and 'is ashamed and sits silent at his beer drinking'.

(The yale is then something of a first cousin to the unicorn; indeed as the illustration from Wood's *Natural History of Man* shows, both legends began in exactly the same way.)

The history of the wodehouse, or wild man of the woods, is even more complex. It has been the subject of a lengthy study by Richard Bernheimer, who says that 'medieval literature is shot through with the mythology of the wild men'. The wild men were hirsute, carried heavy clubs or branches of wood, and instead of clothes, covered their nakedness with foliage. These were the *Homo sylvestris* which Linné included at the head of his catalogue of nature just under *Homo sapiens*.

Today in many parts of Eastern Europe, the wild men still appear at annual festivals. In heraldry they appear on countless coats of arms. But in the light of modern reports of semi-human creatures from several parts of the world, they take on a new interest. They seem to anticipate the creature which Bernard Heuvelmans and Ivan Sanderson discovered in 1968. But before we reach such a modern monster, we must pass by the monsters of literature.

CHAPTER TWENTY-TWO

LITERARY BEASTS

In recent times fabulous and imaginary animals have become the property of literature; and in America, of a somewhat self-conscious folklore.

This movement began with the poets and artists of the late Renaissance. Earlier the monsters and marvellous animals of legend and mythology had a real existence and were really believed in. But for writers and artists from Dante on, they became symbolic. The griffins which Dante imagined as pulling Beatrice's chariot are poetic creatures, and no longer the grim guardians of Central Asian hordes of gold.

The lamia is another example of how these animals were transformed. Originally a person in Greek mythology – she was the paramour of Zeus whose children were destroyed by Hera – she

166

took to killing other people's children. She later became one of the empusae, those incubi who lie with men and suck away their blood. Her beautiful face changed into a gorgon mask of depraved cruelty. Lamia seems to have been a Libyan goddess of some kind, whose cruel cult was suppressed by Greek invaders, Robert Graves suggests. The face came from the gorgon masks worn by her priestesses during rites in which infants were sacrificed. This unpleasant creature became confused with the true gorgons, and with the poisonous reptiles for which Libya was infamous. The lamia had no place in the bestiaries, but later became a favourite of Renaissance poets after the revival of classical learning.

The lamia was now conceived as a scaly four-footed creature with a woman's head. These creatures were said to lead men astray by posing as beautiful seductive creatures only later turning into reptiles. And so the name came to be applied in England to harlots. Poets such as Spenser and Milton delighted in the monsters of the classical tradition, and many familiar shapes haunt the pages of *The Faerie Queene* and *Paradise Lost*. But then the taste for monsters changed. The growing rationalism of the Enlightenment was not in favour of such fantastic beings.

When Captain Gulliver in his travels into several remote regions of the world encounters the Yahoos and the Houynnhnms, there are echoes of both the wild men of the Middle Ages and the wise centaurs of classical myth. But the temper of the time was not in favour of Swift's satire : *Gulliver's Travels* was quickly defused by being relegated to the rank of a children's book. Many would have agreed with the Irish bishop who remarked that *Gulliver's Travels* seemed to be full of improbable statements, and that for his part he scarcely believed half of it.

The idea of using animals as satirical models of human society had a long history. The fables of Aesop, reputedly a slave, were not even the first of the kind, though they are the earliest to survive. Moralising on the lives of animals was the raison d'être of the bestiaries, which drew Christian morals out of even the strangest behaviour of the beasts of the field. The fables of Jean de la Fontaine have, like Aesop's, passed into the stream of Western culture.

The drawings of the French artist Grandville, whose *Private and Public Lives of the Animals* appeared in 1839, were satirising the figures of French public life. In one cartoon he has animals in fashionable clothes examining with curiosity the leading French radicals of the day, all safely behind bars in a special zoo. This was a serious use of animals, as were the monsters which crowd into the last pages of Flaubert's *Temptation of St Anthony*.

A lighter touch was to be found in England in the nonsense of Edward Lear. What zoologist has not at some time dreamt of finding the Dong with the Luminous Nose, or what botanist hoped to cultivate *Nasticreechia Krorluppia*? And who has not wondered what genetic mismatch produced the Pobble Who Had No Toes? And Lewis Carroll, of course, whose manual on cryptozoology *The Hunting of the Snark* has been bedside reading of mine for a quarter of a century. That mysterious animal devours (or otherwise disposes of) the unfortunate Baker. But there was once intended to be a drawing of the monster in the book. No bestiary of the bizarre would be complete without it, or the comments of the artist Henry Holiday who created it :

> Mr Dodgson wrote that it was a delightful monster, but that it was inadmissible. All his descriptions of the Boojum were quite unimaginable, and he wanted the creature to remain so. I assented, of course, though reluctant to dismiss what I am still confident is an accurate representation. I hope that some future Darwin, in a new *Beagle*, will find the beast, or its remains; if he does, I know he will confirm my drawing.

But if the Boojum Snark was suppressed, the Jabberwocky and the other strange creatures of Carroll's mind were not. Tenniel's drawing of the Jabberwocky which Alice is striving to slay was derived from a picture in William Hone's *The Everyday Book* showing St Anthony in the desert beset by two terrible demons. Carroll seems to have drawn Sir John's attention to this illustration, and he based his picture of the Jabberwocky on it. But into that monster also went bits and pieces of the dinosaurs and pterodons which had only recently emerged into the Victorian daylight from the fossilised darkness. Carroll as a Christian had every reason to fear these monsters of Darwinian theory.

Other monsters haunted his dreams as well. These include the Cheshire Cat of English folklore, which slowly vanishes down to its grin; the Gryphon and the Mock-Turtle (from which mock-turtle soup was made, hence the calves' feet, as the soup was made from veal). And the weird creatures mentioned in the Jabberwocky poem itself: the Toves, the Rath, and the Borogoves. Not forgetting the Jubjub bird and the Bandersnatch, and the Unicorn and the Lion.

These creatures were deliberate literary creations; in America such fabulous creatures are often passed off as real folklore. These 'fearsome critters' are said to belong to the native folklore of America. But often this is not so. The legend of the giant woodsman Paul Bunyan and his giant ox Babe, for instance, were dreamt up to advertise the woodpulp industry. Other creatures are also products of the pen rather than of the populace.

One such is the hoop-snake, which puts its tail in its mouth and rolls down the road. This is very like the ancient symbol of eternity which was revived by the alchemists. Another was the guyascutus, which was first reported in 1844 as a large creature which haunted the tops of poplar trees. But in the course of time it shrank to the size of a deer with ears like a rabbit and the teeth of a mountain lion. It had telescopic legs which enabled it to graze on the steep slopes of mountains.

The squonk was a creature which was said to be found in the forests of Pennsylvania. A shy beast because of its horrible warty appearance, it cried continual tears of self-pity. Indeed it was very likely to dissolve into a pool of its own tears.

The hodag from the swamps of Wisconsin was a terrible man-eating creature with horns, bulging eyes and a ridge of sharp spines along its back and a long tail. It slept standing against a tree, and could easily be captured by felling the tree from under it, which made it fall over.

More recently the glawackus appeared in Glastonbury in the state of Connecticut in 1939, and in Frizzleberg in Maine in November 1944. It was said to be something like a mountain lion or a boar.

Among these invented American beasts, Al Capp's shmoo should not be forgotten. This all-providing creature laid eggs, butter and milk, and tasted of best steak when grilled, chicken when fried, and so on. The arrival of the creature upset the economy of Dogpatch, where the *Li'l Abner* comic strip was set, and had to be killed off by the artist to preserve the primitive

Cappitalism of the community from Shmoocialism.

But aside from these creatures, and such modern creations of the cinema as King Kong, Kwangi and the Creature from the Black Lagoon (surely a descendant of the bishop-fishes of the Middle Ages), modern monsters, real monsters in the old tradition, still exist in the haunted hearts and minds of modern man, and in some not so distant parts of the world as well.

CHAPTER TWENTY-THREE

MODERN MONSTERS

Monsters are not merely imaginary creatures from past times. Even today they lurk in the remote, and not so remote, areas of the world. And especially in the depths of the oceans.

It might seem strange to call the sea-serpent a modern monster; but actually the first useful reports date from only the middle of the seventeenth century. And it was not until the nineteenth century that the creature (or rather creatures) gained any wide notoriety outside folklore and legend.

The most famous sightings all date from then : the spate of reports from the New England seaboard, the *Daedalus* affair of 1848, the Dutch and French reports towards the end of the century. The sea-serpent provided a continuing story for many newspapers and magazines. If reports seem to have died away in recent years, this is not from lack of sightings, merely from lack of interest from editors.

Recently there have been a long series of sightings (and even photographs) along the Cornish coast of England. But these events have been surrounded by such an air of mystery that they are not taken seriously by many people. This is a great pity as many genuine reports continue to come in, so it is a shame that these should be lumped in with the results of hoaxes and jokes.

The last great sea-serpent sensation in France turned out to be a hoax. In 1964 a Breton photographer published colour photographs of what he claimed to be a sea-monster which he and his family had encountered at Hook Island on the Great Barrier Reef in Australia. Though widely publicised in France and America, the pictures were undoubtedly a hoax. Before leaving France, Le Serec, the photographer, had mentioned the possibility of an encounter with a sea-serpent as a fund-raising hope.

A lake-monster reported in 1976 from Lake Lucerne also turned out to be a hoax – this time one perpetrated by a television company, who should have known better than to indulge in such tiresome stupidity.

Hoaxes or not, the Loch Ness monster continues on its way, with an annual crop of reports and even the occasional new photograph. When I last wrote on the case (at the end of December 1975), the most recent photographs were yet to be released.

These had been taken by an American group led by Dr Robert Rines, who had earlier photographed what seemed to be the fin of an animal underwater at Loch Ness. This time the party obtained photographs of a large long-necked object diving down towards the camera, and a startling close-up of what Rines said was the animal's head. During December 1975 there was immense interest in these photographs, but this died away in disappointment when they did not seem to merit the large claims made for them in advance.

Though they did little to solve the mystery, the photographs did suggest that underwater photography might eventually provide the answer to the mystery of Loch Ness. But during the following summers further expeditions came away with nothing more. The attempt by Robert Rines and Sir Peter Scott to give a scientific name to the animal was rebuffed by the scientific community. For not merely did other names have priority (notably that suggested by Dr Bernard Heuvelmans in 1965) but there must be a type specimen to examine and display before one can properly name a new species. Only when we have its carcase can we call the monster something other than a monster.

There was world-wide excitement in July 1977 when the Taiyo Fishing Company of Tokyo (the world's largest whaling organisation) announced that early in the year one of their trawlers had fished up off the coast of New Zealand the carcase of what some Japanese scientists thought was a plesiosaur. Had a real sea-serpent been captured at last?

Excitement was premature. A small piece of one 'fin' had been retained when the rotting carcase was thrown back into the sea for fear it would foul the rest of the catch. A biopsy was carried out on this piece. It contained material found only in members of the shark family. Whatever it was, the creature was not a plesiosaur. It could, of course, still have been an unknown monster, for Bernard Heuvelmans has suggested that at least some of the reports of so-called 'sea-serpents' are in fact giant selachians, or eel-like sharks. So the monster of the *Kishu Maru* still remains something of a mystery. And we have still to find a carcase.

This also applies to the Abominable Snowman and his relatives around the world, in the Caucasus, in Central Asia, and the long mountain chain running from British Columbia south to California in the United States, where he is called Sasquatch or Bigfoot.

The long and very involved history of these creatures (reports of which date back to Classical antiquity) would need a book in itself to relate. Sightings, tracks, photos, 'close encounters of the third kind', even a short piece of film taken of a Bigfoot in 1967 by Roger Patterson, have led only to continuing dispute.

Yet strangely enough, the account of the one discovery which would have clinched the matter remains unpublished in the English language. This is Dr Bernard Heuvelmans' remarkable book, written with Boris Porshnev, about his discovery along with Ivan T. Sanderson of the so-called 'Ice-Man' of Minnesota. Scientists in Britain and America have chosen to ignore the book, even though Heuvelmans has conclusively proved that this creature which he has called *Homo pongoides* is a surviving Neanderthaler, the type of early man believed to have been exterminated by our own species in the Old Stone Age.

These are only a few examples of the mysterious creatures of ocean, lake and forest whose existence is well-documented, but which remain uncaptured and therefore unacceptable to science. Until they are properly classified they will remain classed as myth and legend, along with the other creatures in the magic zoo. But just as the phoenix, the unicorn and the mermaid can be shown to have a real natural history, so in time we will be able to prove that these modern monsters also have a real existence.

But their real existence cannot deny the imaginary nature of the fabulous beasts in the magic zoo. Only a part of their strangeness is due to man's imagination. This book has been about animals and man. The last chapter will have to deal with man and animals. Not with the experience of animals. Nor with the exact knowledge of animals. But with the exploration of the imaginary qualities with which man has invested the beasts around him. So 'by a commodious vicus of recirculation' we return at last to the fauna of the mind.

PART THREE
Man and Animals

'. . . a minute contribution to the study of the only subject that deeply and permanently concerns us – human nature and the ways of human thought.'

Odell Shepard: *The Lore of the Unicorn*

CHAPTER TWENTY-FOUR

THE FAUNA OF THE MIND

The symbolism of animals has concerned many leading scientists and artists. But as is often the case, their views are usually opposed, even quite contradictory.

The pioneering psychiatrists Sigmund Freud and C. G. Jung saw such mythical creatures as those collected in this book in quite different ways.

Freud saw monsters as figures from the subconscious of man's mind, redolent with sexual significance. Jung, who broke with Freud very early on, saw imaginary creatures as archetypes representing universal fears and feelings. For Freud all such symbols could be reduced to basic figures of human sexuality – such is the potent secret of the unicorn. For Jung the purity of the noble creature could have been of greater symbolic significance. This contradictory opposition is not new : it appears in the medieval lore of the unicorn.

Scientists, which Freud and Jung would have considered themselves to be, seek certainty. This is easier for the biologist or physicist, but more difficult for those concerned with the manifestations of the mind and the imagination. Kenneth Clark, in his survey of animals in art, gives a broad idea of the varying responses to the natural world over many centuries. Heinz Mode and Francis Klingender, in their studies, see these creatures as reflections, not of the natural world, but of the human social world. Thus the real fauna of the mind is as varied and diverse as man's multitudinous cultures.

For the poet and the painter, it is the lack of certainty, the aura of ambiguity about these creatures, which appeals to them. The monsters do not have to be real, merely interesting and mysterious. Even such efforts at reductionism as this book have not dissipated their mystery.

The unicorn, to take a familiar and classic example, is not merely a creature of man's creation. Earlier we have seen how the natural history of the unicorn developed from a distorted account of the Indian one-horned rhinoceros. 'If it has been distorted systematically,' Bernard Heuvelmans observes

it is obviously to fit a definite pre-existing archetype, a phallic symbol, a dream of ever ready male aggressiveness. But who can say when the unicorn ceased to be a real animal and became mythical? As a matter of fact the real rhino has been slowly and gradually mythicised. I even think that as soon as our knowledge of any animal goes through the prism of our emotional brain and is later confronted with our cognitive map, it is always more or less 'mythicised'. First of all it is impossible for us to grasp reality with our imperfect and limited sense; then our representation of reality is further distorted by our emotions, related to our inner wishes, fears and conflicts, and finally it is filtered in the net of our prejudiced ideas. Even the most common animal – cat, horse, fox, dove, grass snake or snail – is partly 'imaginary'. And reciprocally all 'mythical' animals are partly real.

After surveying the history of the unicorn, it seems clear enough that for the author of the bestiary the unicorn was a real, if rare, animal. By the time of the Renaissance the unicorn had become largely a symbolic creature, if ambiguously deployed in secular and religious art. But strangely the more 'unreal' it became for the zoologist, the more powerful the unicorn became for artists and poets. Some examples will demonstrate this.

Though the legend of the unicorn was very ancient, it was not until the late Gothic era of the Middle Ages that it obtained a special place in Western art. By now it was symbolic of purity and chastity. Sometimes it was intended to represent Christ, but in most cases it was intended to carry a more secular idea of carnal love.

One of the most superb treatments of the unicorn in art is *The Hunt of the Unicorn,* a series of seven tapestries now in the Cloisters of the Metropolitan Museum of Art in New York City. This series of tapestries was made in France about 1500. Their exact origin and early history are unknown. They first came to light when they were inventoried after the death in 1680 of the Duc de la Rochefoucauld, the celebrated author of the *Maxims*. During the Revolution in 1793 the Rouchefoucauld castle at Verteuil in the Charante was looted : sixty years later the tapestries were recovered from a peasant who was using them to cover the potatoes in his barn. However, the tapestries were very little known until 1937 when John D. Rockefeller bought them from the Duc de la Rochefoucauld and presented them to the museum. During the war they were removed to safety, and so it is only since 1944 that their true magnificence has begun to impose itself on the collective imagination.

Margaret Freeman, in her monumental study of the tapestries, has suggested that they were made for a Rochefoucauld marriage. But as the initials AE are prominently woven into the designs, it had previously been thought that they might have been made for the marriage of Anne of Brittany in 1499 to Louis XII at Langeais on the Loire. Later the couple lived at Blois, where they cultivated a celebrated garden. Flowers are the pre-eminent wonder of the tapestries, hence their name 'les millefleurs'.

Mrs Freeman believes that the tapestries were intended as decorations for the bridal chamber : one of them would have been a bedstead, five others would have hung around the wall, and the last, the Unicorn in Captivity, would have covered the ceiling. 'Almost anyone would agee,' she writes, 'that to lie in bed and look up at the Unicorn in Captivity as a ciel would have been a delightful experience indeed.'

This is too coyly put, as the English poet Geoffrey Grigson points out. For 'the young wife would have looked up, from under her husband's shoulder, at spring symbols of what she was experiencing from him in his virility; and of what he was expecting from her, in character, wifeliness, pregnancy and parturition.'

The pure white, goat-headed unicorn, so tamely ensconced within the wooden pale, is an image of secular rather than spiritual love. He is surrounded by sexually symbolic flowers : the erect purple orchis, lords-and-ladies, dame's violet. Beyond the fence grow the virginal madonna lily, stitchwort, milk thistle, columbine and periwinkle. There are also particular flowers of Brittany and the Atlantic sea-board, the bluebell and the arbutus (indicative that the designer or his patron at least came from above the Loire, if not the tapestries themselves).

The flora of the tapestries was studied by E. S. Alexander and C. H. Woodward with the hope of discovering the locale from which the works came. They failed, as did Mrs Freeman who followed them. Yet, as Grigson (himself a skilled botanist) points out, most of the flowers, including a plant called *Cucubalus baccifer*, come from the country north of the Loire.

Here then, in these tapestries is a symbolic conjunction of the 'real' and the 'mythical', by which the love of the young couple was surrounded not merely by the lovely burgeoning tokens of the homeland, but by the symbolic and ambiguous power of the unicorn. There is a sense in which the unicorn is here more 'real' than any mere biological specimen would be.

In the Cluny Museum in Paris today there hangs another set of unicorn tapestries, made in Flanders, also about 1500. These are not so magnificent as those in the Cloisters, but are still striking works of mystery and grace. They are known as *La Dame à la Licorne* (The Lady with the Unicorn), and may have been planned as illustrations of the metrical romance of that name. The scenes are symbolic of the five senses. The full significance of what the artist or his patron intended is as unclear as in the Cloisters tapestries.

This French series, especially the one called *La Vue* (Sight), in which the unicorn rests on the virgin's lap, gazing contentedly at his own reflection in a mirror, inspired one of the poems in Rilke's series *Sonnets to Orpheus*.

> This is the creature there has never been.
> They never knew it, and yet, none the less,
> they loved the way it moved, its suppleness,
> its neck, its very gaze, mild and serene.
>
> Not there, because they loved it, it behaved
> as though it were. They always left some space.
> And in that clear unpeopled space they saved
> it lightly raised its head, with scarce a trace

of not being there. They fed it, not with corn,
but only with the possibility
of being. And that was able to confer
such strength, its brow put forth a horn. One horn.
Whitely it stole up to a maid, – to *be*
within the silver mirror and in her.

Here the poet manages to suggest not only the mysterious manner
in which the unicorn exists as part of the fauna of the mind, but
also the ambiguous elements of both purity and virility that so
appealed to the late Gothic imagination. The unicorn had become by then a perfect creature, so plausible that it was hard to
imagine that it did *not* exist. 'They always left some space':
nowadays we have crowded out these creatures of the mind, and
banished them along with much else, back into the unconscious
or subconscious, or whatever one calls the dark labyrinths of the
mind where the minotaur and all these other creatures wander
still.

These creations, master works of their period and kind, are the
supreme expressions of the unicorn myth in Western art, as that
myth had been current in Western culture for over two millennia.
Preserved in these pieces of art, or in a painting such as Domeni-
chino's of a virgin embracing its pale white neck, the unicorn, like
the other creatures of the magic zoo, remains in the end a creature
of mystery, always a little way beyond explanation.

A Chinese sage realised this many centuries ago. In his an-
thology of Chinese literature Marguolies quotes the following allegory from a ninth-century writer :

It is universally held that the unicorn is a supernatural being
and of auspicious omen; so say the odes, the annals, the bio-
graphies of worthies, and other texts whose authority is unim-
peachable. Even village women and children know that the
unicorn is a lucky sign. But this animal does not figure among
the farmyard animals, it is not always easy to come across, it
does not lend itself to zoological classification. Nor is it like the
horse or bull, the wolf or deer. In such circumstances we may be
face to face with a unicorn and not know for sure that we are.
We know that a certain animal with a mane is a horse and that

a certain animal with horns is a bull. We do not know what a unicorn looks like.

And neither do we. For today the world has grown too small for these mysterious creatures. Monsters have been driven back into the impenetrable regions of the earth. Among these we must count the imagination, the Serengeti of the mind.

Only in art, painting and poetry do the animals of the magic zoo continue to flourish. Presenting man not so much with an image of Nature (the horse or deer of the Chinese sage), but with another kind of world 'entire of it self'. The shaman whom we met earlier may be the ancestor of the scientist, but he is also the ancestor of the painter and the poet.

These responses to just one symbolic animal are only a few of many. Kenneth Clark, Francis Klingender and Heinz Mode give one a more extensive idea of the artistic use of magic animals than I can possibly do here.

In early myth, the idea of an earthly paradise was paramount. We are all familiar with the garden planted 'eastward in Eden' in the opening chapters of Genesis. There Adam, the first man, gave names to all the beasts and birds. The hope of recapturing that ideal place has obsessed the human imagination ever since. The animal paradise features in Roman mosaics, medieval paintings, the expeditions of early explorers. But the *paradise terrestre* has never been found, not in Asia, America or the Antipodes. Least of all in Europe. If it existed, if it still exists, it is in the imagination that we must seek the ruins of Eden, where these magic animals still possess their own territory.

BIBLIOGRAPHY

This bibliography includes not only books quoted by me, but also other works which will be of use to those wishing to investigate further. Extended bibliographies can be found in Carrington (1956), Clarke (1975), Klingender (1969) and Mode (1976); and on cryptozoology in the several works in French and English of Dr Bernard Heuvelmans.

CHAPTER ONE : ANIMALS AND MAN

Allen, Don Cameron : *The Legend of Noah.* Urbana, Ill., 1949; 1963.

Cansdale, G. S. : *Animals and Man.* London, 1952.

Childe, V. Gordon : *What Happened in History,* London, 1942.

Coon, Carleton : *The World of the Hunters.* New York, 1967.

Dembeck, Hermann : *Animals and Men.* New York, 1964.

Guggisberg, C. A. W. : *Man and Wildlife.* London, 1970.

Hyams, Edward : *Animals in the Service of Man.* London, 1972.

Johanson, Donald C. : 'Ethiopia Yields First "Family" of Early Man', *National Geographic* (Washington D.C.), vol. 150, no. 8, December 1976, pp. 791–811.

Katz, D. : *Animals and Men.* London, 1937.

Leakey, Richard with R. Lewin : *Origins.* New York, 1977.

Marchant, R. A. : *Man and Beast.* London, 1968.

Morris, Desmond : *The Naked Ape.* London ,1967, pp. 189–211.

Petter, Francis : *Les animaux domestique et leurs ancêtres.* Paris, 1973.

Singer, Peter : *Animal Liberation.* New York, 1975

Weimer, Bernard R. : *Man and the Animal World.* New York, 1951.

Zeuner, Frederick E. : *A History of Domesticated Animals.* London, 1958.

CHAPTER TWO : SHAMAN INTO SCIENTIST

Adams, Alexander B. : *The Eternal Quest.* New York, 1969.

Arnold, R. : *Das Tier in der Weltgeschichte.* Frankfurt, 1939.

Blankenburg, Vern von : *Heilige und Dämonische Tiere*. Leipzig, 1943.

Brodrick, Alan Houghton (editor) : *Animals in Archaelogy*. London, 1972.

Burkhart, G. : *Die Geschichte der Zoologie*. Berlin, 1921.

Calvert, Jean and Marcel Crupp : *Le bestiaire de l'antiquitié classique*. Paris, 1955.

Carus, Julius Victor : *Histoire de la zoologie*. Paris, 1880.

Cuvier, Georges : *Histoire des sciences naturelles depuis leur origine jusqu'à nos jours, chez tous les peuples connus*. 5 vols. Paris, 1831–1845.

Delauney, Paul : *La zoologie au XVIe siecle*. Paris, 1962.

Denis, Ferdinand : *Le monde enchanté: cosmographie et histoire naturelle fantastique du Moyen-Age*. Paris, 1843.

Fohrmann, Ernst : *Das Tier in der Religion*. München, 1922.

Hays, H. R. : *Birds, Beasts and Men: a Humanist History of Zoology*. New York, 1972.

Hoefer, Ferdinand : *Histoire de la zoologie*. Paris, 1873.

Jennison, George : *Animals for Show and Pleasure in Ancient Rome*. Manchester, 1937.

Keller, Gottfried : *Daten zur Geschichte der Zoologie*. Bonn, 1949.

Keller, Otto : *Thiere des classichen Alterthums*. Innsbrück, 1887.

—— : *Die antike Tierwelt*. 2 vols. Leipzig, 1909 and 1913.

Kerr, John Graham : *A Naturalist in Gran Chaco*. Cambridge, 1951.

Langlois, Charles-Victor : *La connaissance de la nature et du monde au Moyen-Age d'après quelques escrits français a l'usage des laïcs*. Paris, 1911.

Lauchert, Friedrich : *Geschichte der Physiologus*. Strasbourg, 1889.

Lévi-Strauss, Claude : *La pensée sauvage*. Paris, 1962.

Ley, Willy : *Dawn of Zoology*. Englewood Cliffs, N.J., 1968.

Loisel, Gustave-Antoine : *Histoire des menageries de l'antiquité à nos jours*. 3 vols. Paris, 1912.

Meunier, Victor : *Histoire philosophique des progrés de la zoologie de puis l'antiquité jusqu'à nos jours*. Paris, 1891.

Mode, H. : *Fabulous Beasts and Demons*. London, 1975.

Petit, G. and J. Theodoridès : *Histoire de la zoologie, des origines à Linné*. Paris, 1962.

Peyer, Bernhard : *Geschichte der Thierwelt*. Stuttgart, 1949.

Pizetta, Jules : *Galerie des naturalistes*. Paris, 1891.

Pouchet, F. A. : *Histoire des sciences naturelles au Moyen-Age*. Paris, 1853.

Thorndike, Lynn : *A History of Magic and Experimental Science.* 8 vols. New York, 1923–1958.

CHAPTER THREE: THE SCIENCE OF UNKNOWN ANIMALS

***: 'Histoire naturelle des animaux aprocryphes', *Revue Britannique* 3e ser., vol. 15, pp. 264–292, juin 1835.

Anderson, Dr C. : 'The Sea Serpent and its Kind', *Australian Museum Magazine,* vol. 5, no. 6, pp. 204–208, 1934.

Attenborough, David : *Fabulous Animals.* London, 1975.

Ball, Valentine : 'The identification of the Pygmies, the Martikhora, the Griffin, and the Dikarion of Ktesias', *The Academy* (London), vol. 23, no. 572, p. 277, 21 April 1883.

—— : 'The "Parehon" Tree of Ktesias', *The Academy* (London), vol. 25, no. 624, p. 280, 19 April 1884.

—— : 'On the identification of the animals and plants of India which were known to the early Greek authors', *Proc. Royal Irish Academy* (Dublin) – Polite Lit. and Antiquities, vol. II, ser. 2, no. 6, pp. 302–346, 1884.

Burton, Maurice : *Animal Legends.* New York, 1957.

—— : *Phoenix Reborn.* London, 1959.

—— : *The Elusive Monster.* London, 1961.

Carrington, Richard : *Mermaids and Mastodons.* London, 1957.

Clair, Colin : *Unnatural History.* London and New York, 1968.

Dance, Peter : *Animal Fakes and Frauds.* Maidenhead, 1976.

Falconer, Hugh : 'Conclusion of paper on Colossochelys Atlas', *Proc. Zool. Soc.* (London), part XII, p. 86, 1844.

—— : *Palaeontological Memoirs.* Ed. Charles Murchison. London, 1868, vol. I, pp. 373–377.

Fort, Charles : *The Books of Charles Fort.* New York, 1944.

Gosse, P. H. : *The Romance of Natural History.* First and second series. London, 1860–1861.

Gould, Rupert Thomas : *The Sea-serpent; a paper read before ye Sette of Odd Volumes.* London, 1926.

—— : *The Case for the Sea-Serpent.* London, 1930.

—— : *The Loch Ness Monster and Others.* London, 1934.

Heuvelmans, Bernard : *Sur les pistes des bêtes ignorées.* Paris, 1955.

—— : *Dans le sillage des monstres marins.* Paris, 1958.

—— : *On the Track of Unknown Animals.* London and New York, 1958.

—— : *Le grand serpent-de-mer.* Paris, 1965; 1975.

—— : *In the Wake of the Sea-Serpents.* New York, 1968.

——: *L'Homme de Neanderthal est toujours vivant*. Paris, 1974.

Hichens, William : 'African mystery beasts', *Discovery* (Cambridge), pp. 369–373, December 1937.

Krumbiegel, Ingo : 'Gibt es noch unentdeckte Grosstiere?', *Kosmos* (Stuttgart), pp. 161ff. 1943–1944.

——: *Von neuen und unentdeckten tierarten*. Stuttgart, 1950.

Lane, Frank W. : 'Mystery animals of Jungle and Forest', *National Review* (London), pp. 99–103, July 1937.

——: *Nature Parade*. London ,1939; 1944; 1946.

——: Do these animals exist?', *The Field* (London), vol. 173, pp. 672–681, 31 May 1941.

Lehner, E. and J. : *A Fantastic Bestiary*. New York, 1969.

Ley, Willy : *The Lungfish, the Dodo and the Unicorn*. New York, 1948.

Macrae, F. B. : 'More African mysteries', *Nation Review* (London), vol. 111, pp. 791–796, December 1938.

Malten, H. M. : 'Ueber Dasein und Gestalt einiger räthselhafter Thiere', *Bibliothek der neuesten Weltkunde* (Aarau), Band III, heft 9, pp. 99–116, 1835.

Müller, Karl : 'Naturgeschichte der mythischen Thiere', *Die Natur* (Halle), vol. 7, pp. 73–75, 101–104, 129–131, 158–160, 177–180, 1858.

Oudemans, A. C. : *The Great Sea Serpent*. Leyden and London, 1892.

Sanderson, Ivan T. : *Animal Treasure*. New York, 1938.

——: 'Don't scoff at sea monsters', *Saturday Evening Post* (Philadelphia), pp. 22–23, 84–87, 8 March 1947.

——: 'Nature's nightmares', *This Week* (New York), 10 April 1949.

——: *Investigating the Unexplained*. Englewood Cliffs, N.J., 1972.

Smith, Charles Hamilton : *The Natural History of the Human Species*. Edinburgh, 1848, pp. 104–106.

Smith, Grafton Elliot : *Elephants and Ethnologists*. London. 1924.

Tilmans, Henri : 'Raretés zoologiques', *Le Naturaliste canadien* (Quebec), vol. 32, pp. 64–66, 75–77, 1905.

Timbs, John : *Eccentricities of Animal Creation*. London, 1869.

Tylor, Edward Burnet : *Researches into the Early History of Mankind*. London, 1865, pp. 303 ff.

W. : 'Remarks on the histories of the Kraken and Great Sea-Serpent', *Blackwood's Magazine* (Edinburgh), vol. II, no. 12, pp. 645–654, March 1818.

——: 'On the history of the Great Sea-Serpent', *Blackwood's Mazazine* (Edinburgh), vol. III, no. 13, pp. 33–42, April 1818.

Webster, F. A. M.: 'Are there any undiscovered animals', *Badminton Magazine* (London), pp. 255–260, January 1920.
Whyte, Constance: *More Than a Legend*. London, 1957.

Chapter Four: THE BEAST OF LASCAUX

Bataille, G.: *Lascaux, or the Birth of Art*. Lausanne, 1955.
Breuil, Henri: *Four Hundred Years of Cave Art*. Montignac, 1952.
Brodrick, Alan Houghton: *Lascaux, a Commentary*. London, 1949.
Giedion, S.: *The Eternal Present: The Beginnings of Art*. London, 1962.
Laming, Annette: *Lascaux*. Harmondsworth, 1959.
Leroi-Gourhan, André: *The Art of Prehistoric Man in Western Europe*. London, 1968.
Levy, G. R.: *The Gate of Horn*. London, 1946.
Nyblin. Oruar: [article on the Lascaux Beast] *Bulletin de la Société Prehistorique française,* novembre 1965.
Rousseau, Michel: 'La Licorne, enigme liminaire de Lascaux', *Journal de la Société française d'Histoire de la medecine*, pp. 28–40, juin 1966.
Windels, Fernand: *The Lascaux Cave Paintings*. London, 1949.

Chapter Five: THE MINOTAUR

Beazley, John: *Etruscan Vasepainting*. Oxford, 1947, pp. 6, 54; plate 3.
Bevan, William Latham and Henry Wright Phillot: *Medieval Geography; an essay in illustration of the Hereford Mappa Mundi* London, 1873, p. 64.
Bibby, Geoffrey: *Four Thousand Years Ago*. New York, 1961.
Borges, Jorge Luis: *The Book of Imaginary Beings*. New York, 1969, p. 159.
Conrad, Jack Randolph: *The Horn and the Sword; the History of the Bull as Symbol of Power and Fertility*. London, 1959.
Evans, Sir Arthur: *The Palace of Minos*. London, 1921–1936.
Frazer, J. G.: *The Golden Bough*. Abridged edition. London, 1922, pp. 369–370.
Graves, Robert: *The Greek Myths*. Harmondsworth, 1955.
Renault, Mary: *The King Must Die*. London, 1958.
Rose, H. J.: *A Handbook of Greek Mythology*. New York, 1959.

General

Bassett, F. S.: *Legends and Superstitions of Sailors and the Sea.* London, 1885.

Bennett, Alfred Gordan: 'The Mermaid Myth', in *Focus on the Unknown.* London, 1953, pp. 39–64.

Benwell, Gwen and Arthur Waugh: *Sea Enchantress; the tale of the Mermaid and Her Kind.* London, 1961.

Boullet, Jean: 'Symbolisme d'un Mythe', *Aesculape* (Paris), pp. 3–61, fevrier 1958.

Briggs, K. M.: *The Anatomy of Puck.* London, 1959.

Buckland, Frank T.: *The Curiosities of Natural History.* London, 1866.

Carrington, Richard: *Mermaids and Mastodons.* London, 1957, pp. 15–30.

——: 'The Natural History of the Mermaid', *The Saturday Book* (London), vol. 19, pp. 293–301, 1959.

Dance, Peter: *Animal Fakes and Frauds.* Maidenhead, 1976.

Douglas, Norman: *Siren Land.* London, 1911.

Faral, Edmond: 'La queue de poisson des sirènes', *Romania* (Paris), vol. 74, pp. 433–506, 1953.

Gosse, P. H.: *The Romance of Natural History.* Second series. London, 1861.

Grässe, J. G. T.: 'Von den Meermannern und Meerfrauen', *Beiträge zur Literatur und Saga des Mittelalters* (Dresden), vol. 4, 1850.

Hulme, F. E.: *Natural History Lore and Legend.* London, 1895.

Kastner, Georges: *Les Sirènes.* Paris, 1858.

Lampedusa, Guiseppe di: 'Lighea' in *Racconti.* Milano, 1961. Trans. as 'The Professor and the Siren', in *Two Stories and a Memory.* London and New York, 1962.

Lee, Henry: *Sea Fables Explained.* London, 1883.

Lucas, Frederic: 'Modern mermaids', *Natural History* (New York), 1922.

Pontoppidan, Erik: *Det förste Forsög paa Norges Naturlige Historie.* Copenhagen, 1752–1753.

——: *The Natural History of Norway.* London, 1755.

Sebillot, Paul: *Legendes, croyances et superstitions de la mer.* Paris, 1886.

Shepard, Katherine : *The Fish-Tailed Monster in Greek and Etrus-can Art.* New York, privately published, 1940.

Thomson, David : *The People of the Sea.* London, 1954.

Wells, H. G. : *The Sea Lady.* London, 1902.

Sightings

Reports for which no reference is given will be found in Benwell and Waugh (1961), which gives a first class account of the mermaid.

*** : 'Amazing denizen of the sea', *Fate* (Evanston), vol. 15, no. 5, p. 48, May 1962.

*** : 'One that got away was a mermaid', *Evening Press* (Dublin), 4 August 1962.

*** : 'Mermaids yet', *Fate* (Evanston), vol. 20, no. 11, pp. 21–22, November 1967.

Baring-Gould, Sabine : *Iceland, Its Scenes and Sagas.* London ,1863.

—— : *Curious Myths of the Middle Ages.* New and enlarged edition. London, 1869.

Barnum, P. T. : *The Life of P. T. Barnum, written by Himself.* London, 1859.

Bisschop, Eric de : *Tahiti-Nui.* London, 1959.

Carmichael, Alexander : *Carmina Gadelica.* Edinburgh, 1900.

Columbus, Christopher : 'Columbus his first Voyage . . .' in *Purchas His Pilgrimes.* London, 1625.

Cory, Isaac P. : *Ancient Fragments of the Phoenician.* London, 1832.

Glover, Thomas : [Mermaid at Rappahannock], *Phil. Trans. Royal Society* (London), vol. XI, p. 625, 1676.

Hamilton, Dr Robert : *Amphibious Carnivora, Including the Walruses and Seals, Also of the Herbivorous Cetacea.* Volume 8 of *The Naturalist's Library.* Edinburgh, 1839.

Holinshed, Raphael : *Chronicles.* London, 1697.

Hudson, Henry : 'Divers Voyages and Northern Discoveries of Henry Hudson', in *Purchas His Pilgrimes.* London, 1625.

Josselyn, John : *An Account of Two Voyages to New England.* London, 1674.

Lucian : *De dea Syria* (XIV). Trans. W. Tooke. London, 1820.

Maillet, Benoit de : *Telliamed.* London, 1750.

Munro, William : 'The Mermaid seen on the coast of Caithness', *The Times* (London), 8 September 1809.

Pausanias : *Guide to Greece* (VIII, 2 :7). Trans. Peter Levi. Harmondsworth, 1971.

Pliny : *The historie of the world, commonly called, the naturall historie of C. Plinius Secundus.* Trans. Philemon Holland. London, 1634.

Siebold, Dr P. F. von : *On the Manners and Customs of the Japanese in Nineteenth Century.* London, 1841.

Steinmetz, Andrew : *Japan and Her People.* London, 1859.

Thevet, André : *The New Found World or Antarctika.* London, 1568.

Tieck, Johann Ludwig : *Der Wassermensch.* Breslau, 1847.

Timbs, John : *Eccentricities of the Animal Creation.* London, 1869, pp. 33–48.

Valentijn, François : *Oud en Nieuw Oost-Indien.* Dordrecht and Amsterdam, 1724–1726.

Whitbourne, Richard : *Discourse and Discovery of New-Found-Land.* London, 1622.

White, T. H. : *The Book of Beasts.* London ,1954, pp. 134–135.

Zoete, Beryl de : *The Other Mind, a Study of Life and Dance in India.* London, 1953.

Dugongs and manatees

Allen, Glover M. : *Extinct and Vanishing Mammals of the Western Hemisphere with the Marine Species of All Oceans.* Lancaster, Pa., 1942.

Barrett, O. W. : 'Notes concerning manatees and dugongs', *Journal of Mammalogy,* vol. 16, pp. 216–220, 1935.

Bertram, Colin : *In Search of Mermaids.* London, 1963.

Hayman, R. W. : 'Manatees and dugongs', *Zoo Life* (London), no. 10, 1953.

Mohr, E. : *Sirenen oder Seekühe.* Wittenberg, 1957.

Tennent, Sir J. Emerson : *Sketches of the Natural History of Ceylon.* London, 1861.

Williams, J. H. : *In Quest of a Mermaid.* London, 1960, pp. 7–12 .

Aquatic man

Feldmann, Frank : 'L'Homme-sirène de Brighton', *Pour Tous* (Paris), p. 25, 4 aout 1959.

Gorer, Geoffrey : *Africa Dances.* New York, 1935, pp. 50–51 .

Hardy, Alister C. : 'Was man more aquatic in the past?', *New Scientist* (London), vol. 7, pp. 642–645, 17 March 1960.

——— : 'Has man an aquatic past?', *The Listener* (London), vol. 63, pp. 839–841, 12 May 1960.

Heuvelmans, Bernard : *Dans le sillage des monstres marins.* Genève : Editions Famot, 1974, pp. 466–467.

Jones, Frederic Wood : *Man's Place Among the Mammals*. London, 1929, pp. 269–300.
—— : *Hallmarks of Mankind*. London, 1948, pp. 78–80.
Kersh, Gerald : *The Brighton Monster and Others*. London, 1955.
Morris, Desmond : *The Naked Ape*. London, 1967, pp. 39–41.
Sanderson, Ivan T. : *More Things*. New York, 1969, pp. 89–100.

Chapter Seven : SIRENS, CENTAURS AND SATYRS

Borges, Jorge Luis : *The Book of Imaginary Beings*. New York, 1969, p. 198.
Bradford, Ernle : *Ulysses Found*. London, 1963.
Dante : *Commedia: Inferno*. Ed. Arnaldo Momigliano. Roma, 1945.
Douglas, Norman : *Siren Land*. London, 1911.
Dumézil, Georges : *Le probleme des centaurs*. Paris, 1929.
Graves, Robert : *The Greek Myths*. Harmondsworth, 1955.
—— : *The White Goddess*. New edition. London, 1961.
Herodotus : *The Histories*. Trans. Aubrey de Selincourt. Harmondsworth, 1958.
Homer : *The Odyssey*. Trans. E. V. Rieu. London, 1946.
Kerényi, Carl : *The Gods of the Greeks*. London, 1951.
—— : 'Le sage centaure', *Image-Roche* (Bâsle), no. 45, pp. 7–16, 1971.
Lawson, J. C. : *Modern Greek Folklore and Ancient Greek Religion*. Cambridge, 1910.
Lucretius : *De rerum natura*. Trans. R. C. Trevelyan. Cambridge, 1937, pp. 209–211.
Nilsson, Martin P. : *A History of Greek Religion*. Oxford, 1925.
Pliny : *The Natural History* (III, 3 :35). Trans. J. Bostock and H. T. Riley. London, 1855–1857.
Plutarch : 'The Feast of the Seven Sages' (49), in *Moralia*. Loeb edition. London, 1958, vol. II, pp. 365–367.
Pollard, John : *Seers, Shrines and Sirens*. London, 1959.
Rose, H. J. : *A Handbook of Greek Mythology*. New York, 1959.
Strabo : *The Geography*. Trans. H. C. Hamilton and W. Falconer, London, 1854–1857, vol. III, p. 202 ff.

Chapter Eight : THE PHOENIX

Aelian : *On the Characteristics of Animals*. Trans. A. F. Scholfield. London, 1958–1959, vol. 2, p. 58.
Aldrovandi, Ulisse : *De avibus etc*. Francofurti, 1611, bk. 12, pp. 403–410.

Ambrose, Saint: 'Hexameron' in *Opera Omnia*. Ed. Migne. Paris, 1845, col. 238.

Beebe, Charles William : *A Monograph of the Pheasants*. New York, 1918–1922, vol. IV, p. 218, pl. 71.

Blake, N. F. (ed.) : *The Phoenix*. Manchester, 1964.

Bonnet, H. : *Reallexicon der Agyptischen Religiongeschichte*, 1952, s.v. Phönix.

Browne, Sir Thomas : 'Of the Phoenix', *Pseudoxia Epidemica, or enquiries into very many received tenents and commonly presumed truths*. London, 1646, bk. III, ch. 12.

Burton, Maurice : *Phoenix Reborn*. London, 1959.

Clark, R. T. Rundle : 'Legend of the phoenix, a study in Egyptian religious symbolism', *University of Birmingham Historical Journal*, vol. 2, no. 1, pp. 1–29, 105–140, 1949.

Claudianus, Claudius : *Works*. London, 1922, vol. 2, pp. 223–231.

Clement the Roman, Saint : *First Epistle to the Corinthians* (ch. xxv–xxvi) in Migne, *Pat. Grec.* I, col. 261–266. Paris, 1845.

Cuvier, Georges : *La règne animal*. 4 vols. Paris, 1817.

Cynewulf : 'The Phoenix', in *Anglo-Saxon Poetry*. Ed. R. K. Gordan. London, 1926, pp. 265–279.

Cyril of Jerusalem, Saint : *Catechesis* (ch. xviii, viii).

De Kay, Charles : *Bird Gods of Ancient Europe*. New York, 1898, pp. 220–221.

Delacour, Jean : 'The pheasants', *Animals* (London), vol. 9, no. 8, pp. 464–471, 1966.

Epiphanus : *Ancorotus* (ch. lxxxiv).

Erman, Adolph : *A Handbook of Egyptian Religion*. London, 1907.

Festugière, A. J. : 'Le symbole du phénix et le mysticisme hermétique', *Monuments et Mémoires-Fondation Eugène Piot*, vol. 38, pp. 147–151, 1941.

Gesner, Conrad : *Historia animalium*. Frankfurti, 1585–1617.

Gould, Charles : *Mythical Monsters*. London, 1882.

Hachisuka, M. V. : 'The Identification of the Chinese Phoenix', *Journal Royal Asiatic Society* (London), pp. 585–589, 1924.

Helck, W. and E. Otto : *Kleines Wörterbuch der Aegyptologie* (1956), s.v. Phönix.

Henrichsen, Rudolph Johannes Frederick : *De phoenicis fabula apud Graecos, Romanos et populos orientales* etc. Havniae, 1825.

Herodotus : *The Histories* (II, 72). Trans. Aubrey de Selincourt. Harmondsworth, 1960.

Hortus Sanitatis. Quatuor libris quae subsequuntur complectens. Argentorati, 1536.

How, W. W. and J. Wells : *A Commentary on Herodotus*. Oxford, 1912, vol. I, p. 203.

Hubaux, Jean and Maxime Leroy : *Le mythe du Phénix dans les litteratures Greque et Latine*. Paris, 1939.

Ingersoll, Ernest : *Birds in Legend, Fable and Folklore*. New York, 1923.

Jabouille, P. : 'Le Phoenix fabuleaux de la Chine et le Faisan ocelle d'Annam', *Oiseau* (Paris), vol. 11, pp. 220–232, 1930.

Lactantius : 'Carmen de ave phoenice', in A. Riese : *Anthologia Latina*, Leipzig, 1906, vol. I, no. 485a.

Leroy, Maxime : 'Le Chant du Phénix, *L'Antiquité Classique*, vol. I, pp. 213–231, 1932.

Métral, Antoine : *Le Phénix et l'Oiseau du Soleil*. Paris, 1824.

Müller, W. Max : *Egyptian Mythology*. London, 1930.

Pellicer Salas Ossau y Tovar, José de : *El Fenix y su historia natural*. Madrid, 1630.

Pliny : *The Natural History* (X, 2). Trans. J. Bostock and H. T. Riley. London, 1855–1857.

Poole, Reginald Stuart : *Horae Aegyptiacae*. London, 1851 .

Rawlinson, George : *The Histories of Herodotus*. London, 1858, vol. II, p. 122.

Richmond, O. L. : *De ave phoenice*. Edinburgh, 1947.

Sbordone, F. : 'La fenice nel culto di Helios', *Rivista indo-greco-italica*, vol. XIX, pp. 1–46, 1935.

Solinus : *The Excellent and Pleasant Work of Julius Solinus Polyhistor*. Trans. A. Golding. London, 1587, p. 154.

Tacitus : *The Annals* (VI, 28). Trans. G. C. Ramsay. London, 1904.

Wayre, Philip : *A Guide to the Pheasants of the World*. London, 1969.

White, T. H. : *The Book of Beasts*. London, 1954, pp. 125–128.

Wiedemann, A. : *The Religion of the Ancient Egyptians*. London, 1897, p. 193.

Wiedemann, M. : 'Die Phönix-Sage im alten Aegypten', *Zeitschrift für Aegyptische Sprache und Alterthumskunde*, vol. XVI, pp. 89–106, 1878.

CHAPTER NINE : THE GRIFFIN

Aelian : *On the Characteristics of Animals* (IV, 27 :4). Trans. A. F. Scholfield. London, 1958–1959.

Aeschylus : *Prometheus Vinctus* (lines 802–803).

Ball, Valentine : 'The identification of the pygmies, the Martikhora, the griffin, and the Dikarion of Ktesias', *The Academy* (London), vol. 23, no. 512, p. 277, 21 April 1883.

—— : 'On the identification of the animals and plants of India which were known to early Greek authors', *Proc. Royal Irish Acad.* (Dublin), vol. II, series 2 – Polite lit. and antiquities, no. 6, pp. 312–313, 1884.

Bolton, J. D. P. : *Aristeas of Proconnesu.* Oxford, 1962.

Brown, Leslie and Dean Amadon : *Eagles, Hawks and Falcons of the World.* London, 1973.

Brown, Robert : 'Remarks on the gryphon, heraldic and mythological', *Archaeologia* (London), vol. 48, pp. 355–378, 1885.

Browne, Sir Thomas : *Pseudoxia Epidemica.* London, 1645, Bk. III, ch. XI.

Carroll, Lewis : *Alice's Adventures in Wonderland.* London, 1865.

Dalton, O. M. : *The Treasure of the Oxus.* London, 1905.

Dante : *Purgatio* (canto 29, lines 106–114).

Erman, Adolf : *Travels in Siberia.* London, 1848, vol. II, p. 87.

Evans, Sir Arthur : *The Palace of Minos.* London, 1921–1936.

Frankfort, Henri : 'Notes on the Cretan griffin', *Annual of the British School at Athens,* vol. 37, pp. 106–122, 1936–1937.

Fürtwangler, A. : 'Griffin', in *Ausführliches Lexicon der griechischen und romischen Mythologie.* Edited by W. H. Roscher. Leipzig, 1884–1937.

Gill, William : *The River of Golden Sand.* London, 1882.

Hawkes, David : *Ch'u Tz'u. Songs of the South.* Oxford, 1959.

Heeren, Arnold : *Historical Works.* Oxford, 1833, vol. I, p. 45.

Hennig, Richard : *Terra Incognita.* Leiden, 1944–1956.

Herodotus : *The Histories.* Trans. J. Enoch Powell. Oxford, 1949, vol. I, pp. 252, 278.

How, W. W. and J. Wells : *A Commentary on Herodotus.* Oxford, 1912, vol. I, p. 307.

Howorth, H. : 'The Mammoth', *Geological Magazine* (London). September 1880.

Isidore of Seville : *Etymologiarum sive originum libri XX.* Ed. William Lindsay. Oxford, 1911.

Lum, Peter : *Fabulous Beasts.* London, 1952, pp. 46–56.

McCrindle, J. W. : *Ancient India as Described by Ktesias.* Calcutta, 1882, pp. 43–46.

Mandeville, Sir John : *The Travels of Sir John Mandeville.* London, 1906, ch. 87.

Milton, John : *Paradise Lost.* London, 1668, Bk. II, lines 944–948.

Minns, E. H. : *Scythians and Greeks.* Cambridge, 1913.

Mongait, A. L. : *Archaeology in the U.S.S.R.* Harmondsworth, 1961.

Murchison, R. : *The Geology of Russia.* London, 1845, vol. I, pp. 476–491.

Newman, Edward : 'Notes on the Pterodactyl tribe considered as marsupial bats', *The Zoologist* (London), vol. I, pp. 129–132, 1848.

Pausanias : *Guide to Greece.* Harmondsworth, 1971, vol. I, pp. 69–70, 90.

Peacock, Edward : 'The Griffin', *Antiquary* (London), vol. 10, pp. 89–92, 1884.

Perkins, Ann : 'Griffin', in *Encyclopedia Britannica.* Chicago, 1973 edition, vol. 10, p. 924.

Photius : *Myriobiblon* (LXXII). Geneva, 1612.

Pliny : *The Natural History* (X, 7). Trans. J. Bostock and H. T. Riley. London, 1852–1857.

Polo, Marco : *The Travels of Marco Polo.* London, 1908, p. 393.

Read, Sir Charles Hercules : 'Note on a griffin's claw in the British Museum, formerly at Durham', *Proc. Soc. Antiquaries* (London), series 2, vol. 9, pp. 250–251, 1881–1883.

Rice, Tamara Talbot : *The Scythians.* London, 1957.

Rostovtzeff, M. I. : *Iranians and Greeks in South Russia.* Oxford, 1922.

Sayce, A. H. : *The Ancient Empires of the East.* London, 1883, p. 116.

Shan Hai Ching : passages trans. David Hawkes quoted in Bolton (1962).

Suhr, Elmer G. : 'The griffon and the vulcano', *Folklore* (London), vol. 78, pp. 212–224, 1967.

Tomaschek, W. : *Kritik der altesten Nachrichten über den skythischen nordern.* Wien : Kaiserliche Akademie der Wissenschaften, 1888.

Tournier, E. : *De Aristea Proconnesio et Arimaspeo poemate.* Paris, 1863.

Tylor, Edward : *Researches into the Early History of Mankind.* Third edition. London, 1872, pp. 319–320.

Wilson, Horace Hayman : *Notes on the Indica of Ctesias.* Oxford, 1836.

Wittkower, Rudolf : *Allegory and the Migration of Symbols.* London, 1977.

Garuda, the Ziz and the Simurgh

**** : 'The Sacred Kites of Chingleput', *Wide World Magazine* (London), vol. 19, pp. 623–624, September 1907.

Carrington, Richard: *Mermaids and Mastodons*. London, 1956, pp. 85–88.

Graves, Robert and Raphael Patai: *Hebrew Myths*. London, 1964, pp. 54–56.

CHAPTER TEN: THE ROC BIRD

Aldrovandi, Ulisse: *Ornithologiae hoc est de avibus historiae libri XII*. Bologna, 1599, lib. X, p. 610.

Alexander, W. B.: *The Birds of the Ocean*. New York, 1954.

Attenborough, David: *Zoo Quest to Madagascar*. London, 1961.

Barrow, John: *Travels into the Interior of South Africa*. London, 1806.

Bianconi, G. G.: *Degli scritti di Marco Polo e dell' uccello ruc da lui menzionite*. Bologna, 1868.

Bochart, Samuel: *Hierozoicon*. Leyde, 1692, vol. II, p. 854.

Burton, Sir Richard: *A Plain and Literal Translation of the Arabian Nights' Entertainments, now Entitled The Book of the Thousand Nights and A Night*. Benares [i.e. London], 1885–1886, vol. 6, p. 16, n. 1; p. 49, n. 3.

Carrington, Richard: *Mermaids and Mastodons*. London, 1956, pp. 92–96.

Flacourt, Etienne de: *Histoire de la Grande Isle de Madagascar*. Paris, 1658.

Geoffrey-Saint-Hilaire, Isidore: 'Notes sur des ossements et des oeufs trouvés à Madagascar . . . provenent d'un Oiseau gigantesque', *Comptes rendus des Séances de l'Academie des Sciences* (Paris), vol. 65, pp. 476–478, 1867.

Gibb, H. A. R.: *Ibn Battuta. Travels in Asia and Africa. 1325–1354.* London, 1939.

Grandidier, Alfred: *Histoire de la Geographie de Madagascar*. Paris, 1885–1892, vol. I, p. 25, n. 2.

—— : *Histoire Physique, Naturelle et Politique de Madagascar*. Paris, 1875–1879, vol. I, pp. 25–31.

Heuvelmans, Bernard: *On the Track of Unknown Animals*. London, 1958, pp. 499–504.

Ibn Al Wardi: in E. W. Lane, *The Thousand and One Nights*, 1883, vol. III, p. 85 ff.

Ibn Batuta: see Yale and Cordier, *Cathay and the Way Thither*, 1916, vol. IV, p. 146.

Jameson, William: *The Wandering Albatross*. London, 1958.

Kazwini : in Johann Gildemeister, *Scriptorum Arabum de Rebus Indica.* Bonnae, 1883, p. 220.

Komroff, Manuel : *The Contemporaries of Marco Polo.* London, 1928, pp. 311–312.

Lane, Edward William : *The Thousand and One Nights.* London, 1883, vol. III, pp. 85 ff.

Lowes, J. L. : *The Road to Xanadu.* Boston, 1927.

Parkinson, C. : 'The great bird of the Southern Ocean', *The Cornhill* (London), new series, vol. 8, pp. 654–661, May 1900.

Pigafetta, Antonio : in Camillo Manfroni, *Relazione del primo viaggo intorno al mondo de Antonio Pigafetta.* Milan, 1928, pp. 248, 253, 258.

Polo, Marco : *The Travels of Marco Polo.* London, 1908, pp. 393–394.

Wilson, Horace Hayman : *Works.* Collected and edited by R. Rost. 12 vols. London, 1862–1871, vol. I, pp. 192–193.

Wittkower, Rudolf : ' "Roc" : an Eastern prodigy in a dutch engraving', in *Allegory and the Migration of Symbols.* London, 1977.

Yule, Sir Henry : *The Book of Ser Marco Polo.* Third edition. London, 1903, vol. II, p. 409.

——— : *Cathay and the Way Thither.* Revised by Henri Cordier. London, 1916, vol. IV, p. 146.

Zurla, D. P. : *Il Mappamondo di Fra Mauro.* Roma, 1806, p. 62.

CHAPTER ELEVEN : THE GIANT ANTS OF INDIA

Arrian : *Indica* (XV).

Ball, Valentine : 'On the identification of the animals and plants of India which were known to early Greek authors', *Proc. Royal Irish Acad.* (Dublin) – Polite Lit. and Antiquities, vol. II, series 2, no. 6, pp. 302–316, 1884.

Bolton, J. D. P. : *Aristeas of Proconnesus.* Oxford, 1962, p. 81.

Bunbury, E. H. : *A History of Ancient Geography.* London, 1879, vol. I, p. 230.

Busbequius, A. : *Epistles* (IV, 343). Trans. C. E. Forster. London, 1881, p. 219.

Gill, William : *The River of Gold.* London, 1882.

Hawkes, David : *Ch'u Tz'u.* Oxford, 1959, p. 104.

Herodotus : *The History of Herodotus* (III, 102–106). A new English version, edited, with copious notes by George Rawlinson, assisted by Sir Henry Rawlinson. London, 1858.

Hortus Sanitatus. Argentorati, 1536.

Huxley, Julian : *Ants.* London, 1930.

Laufer, B. : 'Die Sage von dem goldgrabenden Ameisen', *T'oung Pao* (Leyde), vol. XI, 1908.

McCrindle, J. W. : *Ancient India as Described by Megasthenes.* Calcutta, 1877.

——: *Ancient India as Described in Classical Literature.* Westminster, 1901, pp. 3, 51.

Minns, E. H. : *Scythians and Greeks.* Cambridge, 1913, pp. 6, 113.

Pliny : *The Natural History* (XI, 3). Trans. J. Bostock and H. T. Riley. London, 1855–1857.

Prester John : in *Mandeville's Travels.* Edited and trans. M. Letts. London, 1953, vol. II, p. 504.

Schwanbeck, E. A. : *Megasthenis Indica.* Bonn, 1846.

Shan Hai Ching : in Bolton (1962), p. 81.

Strabo : *The Geography* (XV, 1 :44). Trans. H. C. Hamilton and W. Falconer. London, 1854–1857.

Tarn, W. W. : *The Greeks in Bactria and India.* Cambridge, 1951, p. 107.

Wheeler, W. M. : *Ants.* New York, 1910.

Wittkower, Rudolf : 'Marvels of the East', in *Allegory and the Migration of Symbols.* London, 1977.

CHAPTER TWELVE : THE UNICORN

*** : 'Unicorn' [report of Dr Dove's experiment]. *Time* (New York), vol. 27, pp. 47–48, 4 May 1936.

*** : 'Biologist produces live unicorn', *Scientific American* (New York), vol. 155, p. 30, July 1936.

Aelian : *On the Characteristics of Animals* (III, 41; IV, 52; XVI, 20). Trans. A. F. Scholfield. London, 1958–1959.

Aristotle : *Historia Animalium* (II, 2 :8; VI, 36; XVI, 20). Trans. D'Arcy Wentworth Thompson. Oxford, 1910.

Baikie, Dr William Balfour : 'In search of a unicorn', *The Athenaeum* (London), no. 1816, p. 212, 16 August 1862.

Ball, Valentine : 'On the identification of the animals and plants of India which were known to early Greek authors', *Proc. Royal Irish Acad.* (Dublin), vol. II, series 2 – Polite Lit. and Antiquities, no. 6, pp. 316–318, 1884.

Barthema, Ludovico : *The Navigations and Voyages of Lewes Vartomannus.* Trans. out of the Latine into Englyshe by Richard Eden. London, 1576, cap. 19.

Bartholini, Thomas: *De unicornu observationes novae*. Patavii, 1645.

Barrow, John: *Travels into the Interior of South Africa*. London, 1806, pp. 267–275.

Beer, Rüdiger Robert: *Einhorn: Fabelwelt und Wirklichkeit*. München, 1972.

——: *Unicorn, Myth and Reality*. London and New York, 1977.

Berg, Bengt: *Meine Jagd nach dem Einhorn*. Frankfurt am Main, 1931.

Berridge. W. S.: *Marvels of the Animal World*. London, 1921. pp. 47 ff.

Boulet, Jean: 'La merveilleuse histoire de la licorne', *Aesculape* (Paris), vol. 42, pp. 3–61, decembre 1959.

Breydenbach, Bernard von: *Reise ins Heilge Land*. Mainz, 1486.

Brown, Robert: *The Unicorn, a Mythological Investigation*. London, 1881.

Browne, Sir Thomas: *Pseudoxia Epidemica*. London, 1646, Bk. III, ch. 23.

Campbell, Rev. John: *Travels in South Africa*. London, 1822, vol. I, pp. 294.

Carrington, Richard: 'The Natural History of the Unicorn', *The Saturday Book*, vol. 20, pp. 273–285. London, 1960.

Clarke, T. H.: 'A European rhino hunt', *The Times* (London), p. 7, 25 September 1975.

Cohn, Carl: 'Zur literarischen Geschichte des Einhorns', supplement to the *Annual Transactions of the Berlin City Realschule*, vol. 11, Easter 1896 and 1897.

Ctesias: 'Indica opera', in Photius: *Myriobiblon*. Geneve, 1612.

Cuvier, Georges: 'Excursus IV' in Pliny: *Historia Naturae*. Paris, 1827.

Dove, Dr William Franklin: 'Artificial production of the fabulous unicorn. A modern interpretation of an ancient myth', *Scientific Monthly* (New York), vol. 42, pp. 431–436, May 1936.

Einhorn, Rev. Dr Jürgen Werinhard: *Spiritualis Unicornis*. München, 1976.

Ettinghausen, Richard: *The Unicorn* (Studies in Muslin Inconography, No. I). Washington, D.C., 1950.

Freeman, Rev.: [article on unicorn], *South African Christian Recorder*, vol. I, no. 1, 1834.

Freeman, Margaret: *The Unicorn Tapestries*. New York and London, 1977.

Fresnel, Fulgence : 'Lettre sur certain quadrupèdes réputés fabuleux', *Journal Asiatique* (Paris), pp. 129–159, mars 1844.

—— : 'Deuxième lettre sur certains quadrupèdes réputés fabuleux', *Journal Asiatique* (Paris), mars 1845.

—— : 'Sur l'existence d'une espèce unicorne de Rhinocéros dans la partie tropicale de l'Afrique, *Comptes rendues de l'Academie des Sciences* (Paris), vol. 26, no. 9, pp. 281–284, 1848.

Galton, Francis : *The Narrative of an Explorer in Tropical South Africa.* London, 1853, pp. 283–284.

Hedin, Sven : *Scientific Results of a Journey in Central Asia.* Stockholm, 1904, vol. VI, pp. 29 ff.

Heuvelmans, Bernard : *On the Track of Unknown Animals.* London, 1958.

Houghton, William : *Gleanings from the Natural History of the Ancients.* London, 1880, pp. 169–173.

Jong, Cornelius de : *Reisen nach dem Vorgebirge der guten Hoffnung.* Hamburg, 1803, vol. I, p. 201.

Katte, A. von : *Reisen in Abyssinien im Jahre 1836.* Stuttgart, 1838, p. 89.

Land, J. P. N. : *Anecdota Syriaca.* Lugd. Batav., 1870, vol. IV, p. 146.

Le Vaillant : *Travels in Africa.* London, 1796.

Ley, Willy : 'Mystic unicorn', *Nature Magazine* (Washington, D.C.), vol. 27, pp. 78–79, 9 February 1936.

—— : 'La legende de l'unicorne', *La Terre et la Vie* (Paris), vol. 8, no. 6, pp. 177–185, 1938.

—— : *The Lungfish, the Dodo and the Unicorn.* New York, 1948.

Lydekker, Richard : 'Unicorn rams from Nepal', *The Field* (London), vol. 118, p. 1447, 1911.

Malte-Brun, Conrad : *Précis de la Geographie Universelle.* Paris, 1817, livre 92, vol. V, p. 71.

Miller, Geneviève : 'The Unicorn in Medical History', *Trans. and Studies of the College of Physicians of Philadelphia*, vol. 28, pp. 80–93. 1960.

Mohammed Ebn Omar, al Tounsy : *Voyage au Darfour.* Preface par M. Jomard. Paris, 1845, pp. xvi–xviii.

Morgan, H. T. : *Chinese Symbols and Superstitions.* South Pasadena, 1942, p. 8.

Oustalet, E. : 'Le narval et la licorne des anciens', *La Nature* (Paris), vol. 18, pp. 134–138, 2 aout 1890.

Pallas, Peter Simon : *Spicilegia Zoologica.* Berlin, 1774, fasc. xii, pp. 35 ff.

Pliny: *The Natural History* (VIII, 21 :33). Trans. J. Bostock and
H. T. Riley. London, 1855–1857.

Plutarch : *Perikles* (VII).

Polo, Marco : *The Travels of Marco Polo.* London, 1908, p. 340.

Prejevalsky, Nicolai : *Mongolia.* London, vol. II, pp. 207 ff.

Reade, William Winwood : *Savage Africa.* London, 1863, pp. 471–
476.

Rüppell, Eduard : *Reisen in Nubien, Kordofan und dem petraischen
Arabia.* Frankfurt, 1829, pp. 161 ff.

Russeger, Joseph : *Reisen in Europe, Asien und Afrika.* Stuttgart,
1843, Band II, p. 474.

Shepard, Odell : *The Lore of the Unicorn.* London, 1930; 1969.

Shipley, Sir Arthur : *Cambridge Cameos.* London, 1924, pp. 64–98.

Smith, Sir Andrew : *Illustrations of the Zoology of South Africa.*
London, 1849.

Smith, Charles Hamilton : 'Reem', in *A Cyclopedia of Biblical
Literature.* Edited by John Kitto. Edinburgh, 1845, vol. II, pp.
605–607.

Sparrman, A. : *Resa till Goda Hoppa-Udden.* Stockholm, 1783.

Timbs, John : *Eccentricities of Animal Creation.* London, 1869, pp.
49–61.

Trouessart, E. : 'La licorne chez les anciens et les modernes', *La
Nature* (Paris), no. 1873, 17 avril 1909.

Urreta, Luis de : *Historia de los Grandes y Remotos Reyos de la
Etiopia, Monarchia del Emperador llamado Preste Juan.* Valencia,
1610, pp. 245 ff.

Vicalji Dinshaw : 'The unicorn', *Journal of the CAMA Oriental
Institute* (Bombay), no. 28, pp. 97–100, 1932.

White, T. H. : *The Book of Beasts.* London, 1954, pp. 20, 44.

Wilhelm, Richard : 'The Unicorn in China', *Der Ostasiatische Lloyd*
(Shanghai), vol. 25, pp. 539 ff, 1911.

Wilson, Alban : *Sport and Service in Assam and Elsewhere.* London, 1924, p. 217.

Wilson, Horace Hayman : *Notes on the Indica of Ctesias.* Oxford,
1836, pp. 48–54.

Wood, John George : *The Natural History of Man.* London, 1868.

Wurm, Ole : *An os illud quod vulgo pro cornu monocerotes vendita-
tur verum sit Unicornu.* A dissertation delivered at Copenhagen in
1638, quoted in Thomas Bartholini, *De unicornu* (1645).

Wurmb, Baron von : *Briefe der Herrnvon Wurmb und der Herrn
Baron von Wollzogen auf ihren Reisen nach Afrika und Ostindien
den Jahren 1774 bis 1792.* Gotha, 1794, pp. 412–416.

Chapter Thirteen : THE MANTICORA

*** : 'Aristotle's *History of Animals*', *Edinburgh Review*, vol. 160, pp. 460–489, October 1884.

Aelian : *On the Characteristics of Animals* (VI, 21). Trans. A. F. Scholfield. London, 1958–1959.

Aristotle : *Historia Animalium* (II, 1 :53). Trans. D'Arcy Wentworth Thompson. Oxford, 1910.

Ball, Valentine : 'On the identification of the animals and plants of India which were known to early Greek authors', *Proc. Royal Irish Acad.* (Dublin) – Polite Lit. and Antiquities, vol. II, series 2, no. 6, pp. 302–316, 1884.

—— : 'The identification of the pygmies, the Martikhora, the griffin, and the Dikarion of Ktesias', *The Academy* (London), vol. 23, no. 572, p. 277, 21 April 1883.

Corbett, Jim : *Man-Eaters of Kumaon.* London, 1946.

Ctesias : 'Indica opera' (cap. 7), in Photius : *Myriobiblon.* Geneva, 1612.

Garnett, David : *The White/Garnett Letters.* London, 1960, pp. 254–255.

Gesner, Conrad : *Historia animalium.* Zürich, 1551–1587.

Hulme, Edward : *Myth-Land.* London, 1886, pp. 1–93.

Hunt, Leigh : *The Autobiography of Leigh Hunt.* New edition. London, 1878, pp. 30–32.

Jonston, John : *Historia naturalis de quadrupedibus.* Amsterdam, 1657, plate 52.

McCrindle, John Watson : *Ancient India as Described by Ktesias the Knidian.* Calcutta, 1882, pp. 40–42.

—— : *Ancient India as Described by Megasthenes.* Calcutta, 1884, p. 56.

—— : *Ancient India as Described in Classical Literature.* Westminster, 1901, pp. 137, 184, 210.

Mâle, Emile : *L'Art religieux du XIIe siecle en France.* 2e edition. Paris, 1924, p. 324.

Pausanias : *Description of Greece* (IX, 21 :4). Trans. J. G. Frazer. London, 1898, vol. I, p. 470.

Photius : *Myriobiblon.* Geneva, 1612.

Pliny : *The Natural History.* Trans. J. Bostock and H. T. Riley. London, 1855–1857.

Reland, Adrian : *Dissertationum Miscellanearum.* Trajecti ad Rhenum, 1706–1708, vol. I, p. 223.

Solinus : *The excellent and pleasant worke of Julius Solinus Poly-histor*. Trans. A. Golding. London, 1587, p. 198.

Strabo : *The Geography* (XV, 1 :37). Trans. H. C. Hamilton and W. Falconer. 3 vols. London, 1854–1857.

Thévenot, Jules de : *The Travels of Monsieur de Thévenot into the Levant.* London, 1687, Part III, Ch. iv, p. 7.

Thévet, André : *Cosmographie universelle.* Paris, 1575, vol. I, p. 52.

Thoby-Marcelin, Philippe and Pierre Marcelin : *The Beast of the Haitian Hills.* New York, 1946. A trans. of *La Bête de Musseau.*

Tod, Col. James : *Travels in Western India.* London, 1839, pp. 82 ff.

Topsell, Edward : *The Historie of foure-footed beasts.* London, 1607.

Weerth, Aus'm : *Der Mosaikfussboden in St Gereon zu Cöln.* Bonn, 1873, pp. 15 ff.

White, T. H. : *The Books of Beasts.* London, 1954, pp. 51–52.

Wilson, Horace Hayman : *Notes on the Indica of Ctesias.* Oxford, 1836, pp. 39–43.

CHAPTER FOURTEEN : THE CATOBLEPAS

Allamand, Prof. : 'Du Gnou', in Buffon, *Supplement*, vol. 6, pp. 93–100.

Aelian : *On the Characteristics of Animals* (VIII, 105). Trans. A. F. Scholfield. London, 1958–1959, p. 99.

Buffon, George : *Histoire naturelle generale et particuliere* (Supplement VI, pl. VIII et IX). Paris, 1882, pp. 89–100.

Carey, Max and E. H. Warmington : *The Ancient Explorers.* New edition. Harmondsworth, 1965, p. 214.

Cosmas : *The Christian Topography of Cosmas Indicopleustes* (XI). Ed. E. O. Winstedt. Cambridge, 1909.

Cuvier, Georges : *Le regne animal.* 2 vols. Paris, 1817, tome I, pp. 264–265.

—— : *The Animal Kingdom.* 2 vols. London, 1834, vol. I, p. 176.

Flaubert, Gustave. *La Tentation de Saint Antoine.* Paris, 1874.

Lobo, R. P. : *Voyage d'Abyssinie.* Amsterdam, 1728, tome I, p. 292.

Pliny : *The Natural History* (VIII, 132). Trans. J. Bostock and H. T. Riley. London, 1855–1857.

Ptolemy : 'Guide to Geography' (I, 9 :3–4) in *The Works of Ptolemy.* Ed. J. L. Heiberg. London, 1898–1907.

Solinus : *The Excellent and Pleasant Work of Julius Solinus Poly-histor.* Trans. A. Golding. London, 1578, p. 140.

Topsell, Edward : *The Historie of Four-Footed Beasts.* London, 1607.
White, T. H. : *The Book of Beasts.* London, 1954, pp. 55, 267.

Chapter Fifteen : LEVIATHAN AND BEHEMOTH

*** : 'Leviathan', in *Encyclopedia Britannica.* 9th edition. London, 1899.
Bible : *Job* III, 8; XL, 15–24; XLI, 1–34; *Isaiah* XXVII, 1; XXXIV, 16; *Psalms*, LXXIV, 14; CIV, 26.
Bochart, Samuel : *Hierozoicon.* Leyde, 1692.
Calvert, Jean and Marcel Crupp : *Les animaux dans la littérature sacré.* Paris, 1956.
Chasles, R. and M. : *De la Bête à Dieu: le mystère animal dans la Bible et les initiations antiques.* Paris, 1949.
Clark, Kenneth : *Animals and Men.* London, 1977, p. 170.
Gesenius, H. F. W. : *Thesaurus philologicus criticus hebraeae et chaldaeae Veteris Testementi.* Leipzig, 1829–1888, p. 747.
—— : *A Hebrew and English Lexicon of the Old Testament.* London, 1907.
Graves, Robert and Raphael Patai : *Hebrew Myths.* London, 1964.
Harris, Thaddeus Mason : *The Natural History of the Bible.* London, 1824.
Hart, Henry Chichester : *Scripture Natural History* (vol. 2 : 'The Animals Mentioned in the Bible'), London, 1888.
Hooke, H. S. : *Middle Eastern Mythology.* Harmondsworth, 1963.
Knight, Alfred E. : *Bible Plants and Animals.* London, 1889.
Lathorp, Dorothy and Helen French : *Animals in the Bible.* New York, 1937.
Pinney, Roy : *The Animals in the Bible.* Philadelphia, 1964.
Tristram, H. B. : *The Natural History of the Bible.* London, 1867.
Vigouroux, F. : *Dictionnaire de la Bible.* Paris, 1928.
Wiley, Lulu Ramsey : *Bible Animals.* New York, 1957.
Wood, John George : *Bible Animals.* London, 1869.

Chapter Sixteen : THE DRAGON
General

Aelian : *On the Characteristics of Animals.* Trans. A. E. Scholfield. London, 1958–1959.
Aldrovandi, Ulisse : *Serpentum et draconum historiae.* Bologna, 1640.
Aristotle : *The Works.* Trans. W. D. Rouse. Oxford, 1908–1931.

Baring-Gould, Sabine : *Curious Myths of the Middle Ages*. London, 1877.

Bölsche, Wilhelm : *Drachen: Sage und Naturwissenschaft*. Stuttgart, 1929.

Broderip, William John : 'Dragons' in *Zoological Recreations*. London, 1847, pp. 326–338.

Campbell, John F. : *The Celtic Dragon Myth*. Edinburgh, 1911.

Carrington, Richard : *Mermaids and Mastodons*. London, 1956.

Dacqué, Edgard : quoted in Carrington (1956).

Davidson, H. R. Ellis : *Gods and Myths of Northern Europe*. Harmondsworth, 1964, pp. 159–162.

Doderer, Heimito von : 'Die Wiederkehr der Drachen', *Atlantis* (Zürich), vol. 31, no. 3, pp. 101–112, 149–150, März 1959.

Dorfeuille, C. L. M. : *Dissertation sur l'existence des dragons*. Saint-Maixent, An VII [1795].

Douglas, Norman : 'Dragons' in *Old Calabria*. London, 1912, pp. 100–104.

Gesner, Conrad : *De serpentibus*. Heydelberg, 1613.

Gould, Charles : *Mythical Monsters*. London, 1886.

—— : *Dragons*. London, 1977.

Gould, M. M. : *Dragons and Sea-Serpents*. London, 1886.

Graupner, Heinz : 'Lindwurm : Fabel oder Wirklichkeit?', *Koralle* (Berlin), neue folge, vol. 4, pp. 930–932, 12 Juli 1936.

Graves, Robert : *The Greek Myths*. Harmondsworth, 1955.

Ingersoll, Ernest : *Dragons and Dragon Lore*. New York, 1928.

Lankester, Sir Edwin Ray : *Science from an Easy Chair*. London, 1910.

Leach, E. R. : 'St George and the Dragon', in Glyn Daniel : *Myth or Legend?* London, 1955, pp. 79–87.

London, Hugh : *The Queen's Beasts*. London, 1954.

Münster, Sebastian : *Cosmographia universalis*. Basle, 1552, p. 1096.

Panthot, Jean-Baptiste : *Traité des dragons et des escarboncles*. Lyon, 1691.

Philostrate, Flavius : *Le merveilleux dans l'antiquité*. Paris, 1862, pp. 92–102.

Pliny : *Natural History*. Trans. J. Bostock and H. T. Riley. London, 1855–1857.

Reese, David S. : 'Men, Saints, or Dragons', *Folklore* (London), vol. 87 (1), pp. 89–95, 1976.

Sagan, Carl : *The Dragons of Eden*. New York, 1977.

Salverte, Eusèbe : *Des dragons et des serpents monstreux qui figur-*

205

ent dans un grand nombre de récits fabuleux et historique. Paris, 1826.

Scott-Stokes, Henry Folliot : *Perseus; or, Of Dragons.* London, 1924.

Siecke, Ernst : *Drachenkämpfe: Untersuchungen zur indogermanischen Sagenkunde.* Leipzig, 1907.

Smith, Grafton Elliot : 'Dragons and Rain-Gods', *Bulletin of the John Rylands Library* (Manchester), vol. 5, pp. 317–380, 1918–1920.

—— : *The Evolution of the Dragon.* Manchester, 1919.

Vinycomb, John : *Fictious and Symbolic Creatures in Art.* London, 1906.

White, T. H. : *The Book of Beasts.* London, 1954, pp. 165–167.

Williams, Gwynn : 'The Dragon of Cyrenaica', *The Listener* (London), vol. 64, pp. 512–513, 29 September 1960.

—— : *The Green Mountain.* London, 1963.

Zahn, Joannes : *Specula physico-mathematico-historica notabilium ac mirabilium sciendorum et mundi mirabilis oeconomia.* 2 vols. Norimbergae, 1696, vol. II, pp. 433–439.

Dragon banners

Dlugosz, J. : *Historia polonica.* Leipsig, 1711–1712, col. 679.

Hart, Clive : *The Dream of Flight.* London, 1972, pp. 32–48.

Lucian : *How to Write History.* London : Loeb Library, vol. 6, pp. 42–43.

Renel, C. : *Cultes militaires de Rome: les enseignes.* Paris, 1903, pp. 206–211.

Tatlock, J. S. P. : 'The Dragons of Wessex and Wales', *Speculum*, vol. 18, pp. 223–235, 1933.

Wissowa, G. (ed.) : *Paulys Realencyclopädie der Classischen Altertumswissenschaft*, article 'Draco'. Stuttgart, 1893.

The Tarasque

Dumont, Leon : *La Tarasque.* Abbeville, 1949.

Dumont, Louis : *La Tarasque.* Paris, 1951.

Floret, Jean Marie : *La Tarasque.* Tarascon, s.d.

Oriental dragons

Binyon, Laurence : *The Flight of the Dragon.* London, 1911.

Crump, James Irving : *Dragon Bones in the Yellow Earth.* New York, 1963.

Daniels, Frank James : 'Snake and dragon lore of Japan', *Folklore* (London), vol. 71, pp. 145–164, 1960.

Dennys, N. B. : *The Folklore of China.* London, 1896.

Groot, J. J. M. de : *The Religious System of China.* Leyden, 1892–1910.

Hayes, L. Newton : *The Chinese Dragon.* Shanghai, 1922.

Hopkins, L. C. : 'The Dragon Terrestrial and the Dragon Celestial', *Journal of the Royal Asiatic Society* (London), Oct. pp. 791–806, 1931; Jan., pp. 91–97, 1932.

Lum, Peter : *Fabulous Beasts.* London, 1952.

Visser, M. W. de : *The Dragon in China and Japan.* Amsterdam, 1913.

Werner, E. T. C. : *Myths and Legends of China.* London, 1924.

Wittkower, Rudolf : 'East and West : the Problem of Cultural Exchange', in *Allegory and the Migration of Symbols.* London, 1977, pp. 10–14.

Yetts, W. Perceval : *Symbolism in Chinese Art.* Leyden, 1912.

Komodo dragons

Arnold, Peter : 'In search of dragons', *Animals* (London), vol. 15, no. 8, pp. 364–369, August 1973.

Attenborough, David : *Zoo Quest for a Dragon.* London, 1957.

Broughton, Lady : 'A modern dragon hunt on Komodo', *National Geographic Magazine* (Washington, D.C.), September 1936.

Burden, William Douglas : *Dragon Lizards of Komodo.* New York, 1927.

Hoogerwerf, A. : 'Le lézard géant de Komodo', *Science et Nature* (Paris), no. 9, mai–juin 1955.

—— : 'The Indonesian giant', *Natural History* (New York), vol. 67, no. 3, March 1958.

Ouwens, P. A. : 'On a Large Varanus Species from the Island of Komodo', *Bull. Jard. bot. Buitenz.* (Buitenzorg), vol. 2, no. 6, pp. 1–3, 1912.

Reittich, M. : 'Wie der Drache von Komodo Entdeckt winde', *Arche Noah* (Hamburg), vol. 1, p. 188, 1949.

CHAPTER SEVENTEEN : BASILISK AND SALAMANDER

Basilisk

Browne, Sir Thomas : *Pseudoxia Epidemica.* London, 1646, Bk. III, ch. 7.

Dance, Peter : *Animal Fakes and Frauds.* Maidenhead, 1976, pp. 17–30.

Ditmars, Raymond : *Reptiles of the World.* New York, 1946.

Evans, Edward Payson: *The Criminal Prosecution and Capital Punishment of Animals.* London, 1906, pp. 162–164.

Galton, Sir Francis: *The Narrative of an Explorer in Tropical South Africa.* London, 1853, pp. 283–284.

Gosse, P. H.: *A Naturalist's Sojourn in Jamaica.* London, 1851, pp. 374–384.

——: *The Romance of Natural History.* Second series. London, 1861, pp. 211–219.

Gudger, E. W.: 'Jenny hanivers, dragons and basilisks in the old natural history books and in modern times', *Scientific Monthly* (New York), June 1934, pp. 511–523.

Lucan: *Pharsalia.* Trans. Robert Graves. Harmondsworth, 1956, p. 215 (IX, 703).

Ley, Willy: *The Lungfish, the Dodo and the Unicorn.* New edition. New York, 1952, pp. 61–67.

Malleus Maleficarum. Trans. Montague Summers. London, 1928, p. 18.

Münster, Sebastian: *Cosmographia universalis.* Colonna, 1575.

Neckham, Alexander: *De rerum naturis.* Trans. Thomas Wright. Rolls Series, vol. 34. London, 1863.

Pepys, Samuel: *The Diary of Samuel Pepys Esquire F.R.S.* Ed. Lord Braybrooke. Abridged edition. London, 1902, p. 131.

Phillips, Henry: *Basilisks and Cockatrices.* Philadelphia, 1882.

Pliny: *The Natural History.* Trans. J. Bostock and H. T. Riley. London, 1855–1857.

Robin, P. Ansell: *Animal Lore in English Literature.* London, 1932.

Seba, Albert: *Locupletissimi rerum naturalium thesauri accurata descripto.* Amsterdam, 1734–1765; vol. II, plate 40.

White, T. H.: *The Book of Beasts.* London, 1954, pp. 168–169.

Whitley, Gilbert P.: 'Jenny Hanivers', *Australian Magazine*, vol. 3, pp. 262–264, 1928.

Salamander

***: [Experiment on salamander]. *Phil. Trans. Royal Society* (London), vol. 2, p. 816, 1716.

Aldrovandi, Ulisse: *De quadrupedib' digitalis viviparis libri tres et de quadrupedib' digitalis oviparis.* Bonon, 1637, pp. 639–644.

Aristotle: *On the Parts of Animals.* Trans. W. Ogle. London, 1882.

——: *Historia animalium* (V, 17 : 12, 13). Trans. D'Arcy Wentworth Thompson. Oxford, 1910.

Browne, Sir Thomas: *Pseudoxia Epidemica.* London, 1646, Bk. III, ch. 12.

Cardano, Girolamo : *De subtilitate*. Norimbergae, 1550.

Cellini, Benvenuto : *Life, written by himself*. London, 1949, p. 6.

Gesner, Conrad : *Historia animalium*. Frankfurti 1585–1617, Bk. II.

Owen, Rev. Charles : *Essay Towards a Natural History of Serpents*. London, 1742, pp. 92–96.

Pierrii, Joannis : *Hieroglyphicae*. cap. 21–26, pp. 195–197.

Pliny : *The historie of the world; commonly called, the naturell historie of C. Plinius Secundus*. Trans. Philemon Holland. 2 vols. London, 1634.

——: *The Natural History* (VIII, 33). Trans. J. Bostock and H. T. Riley. London, 1855–1857.

Polo, Marco : *The Travels of Marco Polo*. London, 1908, p. 109.

Vinden, John : 'The Unnatural History of the Salamander', *The Saturday Book*, vol. 22, pp. 172–184. London, 1962.

White, T. H. : *The Book of Beasts*. London, 1954, pp. 182–183, 186.

CHAPTER EIGHTEEN : THE BARNACLE GOOSE

*** : 'History of the Bernacle and the Macreuse', *Blackwood's Magazine* (Edinburgh), vol. 3, no. 18, pp. 671–679, September 1818.

Albertus Magnus : *De animalium historia*. Roma, 1478, lib. 23, cap. 4, p. 186.

Armstrong, Edward Allworthy : *The Folklore of Birds*. London, 1958, pp. 225–239.

Boece, Hector : *Scotorum historiae*. Paris, 1526, fol. xiii verso.

Colonna, Fabius : *Phytobasanos*. Napoli, 1592, pp. 14–18.

Diamant, J. : *Jubilee Volume for M. Bloch*, cited in *Transactions of the Jewish Historical Society of England*, vol. 12, p. 110, 1905.

Dineen, Patrick : *An Irish–English Dictionary*. Dublin, 1929, p. 539.

Frederick II of Hohenstaufen : *The Art of Falconry, being the De arte venandi cum avibus*. Trans. and ed. Casey A. Wood and F. Marjorie Fyfe. Stanford, Calif. : Stanford University Press, 1943.

Gerald de Barri : *The First Version of the Topography of Ireland*. Trans. John J. O'Meara. Dundalk, 1951.

Gerard, John : *The Herball or generall historie of plantes . . . enlarged and amended by T. Johnson*. London, 1636, p. 1587.

Goblet d'Alviella, Eugène : *La migration des symbols*. Paris, 1891.

——: *The Migration of Symbols*. London, 1894.

Guettard, J. E. : *Memoires sur différents parties des Sciences et Arts*. Paris, 1768–1783, in vol. IV (1787), pp. 238–303.

Heron-Allen, Edward : *Barnacles in Nature and Myth*. Oxford, 1928.

Hill, John : *Review of the Works of the Royal Society of London.* London, 1751, p. 105.

——— : *Natural History of Animals.* London, 1752, p. 422.

Houssay, Frédéric : 'Les theories de la genese à Mycènes', *Revue Archeologique* (Paris), ser. iii, vol. XXVI, pp. 1–27, 1895.

Jacobs, G. : 'Arabische Berichte von Gesandten an germanische Fürstenhöfe aus dem 9 v. 10 Jhadt.' *Quellen zur Deutschen Volskunde,* I. Berlin und Leipzig, 1927.

Lankester, Sir Edwin Ray : *Diversions of a Naturalist.* London, 1915, pp. 100–141.

Lynch, John : *Cambrensis Eversus.* Ed. with trans. and notes by the Rev. Matthew Kelly. 3 vols. Dublin, 1848–1852, vol. 3, pp. 457–471.

Moray, Sir Robert : 'Account of the Barnacle Goose'. *Phil. Trans. Royal Society* (London), vol. 12, no. 137, 1677–1678.

Müller, Frederick Max : *Lectures on the Science of Language.* London, 1871; 1885 ed., p. 573.

Neckham, Alexander : *De naturis rerum.* Ed. Thomas Wright. Rolls Series, vol. 34, London, 1863.

Perrot, G. and C. Chipiez : *Histoire de l'art dans l'Antiquité.* Paris, 1882–1914. Vol. VI, *La Grèce primitive: l'art Mycenien.*

——— : *History of Art in Primitive Greece.* London, 1894, vol. III, p. 386–407.

Piccolomini, Aeneas Sylvius : 'Historia de Europe', in *Opera quae extant omnia.* Basle, 1571, p. 443.

Raven, C. E. : *English Naturalists from Neckham to Ray.* Cambridge, 1947.

Robinson, Dr Tancred : 'Some observations on the French Macreuse, and the Scotch Bernacle', *Phil. Trans. Royal Society* (London), vol. 15, no. 172, p. 1036, 1685.

Schliemann, H. : *Mycenae.* London, 1878, pp. 130–137; fig. 214.

Vincent of Beauvais : *Bibliotheca mundi.* Antwerp, 1624.

Zimmels, H. J. : 'Fowls growing on trees' [in Hebrew]. *Minhat Bikurum. Festschrift Schwartz.* Wien, 1926.

Barnacle goose riddle

Baum, Paull F. : *Anglo-Saxon Riddles of the Exeter Book.* Durham, N.C. : Duke University Press, 1963, p. 23.

Crossley-Holland, Kevin : *The Riddles of the Book of Exeter.* London, 1978.

Krapp, George Philip and Elliot van Kirk Dobbie : *The Exeter Book.* New York, 1936.

Tupper, F. : *Riddles of the Exeter Book.* Boston, 1910.

White, B. : 'Three Notes on Old and Middle English : II. The Barncle Goose Legend', *Modern Language Review*, vol. 40, pp. 205–206, 1946.

CHAPTER NINETEEN : THE VEGETABLE LAMB

Bennet, Josephine Waters : *The Rediscovery of Sir John Mandeville.* New York, 1954.

Breyn, Dr John Philip : 'Dissertatiuncula de Agno Vegetabli Scythico, Borametz vulgo dicto', *Philosophical Transactions of the Royal Society* (London), vol. 33, no. 390, pp. 353–360, 1725.

Cardano, Girolamo : *De rerum varietate.* Basileae, 1557, VI, 22.

Conway, D. Moncure : 'Monsters', *Harper's New Monthly Magazine* (New York), vol. 64, pp. 97–106, 1881.

Darwin, Erasmus : *The Botanic Garden.* London, 1781.

De La Croix, Dr : *Connubia Florum, Latino Carmine Demonstrata.* Bath, 1791.

Du Bartas, Saluste Guillaume : *La Semaine.* Paris, 1578.

—— : *Du Bartes his Divine Weekes and Workes.* Trans. Joshua Sylvester. London, 1584.

Duret, Claude : *Histoire admirable des plantes et des herbes.* Paris, 1605, cap. 29.

Exell, A. W. : 'Barometz, the Vegetable Lamb of Scythia', *Natural History Magazine*, vol. 33, pp. 194–200, 1932.

Herberstein, Baron von : *Rerum moscoviticarum commentarii.* 1549.

Herodotus : *The Histories.* Book III, ch. 106.

Kaempfer, Dr Engelbrecht : *Amoenitatum Éxoticarum politico-physico-medicarum fasciuli.* Lemgo, 1712, X, lib. 3. obs. 1.

Kircher, Athanasius : *Magnes, sive de arte magnetica opus tripartitum.* Paris, 1641, p. 730.

Lee, Henry : *The Vegetable Lamb of Tartary; a curious fable of the cotton plant, to which is added a sketch of the history of cotton and the cotton trade.* London, 1887.

Ley, Willy : 'Vegetable Animals', in *The Lungfish, the Dodo and the Unicorn.* New York, 1949.

Libellus de natura animalium. Edited by J. I. Davis. London, 1958.

Liceti, Fortunio : *De spontaneo viventium ortu.* Padua, 1518, lib. III, cap. 45.

Mandeville, Sir John : *The Travels of Sir John Mandeville.* Edited by A. W. Pollard. London, 1905.

——: *The Voyage and Travaile of Syr John Maundeville*. London, 1932.

Nieremberg, Juan Eusebio: *Historia naturae*. Antwerp, 1605.

Odoric of Friuli, in *The Contemporaries of Marco Polo*. Edited by Manuel Komroff. London and New York, 1928.

Parkinson, John: *Paradisi in sole, paradisus terrestris*. London, 1656.

Pliny: *Natural History*.

Rymsdyk, John and Andrew: *Museum Brittannicum*. London, 1778, plate XV.

Scaliger de Julius Caesar: *Exotericarum exercitationum liber quintus decimus de subtilitite*. Edited by H. Cardanum. Francofurti, 1665, lib. XV, cap. 29, p. 567.

Seymour, M. C. (ed.): *Mandeville's Travels*. Oxford, 1967, p. 191.

Sigismund von Herberstein: *Rerum muscoviticarum commentarii*. Antwerp, 1549.

Sloane, Sir Hans: 'Account of a China Cabinet', *Philosophical Transactions of the Royal Society* (London), vol. 20, no. 247, p. 461, 1698.

Strauss, Jans Janszoon: *Voyages de Jean de Struys en Muscovie, en Tartarie et en Perse*. Amsterdam, 1681, ch. XII, p. 167.

Theophrastus: *De historia plantarum*. Book IV, ch. 9, 45.

Tryon, H. F.: 'The Vegetable Lamb of Tartary', *Missouri Botanical Garden Bulletin*, vol. 43, pp. 25–28, 1935.

Chapter Twenty: THE CARRABUNCLE

Barco Centenera, Martín del: *Argentina y Conquista del Rio de la Plata, con otros acaecimiento de los regnos del Peru, Tucumen y estado del Brasil*. Lisboa, 1602.

Borges, Jorge Luis: *The Book of Imaginary Beings*. New York, 1969, pp. 51–53.

Colgan, Nathaniel: 'Field Notes on the Folklore of Irish Plants and Animals', *Irish Naturalist* (Dublin), vol. 23, p. 59, March 1914.

Costello, Peter: *In Search of Lake Monsters*. London, 1974, pp. 184–186.

Fernandez de Oviedo y Valdés, Gonzalo: *Historia general y natural de las Indies*. Toledo, 1526.

Hart, Henry: 'Plants of some of the mountain ranges of Ireland', *Pro. Royal Irish Academy* (Dublin), second series, vol. IV-science, p. 220, 1884.

Isidore of Seville: 'Etymologiarum' (XII, 2–7) in *Opera Omnia*. Ed. J. P. Migne. Paris, 1850.

Praeger, Robert Lloyd : *The Way That I Went*. Dublin, 1934, pp. 364–366.

Shakespeare, William : *As You Like It* (Act II, scene i, line 13).

Smith, Charles : *History and Present State of the County of Kerry*. Dublin, 1756, p. 124.

Wallace, Alfred Russell : *A Narrative of Travels on the Amazon and Rio Negro*. London, 1853, p. 495.

Chapter Twenty-one HERALDIC CREATURES

Allen, John Romilly : *Early Christian Symbolism in Great Britain and Ireland*. London, 1887.

Anderson, Mary D. : *Animal Carvings in British Churches*. Cambridge, 1938.

—— : *Imagery in British Churches*. London, 1955.

Bellew, George : *The Queen's Beasts*. London, 1953.

Bernheimer, Richard : *Wild Men in the Middle Ages*. London, 1952.

Collins, Arthur Henry : *The Symbolism of Animals and Birds Represented in English Church Architecture*. London, 1913.

Davies, Arthur Charles Fox : *The Art of Heraldry*. London, 1904.

Evans, E. P. : *Animal Symbolism in Ecclesiastical Architecture*. London, 1896.

London, Hugh Stanfield : 'Minor Monsters', *Coat of Arms* (London), issues 3–4, 1954–1956.

—— : *Royal Beasts*. East Knoyle, 1956.

Lower, Mark A. : *The Curiosities of Heraldry*. London, 1845.

Neubecker, Ottfried and J. P. Brooke-Little : *Heraldry: Sources, Symbols, and Meaning*. London, 1977.

Robin, Percy Ansell : *Animal Lore in English Literature*. London, 1932.

Shipley, Sir Arthur : 'The Hunting of the Yale', in *Cambridge Cameos*. London, 1924, pp. 64–88.

Vinycomb, John : *Fictious and Symbolic Creatures in Art, With Special Reference to Their Use in British Heraldry*. London, 1906.

Wood, J. G. : *The Natural History of Man*. London, 1868.

Chapter Twenty-two : LITERARY BEASTS

Barber, Richard and Anne Riches : *A Dictionary of Fabulous Beasts*. London, 1971.

Borges, Jorge Luis : *The Book of Imaginary Beings*. New York, 1969, pp. 68–69.

Botkin, B. A.: 'Fearsome Critters', in *The Standard Dictionary of Folklore, Mythology and Legend* (ed. Maria Leech). New York, 1949, pp. 373–374.

Gardner, Martin: *The Annotated Alice.* New York, 1960.

——: *The Annotated Snark.* New York, 1962.

Grandville: *Scènes de la Vie publique et privée des Animaux.* Paris, 1839.

Graves, Robert: *The Greek Myths.* Harmondsworth, 1955.

Holiday, Henry: *Reminiscences of My Life.* London, 1914.

Hone, William: *The Every-Day Book.* London, 1831.

Huxley, Francis: *The Raven and the Writing Desk.* London, 1976.

Lear, Edward: *A Book of Nonsense.* London, 1854.

Moore, Clifford B.: 'America's mythical snakes', *Scientific Monthly* (New York), vol. 68, pp. 52–58, January 1949.

Skinner, Charles: *American Myths and Legends.* Philadelphia, 1903.

Swift, Jonathan: *Travels into Several Remote Nations of the World.* London, 1726.

Chapter Twenty-three : MODERN MONSTERS

***: 'South Pacific Nessie?', *Newsweek* (New York), 1 August 1977, p. 41.

Costello, Peter: *In Search of Lake Monsters.* Revised edition. London, 1975.

——: *A la recherche des monstres lacustres.* Paris, 1977.

Heuvelmans, Bernard: *On the Track of Unknown Animals.* Revised edition. London and New York, 1962.

——: *L'homme de Neanderthal est toujours vivant.* Paris, 1974.

——: *Le grand serpent-de-mer.* Paris, 1975.

Hunter, Don, with Rene Dahinden: *Sasquatch.* Toronto, 1955.

Mawnan-Peller, A.: *Morgawr.* Ponsanooth, Truro, Cornwall, 1976.

Napier, John: *Bigfoot, the Yeti and the Sasquatch in Myth and Reality.* London, 1972.

Sanderson, Ivan T.: *Abominable Snowmen: Legend Come to Life.* Philadelphia, 1962.

Scott, Peter and Robert Rines: 'Naming the Loch Ness Monster', *Nature* (London), vol 258, 11 December 1975, pp. 466–468.

Slate, B. Ann and Alan Berry: *Bigfoot.* New York, 1976.

Alexander, E. J. and C. H. Woodward : *The Flora of the Unicorn Tapestries*. New York, 1941.

Beer, Rüdiger Robert : *The Unicorn*. London, 1977.

Berger, John : 'Animal World', *New Society* (London), 25 November, p. 1043, 1971.

Borges, Jorge Luis : *The Book of Imaginary Beings*. New York, 1969.

Clark, Kenneth : *Animals and Men*. London, 1977.

Freeman, Margaret : *The Unicorn Tapestries*. London, 1977.

Graves, Robert : 'The language of monsters', in *The Crane Bag*. London, 1969.

Grigson, Geoffrey : 'A beast in the bedchamber', *Times Literary Supplement* (London), 6 January, p. 8, 1978.

Hudson, Liam : *The Cult of the Fact*. London, 1972.

Jung, C. G. : *Alchemie und Psychologie*. Zurich, 1952.

—— : *Man and His Symbols*. London, 1964.

Klingender, Francis : *Animals and Art*. London, 1969.

Marguoliès, George : *Anthologie raisonnée de la littérature chinoise*. Paris, 1948.

Mode, Heinz : *Fabulous Beasts and Demons*. London, 1975.

Rawson, Jessica : *Animals in Art*. London, 1977.

Rilke, Rainer Marie : *Sonnets to Orpheus*. Trans. J. B. Leishman. London, 1949.

Rorimer, James J. : *The Unicorn Tapestries at the Cloisters*. New York, 1962.

Shepard, Odell : *The Lore of the Unicorn*. London, 1930.

Verlet, Pierre and Francis Salet : *La Dame à la Licorne*. Paris, 1960.

—— : *The Lady and the Unicorn*. London, 1961.

Willis, Roy : *Man and Beast*. London, 1974.

Wittkower, Rudolf : *Allegory and the Migration of Symbols*. London, 1977.

INDEX

INDEX

Abominable Snowman, 24, 173
Aelian, 36, 77, 96, 112
Aepyornis, 86–7
Aeschylus, 75, 80, 81
Albatross, 87–9
Aldrovandi, Ulisse, 14, 40, 67, 86
Alicorn, 94
Alligator, 124
American monsters, 169–70
Animals, and man, 7–16; in art, 177–82
Anting, in birds, 63–70
Ants, giant, 75, 76, 90–3
Archaeopteryx, 81
Arimaspi, 74, 79
Aristeas, 73–4, 75, 76, 78, 79, 80
Aristotle, 11, 12, 96, 105, 129, 131
Asbestos, 132
Aurochs, 96–7

Ball, Valentine, 21, 28, 92, 107
Baring-Gould, Sabine, 38, 55–6, 120
Barnacle Goose, 13, 42, 135–47
Barometz, see Vegetable Lamb
Basilisk, 127–9
Beebe, William, 11, 69
Behemoth, 117–18
Belon, 14, 139
Benbecula, mermaid found at, 49–50
Benu, 68–9
Bestiary, 12, 14, 37, 60, 61, 97, 122, 127, 129, 165

Bishop-fish, 41, 170
Brahminy kite, 81–2
Brontosaurus, reported in Congo, 22
Browne, Sir Thomas, 14, 68, 78, 128, 133
Buffon, George, 113
Bulls, 30–33
Burton, Maurice, 12, 23, 68, 69–70
Byrne, Peter, 24

Cardan, Jerome, 133, 151
Carrabuncle, 159–62
Carrington, Richard, 23, 81, 124
Catoblepas, 111–14
Cellini, Benvenuto, 130
Centaurs, 60–61, 167
Chimaera, 62
Chinese legends, 93
Clark, Kenneth, 13, 177, 182
Cobra, 129
Cockatrice, 129
Coelecanth, 17
Condor, 87
Corbett, Jim, 106, 108
Cotton plant, 154–8
Crete, 30–33
Crocodiles, 116–17
Cryptozoology, 2, 17–24, 168
Ctesias, 12, 13, 21, 76–7, 95–6, 102, 103, 104–7, 108, 157
Cuvier, Georges, 15, 17, 18, 68, 99, 103, 113

Darwin, Charles, 11, 15, 17
Dinosaurs, 19, 22, 124, 168
Diogenes, 114
Domestication, 1
Dove, W. F., 102–3
Dragon, 18, 119–26
Dragon banners, 122
Dragon bones, 123
Dragon, Chinese, 123

Ergot, 131
Evans, Sir Arthur, 32, 73
Exeter, Book of, 66, 147

Falconer, Hugh, 19
Feng-whang, 69
Flaubert, Gustave, 111, 168
Fort, Charles, 22
Fossils, 15
Frederick II, 13, 138
Freeman, Margaret, 97, 179, 180

Galton, Francis, 100, 129
Garuda, 79, 81
Gasr Silina, 121
Gerald de Barri, 136
Gesner, Conrad, 14, 40, 67, 105,
    112, 133
Gnu, 112–14
Gold, in India, 78–9
Gorer, Geoffrey, 54
Gorgons, 74, 112
Gorilla, 17
Gosse, P. H., 20, 23, 43, 56, 129
Gould, Charles, 124–5
Gould, R. T., 22
Grandidier, Alfred, 84, 86
Graves, Robert, 30, 60, 62, 117,
    118, 167
Griffin, 71–82, 166

Hachisuka, M. V., 69
Hardy, Alister, 51–3

Heliopolis, 63–6
Heraldry, 163–5
Herodotus, 12, 13, 21, 62, 91,
    114, 157
Heron, Purple, 69
Heron-Allen, Edward, 138, 140
Heuvelmans, Bernard, 18, 23,
    101, 165, 173
Hippopotamus, 117
Hitchens, William, 22
Holy Hunt, 97
Horns, manipulation of, 98, 102,
    165
Hunt, Leigh, 107–9

Iceland, mermaid in, 56
Imaginary animals, 177–82
India, 90–91
Indris, 110
Ireland, mermaid in, 38, 58
Isidore, Saint, 12, 77, 159

Jenny Hanivers, 41

Kerr, John Graham, 10, 13
Klingender, Francis, 177, 182
Komodo lizards, 125
Krumbiegal, Ingo, 23

Lactantius, 66
Lamia, 166–7
Lämmergeier, 80–81
Lane, Frank, 23, 85
Lankester, Ray, 143, 145
Lascaux, Beast of, 8, 27–9, 95
Lee, Henry, 158
Lemur, 110
Levi, Peter, 36
Leviathan, 115–17
Ley, Willy, 23
Linné, Carl, 14, 17, 165
Literary beasts, 166–70

Loch Ness monster, 22, 24, 172
Lydekker, Richard, 101, 102

Magic, 1–2
Malten, H. M., 19, 20
Man, Isle of, 58
Manatees, 41
Mandeville, Sir John, 13, 67, 77, 139, 148, 158
Manticora, 104–10
Marmot, 92–3
Megasthenes, 42, 91, 108
Melusina, 40
Mermaids, 34–58
Milton, John, 35, 75, 167
Minos, 30–32
Minotaur, 30–33
Modern monsters, 171–4
Mode, Heinz, 177, 182
Mosasaurus, 18
Müller, Karl, 20
Müller, Max, 139, 140, 143, 160
Mycenae, 143–6

Nandi Bear, 22
Narwhal, 98
Neanderthal Man, 23, 165
Nearchus, 91–2, 157
Neckham, Alexander, 128, 137
Nicholas the Fish, 53
Nzoo-Dzoo, 100

Okapi, 17, 22, 101–2
Onager, 96
Orford, merman at, 39
Oryx, 94, 100
Oudemans, A. C., 21
Owen, Richard, 20
Oxus, Treasure of, 70

Pan, 61
Panda, 17, 22
Parthenon, 60

Pasiphae, 31
Patterson, Roger, 173
Pausanias, 36, 105–7
Pegasus, 62
Persepolis, 95, 108
Pheasant, Golden, 68
Phoenix, 12, 15, 63–70
Physiologus, 12, 18, 97, 118, 128
Pliny, 12, 37, 64, 96, 103, 105, 112, 123, 127, 151, 157
Polo, Marco, 77, 83, 98, 149
Pontopiddan, Erik, 18, 47–8
Prester John, 91, 132, 163
Pterodactyl, 18, 81

Rams, as unicorns, 102
Reem, 115
Rhinoceros, 99–101
Riddle, Anglo-Saxon, 147
Robin, Ansell, 129
Roc, 82, 83–9
Rondelet, G., 14
Rose, H. J., 30, 61
Royal Society, 42, 133, 140

St George, 119–21
Salamander, 129–34
Sanderson, Ivan T., 22, 23, 165, 173
Satyrs, 61–2
Scythians, 72–81
Sea-eagle, 87
Sea-serpent, 20, 22, 171
Seals, 34–58
Septuagint, 96, 115
Shepard, Odell, 23, 94ff, 97, 102
Simurgh, 82
Sinbad, 84–5
Sirens, 59–60
Slick, Tom, 24
Sloane, Sir Hans, 153–4
Sloth, Giant, 21
Smith, Charles Hamilton, 20, 99

Smith, Grafton Elliot, 22
Snark, 168
Snowman, *see* Yeti
Strachey, Richard, 109

Tanagra, 36
Tarasque, 19, 121
Theseus, 31
Thévét, André, 42, 110
Tigers, 106–8
Toadstones, 159
Topsell, Edward, 106, 108, 112
Tritons, 36
Trois Frères, 29, 32
Turtle, giant, 19
Tylor, Edward Burnet, 21, 22

Unicorn, 1, 12, 14, 15, 20,
    94–103, 178–81

Valentyn, François, 46
Vegetable Lamb, 42, 135–47
Vincent of Beauvais, 139

'Walkers for Water', 54
Waugh, Arthur, 49–50
White, T. H., 12, 67, 109
Wild Man, 15, 62, 165, 167
Williams, Gwyn, 120

Yahoo, 167
Yale, 164–5
Yell, mermaid at, 50
Yeti, 15, 62
Yule, Henry, 84

Ziz bird, 82
Zoete, Beryl de, 57
Zoology, 10–16